LORI

LORI

MY DAUGHTER, WRONGFULLY IMPRISONED IN PERU

RHODA BERENSON

WITH A NEW EPILOGUE

FOREWORD BY NOAM CHOMSKY
AFTERWORD BY RAMSEY CLARK

NORTHEASTERN UNIVERSITY PRESS   BOSTON

Originally published in 2000 by Context Books.
Published in 2002 by Northeastern University Press
by agreement with Context Books.

Library of Congress Cataloging-in-Publication Data

Berenson, Rhoda.
Lori : my daughter, wrongfully imprisoned in Peru / Rhoda Berenson ;
foreword by Noam Chomsky ; afterword by Ramsey Clark ;
with a new epilogue.
p. cm.
ISBN 1-55553-498-8 (pbk. : alk. paper)
1. Berenson, Lori. 2. Prisoners, Foreign—Peru—Biography.
3. Prisoners—Peru—Biography. 4. Americans—Peru—Biography.
5. Prisoners, Foreign—Civil rights—Peru. 6. United States—Foreign
relations—Peru. 7. Peru—Foreign relations—United States. I. Title.
HV9622.5.B47 2002
364.1′092—dc21
[B]   2001044991

Printed and bound by The Maple Press Company in York, Pennsylvania.
The paper is Sebago Antique, an acid-free sheet.

Manufactured in the United States of America
06 05 04 03 02   5 4 3 2 1

THIS BOOK IS DEDICATED TO ALL THOSE

WHO, UPON RECOGNIZING INJUSTICE,

REFUSE TO REMAIN SILENT.

■

. CONTENTS

PART FOUR

DECEMBER 1996 TO DECEMBER 1998
CRISIS, HOPE, AND DISAPPOINTMENT

PART FIVE

JANUARY 1999 TO JULY 2000
WILL THE NIGHTMARE END?

EPILOGUE

AFTERWORD BY RAMSEY CLARK

.FOREWORD

Lori Berenson has been subjected to a travesty of justice and a grim exercise of state terror. The victim in this case is a young North American woman of remarkable courage and integrity, who has chosen to accept the fate of all too many others in Peru. She is also—and not so indirectly—a victim of Washington's policies, in two respects: because of its support for the Peruvian terror state and the conditions it imposes on its population, and because of its evasiveness in coming to her defense, as it can readily do, with considerable if not decisive influence. Also not so indirectly, she is a victim of all of those— in all honesty, I cannot fail to include myself—who have done far too little to rescue her from the suffering she has endured for her refusal to bend to the will of state terrorist authorities.

Lori Berenson eminently qualifies as a prisoner of conscience. She has rightly received the support of the U.N. High Commission on Human Rights and Amnesty International. With immense courage and self-sacrifice, she is not only standing up with honor and dignity for her own rights, but for the great number of people of Peru who are suffering severe repression and extreme economic hardship as a consequence of policies that sacrifice much of the population to the greed and power of small sectors of privilege—in Peru itself, and in the deeply unjust and coercive global system that has been constructed to yield such outcomes.

Lori Berenson is not only a wonderful person whose rights are under savage attack, but also an inspiring symbol of the aspirations of countless people throughout the world who seek a measure of the freedom and rights that they deserve, in a world that is more humane and more just, and that we can help create if we are willing to devote to this cause a fraction of the heroism that Lori Berenson has so impressively demonstrated in her honorable and far too lonely struggle.

Noam A. Chomsky
Institute Professor
Linguistics and Philosophy
Massachusetts Institute of Technology

. ACKNOWLEDGMENTS

I would like to thank Bob McIndoe, Beau Friedlander, and Blake Ferris for encouraging me to write this book, and Kathy, Mark, Ramsey, Tom, and Beau for their comments on the manuscript.

I wish there was space to thank individually the thousands of people across the United States and around the world who have worked so hard to free Lori and who, through their expressions of concern, have given me and my family the strength to carry on. This book, and the story it tells, would not be possible without them. I will always be indebted to Ramsey, Tom, and Blase for their advice and encouragement, to Kristen, Gail, Ken D., and Maurice for their tireless efforts, to Judy and Ken B. for always being there, and to the steering committee and regional coordinators of the Committee to Free Lori Berenson.

Similarly, there is not space to list the more than three hundred members of the United States Congress who over the years have supported initiatives on Lori's behalf. But special thanks go to Congresswomen Carolyn Maloney and Maxine Waters for their commitment to bring Lori home, and to those who have spoken publicly or sponsored letters for Lori's freedom—Representatives Jim Leach, Jim McGovern, Cynthia McKinney, and Constance Morella, as well as Senators Christopher Dodd, Jim Jeffords, Patrick Leahy, Daniel Patrick Moynihan, Charles Schumer, and Paul Wellstone.

PART ONE

DECEMBER 1, 1995

TO JANUARY 11, 1996

■

THE

NIGHTMARE

BEGINS

■ Friday, December 1, 1995

It was Friday, December 1, 1995. I had been teaching physics at Nassau Community College for twenty years. December 1 could only mean one thing: the end of the fall semester was fast approaching. My typical workweek was four days of teaching, one day of research. In fall 1995, Mondays were my non-teaching days, and I spent them at the City College of New York, where I was a member of the Theoretical Condensed Matter Physics Research Group. I was fortunate that Nassau Community College was not a "publish or perish" institution. But I published anyway, simply for the joy of doing the research. I studied properties of crystalline materials, and I loved in particular the idea that so much could be explained by mathematics and logic. It was particularly exciting when, occasionally, I was able to use mathematics and general principles of physics to predict something that no one had ever predicted before, and even more exciting when the predictions were actually confirmed by further experiments.

But I loved the work Tuesday through Friday as well. Even though it was standard practice to join with my colleagues to complain about the students, I could think of no career I would prefer to teaching. On Friday, December 1, I taught a morning laboratory class on "The Science of Light and Color," a course I specifically created for liberal arts students who wouldn't ordinarily take a course in Physics. It was very popular. I enjoyed teaching the material, and the students enjoyed studying it. In the afternoon, I met with my introductory physics class, a course somewhat like the one that convinced me to become a physicist in the first place. Unfortunately, my students didn't enjoy taking this course as much as I enjoyed teaching it. However, they were committed to passing, and my office hour after class was always filled with students who were filled with questions.

The students left at about 3:30, and I prepared for the drive home. The college is in Long Island, about thirty miles east of our Manhattan apartment. The commute along the Long Island Expressway, nicknamed "the world's longest parking lot," could take forty minutes or it could take two hours. I had left my apartment that morning, as I did every teaching day, at 6:45 a.m. Although my Friday classes ended earlier than other days, by 3:30 I was definitely ready for the weekend.

As I packed up my papers, I gave some thought to the evening. My husband, Mark, had left that afternoon for a conference at Harvard University. Mark taught at Baruch College in New York, and in recent years he had applied his knowledge of statistics to the study of health-care management. This weekend's conference was focused on health-care research. Mark's time was consumed with his teaching duties, his research, and his textbooks. He had coauthored several statistics books that were used at colleges and universities around the world. In fact, when my daughter Lori was living in El Salvador, people would ask if she was related to the Berenson of the "Berenson and Levine" statistics textbook they used at the university.

So Mark wouldn't be there for dinner, and I had to make my usual Friday night decision, whether or not to go to dance class. I had studied modern ballet all of my adult life, certainly not to become a dancer, but simply to dance. There was something about using dance to create images or express emotions that I found enormously appealing. For several years I had been taking class at the Martha Graham School of Dance, two or three nights a week. That third "iffy" night was Friday. And on this particular Friday I decided to forgo the class for a long nap.

It was about 6 p.m. when the phone woke me. My memory of the conversation is a bit fuzzy, perhaps because I had been sleeping but more likely because the gist of it was so disorienting. Conveyed by the Peru desk at the U.S. Department of

State in Washington—and again by the U.S. embassy in Lima, Peru—the message, as I understood it, was that my twenty-six-year-old daughter had been arrested the previous day. Lori was being held at the antiterrorist police headquarters. The probable charge was treason.

I found myself alone and in a daze, trying to make sense of it all. Things like this don't happen to my family, don't happen to me. I'm a physicist, an academic. I lead an organized, quiet life. I wasn't someone who received calls from U.S. government officials. But I had just spoken with Washington consular officer Marti Melzow, and she "patched me through" to Consul General Thomas Holladay and Consular Officer Julie Grant in Peru. That morning, Peruvian president Alberto Fujimori had waved Lori's passport on TV, and someone at the American embassy had seen it. The president of Peru was accusing my daughter of assisting a rebel group, Movimiento Revolutionario Túpac Amaru (MRTA), which had been involved in a shoot-out with police the night before. She faced charges of treason against Peru—even though she wasn't a Peruvian citizen. I needed to find a Peruvian lawyer to represent her. Embassy officials only had a list of lawyers who handled drug charges, not treason. They suggested I ask my friends if they knew any Peruvian lawyers.

Ask my friends if they knew any Peruvian lawyers? That didn't make any more sense than accusations of treason or Lori assisting a rebel group.

I had been told by Tom Holladay and Julie Grant that they visited Lori at the DINCOTE prison. DINCOTE (Dirección Nacional Contra el Terrorismo) are the Peruvian antiterrorism police. Lori explained to them that she had been on a bus when a plainclothes officer boarded and pulled her off. He didn't identify himself, and Lori struggled with him, thinking she was being kidnapped. She had been roughed up and was given first aid at DINCOTE. She asked Mr. Holladay to tell us she was okay and that she hadn't been harmed. She asked him to tell us not to worry.

They gave me an emergency number, should I need it, because the embassy would be closed for the weekend. Tom Holladay even gave me his home phone number.

I hung up the phone and stared into space. I was terrified.

It was hard to believe that this wasn't a nightmare. I wanted to scream, because sometimes, in nightmares, when you scream you awaken. But I knew that I was already awake and that screams wouldn't help, and that, terrified or not, I had to focus on what to do next.

Mark was at a conference dinner and wouldn't be reachable until much later that night, so my first call was to my daughter Kathy. Kathy was then a graduate student in Clinical Psychology at New York University and lived in Brooklyn. She is only two years older than Lori, and the two have always been very close. Even during the years that they were separated geographically, they kept close through letters. Kathy immediately came to my apartment, and we agonized over whether or not we should tell Mark anything that night. We decided it might be too painful to cope with this news while he was alone in Boston. It would be better to wait until the next morning, when he'd be able to catch a flight home. I spent the rest of the evening telephoning friends and relatives, looking for anyone who might know a Peruvian lawyer—although I couldn't imagine why any of them would. When it became too late to make further calls, I wandered around the apartment in a fog.

This was the apartment where Lori grew up, and although she was thousands of miles away, she was everywhere. Shelves housed the clay sculptures Lori made as a child, walls displayed her needlepoints, cassette racks held the tapes of her playing guitar and singing, and there were photographs everywhere. There was six-month-old Lori, making funny faces for the camera, five-year-old Lori atop the Empire State Building with the World Trade Center in the background and the wind blowing her long hair across her face, and Lori in 1991 dancing with Mark at his fiftieth birthday party.

I stopped in front of a picture of thirteen-year-old Lori dressed for the role of Vera in a school performance of *Auntie Mame*. She was wearing a powder-blue gown and a white boa, and held a champagne glass in her white-gloved hand. Lori loved performing in those junior high school shows, and in the chamber chorus in high school. But a glance at her bookshelf reminded me that music was just a diversion. The texts on cultural anthropology and indigenous peoples of the Americas reflected the adult Lori, who had decided to devote her life to issues of peace and justice.

Lori had lived in Latin America on and off for seven years, and although the separation had been difficult and I often worried about the dangers she might encounter there, I knew that this was the only life she wanted. Lori was deeply affected by conditions of poverty and hunger, and refused to remain silent when she saw abuse or the denial of basic human rights. She had recently obtained press credentials in Peru in order to write articles about poverty and women's issues for two small magazines, and she was conducting interviews with members of the Peruvian government and other Peruvians.

As exhausted as I was, I didn't sleep much that night. I was too frightened and there were so many questions. Why was she arrested? Did this have something to do with the articles she was writing or the interviews she was conducting? How could a U.S. citizen be accused of treason against Peru? How would I find a Peruvian lawyer? What airlines fly to Peru? How quickly can I arrange to go there? Who do I know who has political connections?

Worst of all, I kept seeing Lori in prison. The only prison I could picture was from movies I had seen, and I imagined it was crowded, dark, and dirty. But she was in prison in South America, so rape, torture, and "disappearance" were also in my thoughts. She had told Tom Holladay she hadn't been harmed and that we shouldn't worry. But was she really "okay" or was she simply trying to ease our anxiety? It was true that the embassy officials said she looked all right. But they didn't know what she was supposed to look like. They didn't know her. How could they recognize the signs of tension or stress that Lori could never conceal from me? And besides, embassy officials had seen her hours ago. What had happened since their visit? What would happen over the weekend when the embassy was closed and no one would be there to check on her? I waited nervously for 5 a.m., when I would call Mark.

▪ Saturday, December 2 to Tuesday, December 5

Mark was devastated by the news. In fact, on the plane ride home from Boston he feared that Lori was dead and that I had not wanted to tell him such horrible news by phone. He had heard news reports that there was a shoot-out in Lima and that several people had died. When he arrived home, he was relieved when I told him Lori was alive, but distraught at the thought of her being held by secret police in a regime known for its brutality.

We spent that weekend on the phone trying to find anyone who knew a Peruvian lawyer. My neighbors came to help answer calls. Our friends and relatives called their friends and relatives. We were learning more about Peru, the kinds of things you don't read about in the newspapers. We heard from Peruvians who warned us about the horrors of the secret military tribunals that deny those accused any right to defend themselves. We were told that human rights groups had documented hundreds, if not thousands, of innocent Peruvians serving long terms under extremely harsh conditions after having been sentenced by those secret tribunals. We learned of the brutality of the Peruvian prisons, particularly the one in the DINCOTE headquarters. A representative of Amnesty International called to say that Peru is "a military dictatorship, thinly veiled as a democracy."

Mark had brought home a copy of the *Boston Globe* that reported on the Lima shoot-out that was supposed to be somehow related to Lori's arrest. The embassy had made it clear to me that Lori was arrested while on a bus, not at this shoot-out. According to the article, five people—four rebels, and one policeman—were killed and nine were wounded during an eleven-hour police siege of a rebel hideout in the upscale La Molina neighborhood of Lima. The second-ranking commander of the MRTA, Miguel Rincón, was captured along with fourteen others. Hundreds of police and soldiers, backed by helicopters and armored vehicles, had surrounded the house, which police claimed held an arsenal of weapons. The rebels escaped and moved through six adjoining homes before their surrender was negotiated. No local residents were injured. The article identified the MRTA as the smaller of Peru's rebel groups, not to be confused with the more notorious Maoist Shining Path.

At about midday Monday, I called Julie Grant at the embassy only to learn that she hadn't visited Lori since Friday and, incredibly, didn't plan to see her for a while. She explained that the embassy normally makes monthly visits to American citizens who are being held but who have not yet had a trial. When she had seen Lori on Friday, she left her card and told Lori to call if she needed anything. She also reminded me that we needed to hire a Peruvian lawyer, but when I told her that Mark and I wanted to come to Peru for that purpose, she discouraged us.

I hung up the phone, completely bewildered. Given what I had heard all weekend, I couldn't believe that Lori would be allowed to call Julie Grant if she were being mistreated by the infamous DINCOTE officials. So, what good was the calling card? And I couldn't understand how the embassy expected us to hire a Peruvian lawyer without coming to Peru. It dawned on me that I would be faced not only with trying to understand the actions of the Peruvian government, but the U.S. government as well.

Later that afternoon, we received a surprise phone call from Lori. She had been taken by the police to her apartment in the San Borja region of Lima. She was brought there to witness the search of her apartment and was allowed to place a thirty-second phone call to us in New York. She sounded frightened and frantic, telling us: "They're accusing me of the most unbelievable things. I am completely innocent of these preposterous charges. I need a lawyer. I need underwear and shoes. Most of all I need a lawyer. Cancel my American Express card immediately, because the military police have taken it and I don't trust them."

We called American Express, and sure enough, $440 had been charged on Saturday—while Lori was in prison. Lori also had told us that the police had taken her latest bank statement. This was an account she held jointly with me in New York. Lori was afraid the police would find a way to access the money.

Lori never could have guessed that the Peruvians would later claim that this bank statement provided definitive proof that Lori was, of all things, an arms dealer.

Although we were told that the Peruvian justice system had many shortcomings, it still seemed crucial that we find the correct lawyer. We knew Lori couldn't possibly be guilty of the charges against her, and we were confident that if she presented her side, countered the supposed evidence, and had her lawyer cross-examine witnesses—in other words, if she had a fair trial—she would be found innocent and released. We were very naive. We did not know then what we know now: Peruvian military tribunals convict whomever they want—and they nearly always convict. Once arrested, there is no way out. The right to a defense is only a pretense, and the role of the lawyer is solely intended to support that pretense.

Our telephone networking led us to two terrific resources. One chain of calls led to a journalist, Frank Smythe, who had been held by the Iranian government and was released with the help of former U.S. Attorney General Ramsey Clark. Frank suggested we contact Ramsey at his office in New York City. We met with him that afternoon.

Among all the other sudden changes in my life, I could now add that I personally met a former U.S. attorney general. Ramsey did not look very different from his photos in 1967, when President Lyndon B. Johnson appointed him. He was still tall and slim, with brown hair. And with his flannel shirt and soft drawl, he brought a touch of Texas to New York. He listened to our story carefully, responding in his characteristic slow, deliberate, thoughtful way. He advised that either Mark or I go to Peru immediately to select a lawyer. Ramsey offered to go along and help with the selection, but due to a prior commitment he could stay at most three days. He also thought it imperative that we contact members of the U.S. Congress and the U.S. Department of State to urge them to pressure the government of Peru to release Lori. He described another case in which he had helped a young American woman, Jennifer Casolo, who had been arrested in El Salvador and who was released after an outcry from Senator Christopher Dodd of Connecticut.

On a separate branch of our newly formed network, we were reminded that one of our neighbors, Thomas Nooter, was active in the local Democratic club and might be able to speak to Congresswoman Carolyn Maloney on our behalf. When we met with Tom he readily agreed to do so, and he also offered his expertise as a criminal lawyer. Tom is fluent in Spanish, having spent his teenage years in Uruguay. He had also worked previously with Ramsey Clark.

By Monday night it was decided that Mark, Ramsey, and Tom would leave on Wednesday for Peru. I was to pressure members of Congress for help and continue gathering information about Peruvian lawyers. I had already spoken to my colleagues, who had readily agreed to cover my classes for that week, and longer if necessary. Mark had made similar arrangements.

Tuesday was spent making plans for the trip to Peru. By this time, many of our friends and their friends had called their congressional representatives and senators, and they in turn called the State Department. Word had reached the embassy in Peru that there was a lot of concern about Lori. At a press briefing, a State Department spokesman said the United States would stay involved in the case and ensure that Peruvian authorities treat Berenson "according to international standards."

So when I called Peru on Tuesday, I noted a new, more helpful attitude. Julie Grant had already visited Lori. She reported that Lori was not being mistreated. She was being held alone in a cell furnished only with a mattress and an overhead light that was controlled from the outside. She had seemed tired but in good humor, and she had expressed concern over interrogators' statements that she would be imprisoned in the notorious Yanamayo Prison in Puno. Julie later spoke with Colonel Juan Gonzales Sandoval, the DINCOTE officer in charge of the case, and was assured that this would not occur. Lori was also most anxious for information about what charges and/or accusations were being made, since she was being held incommunicado and had not been formally charged. Julie made it clear that the embassy role was to look after her welfare, but not to investigate her case. Lori brightened with the news that Mark was coming. She was anxious to see him and was relieved to know that he was going to hire a lawyer. Julie told us that she asked for clothing, shoes, toiletries, and, if we could find it, an old pair of eyeglasses. The police had taken her glasses and claimed to have lost them. She had disposable contact lenses, but she wasn't allowed to use the necessary disinfectant solution.

Consular officials were preparing for the visit from Mark, Ramsey, and Tom. The officials had spoken to Colonel Gonzales and confirmed that they all would be allowed to visit Lori. These officials were also gathering information about Peruvian lawyers, even though, as they indicated in a later report, finding an attorney to represent anyone up on such charges would be very difficult.

Although Lori had made front-page news in Peru ever since her arrest, it wasn't until Tuesday that articles appeared in the *New York Times* and the New York *Daily News*. The *Times* article included our home address, making it easy for reporters to call without having to go through all of the Berensons in

the phone book. We were barraged with calls and had to in-
stall "call-waiting," which we had managed to do without even
when there were two teenaged girls at home.

It was time for a crash course on the media. We learned
very quickly how easily we could be misquoted or quoted out
of context, and how aggressive and how insensitive reporters
can be. I'll always remember the call from a journalist at *People*
magazine who told me he wasn't planning to write a story
immediately, but should Lori be found guilty and given a harsh
sentence, he would very much like to write one.

I started visualizing vultures hovering over a corpse.

Meanwhile, Mark packed his clothes and Lori's, although
we could not locate the eyeglasses. Mark had slept very little
for days, and I hoped that the long trip to Peru would allow
some time for rest. I also hoped, as did Mark, Ramsey, and
Tom, that by the time they reached Lima, the Peruvian government would realize that they made a mistake; that the police would realize she was innocent; that the U.S. government
would convince the Peruvian government to release Lori; that
she'd come home with Mark.

▪ Wednesday, December 6 to Sunday, December 10

At 10 a.m. on Wednesday, Tom and Mark left for the airport, where they were joined by Ramsey. We stayed in frequent phone contact over the next several days, starting with a call when the plane from New York City landed in Miami. Ramsey had called his office and was distressed to learn that officials from the State Department had chosen to treat Lori's case as a consular rather than a political matter. Although Tom and Ramsey tried to explain this in a way that wouldn't further upset Mark, the decision meant that the U.S. government would try to ensure that Lori was well treated, but they were not working behind the scenes for her immediate release. The odds that she'd come home in a few days had diminished considerably.

Meanwhile in New York the phone rang all day as U.S. and Peruvian reporters wanted Mark's flight schedule and hotel destination. I didn't provide information, but I knew they wouldn't have any difficulty locating him. We now had two phone lines, call-waiting, and access to my neighbor's fax. A schedule was set up with Kathy, Mark's brother, Ken, our sister-in-law, Judy, and several neighbors so that there were always at least two people besides me to answer the phones. In addition to calls from the media, there were many from friends, some of whom we hadn't heard from in years. And more amazing were the messages from total strangers who had read about Lori's arrest, and wanted to help. I kept hearing "it could have been me" or "it could have been my daughter." We also had a call from Congresswoman Maloney, who said she was staying in close touch with the State Department, had spoken with the embassy in Peru, and would help in any way possible.

My neighbors were really wonderful. One brought me bagels every morning, another takeout dinner, and another homemade soups. Unfortunately, I hardly found time to eat. In addition to answering the continuous stream of incoming calls, we were busy sending messages out. We put together a flyer explaining the little we knew about Lori's arrest, asking all our friends and their friends to phone or fax their congressional representatives and senators. I faxed one to Nassau Community College, where it was quickly reproduced and circulated. I was told the school fax machines were overloaded with messages to New York Senators Daniel Patrick Moynihan and Alfonse D'Amato. Senator D'Amato was a Nassau County resident, and some of the messages were from people who were his friends as well as his constituents. Similar messages went to Mark's colleagues at Baruch College, my research associates at City College, and friends and relatives across the country. All of this was exhausting, but I felt I was doing something constructive. The flurry of activity kept me from dwelling on thoughts of Lori in a prison cell. The worst times were the lulls, those few quiet moments when I wondered when it would end.

The mail brought letters from movie producers, asking for the rights to Lori's story. I had not yet gotten used to seeing my name in the paper or hearing news reports about Lori on local radio, and certainly the idea of *Lori's Story* on a big screen seemed about as bizarre as the thought of Lori in prison. Lori has always been a very private person, and I was sure she wouldn't want any part of her life acted out for all to see. However, the prospect did provide a source of entertainment as we sat around and chose the actors and actresses we wanted to have play us. Mark's brother, Ken, always in good physical shape, would have no one but Sylvester Stallone, and Kathy's preference was Winona Ryder. I thought Meryl Streep would be fine for me. Jack Lemmon had played Ed Horman, the father of an American who disappeared in *Missing,* a movie based on a true story that had parallels to ours. So Jack Lemmon would play Mark. This was a fun game, but when I spoke to Mark at 1:30 a.m. from his hotel in Lima, I realized that our lives were indeed becoming less and less those of an ordinary family and more and more like a family in a movie, in fact a movie complete with car chases.

Mark's flight landed in Lima at 11:30 p.m. The U.S. embassy had not sent anyone to meet the plane, but the Peruvian press was there in force. As Mark was walking with Tom and Ramsey toward the terminal building, they were surrounded by civilian and military police who helped them clear the last of the customs hurdles and escorted them to taxis directly in front of the airport enclosure.

Instead of the usual crowd of family and friends waiting to welcome the arriving passengers, there were hundreds of journalists and TV crews, all screaming for interviews and photos. In spite of the security escort, they were quickly engulfed by reporters, microphones, and cameras. In the crush, Mark was separated from Tom and Ramsey, and pushed by security into a waiting taxi. There were people all over the taxi, on the roof and on the hood; faces were pressed to the windshield and all of the windows. At one point the door of the taxi opened and camera crews and journalists jumped in, snapping photos and asking questions. One of the cameras smacked against Mark's forehead, scraping a two-inch line of skin from his scalp. It was an accident, but nobody even bothered to apologize. He was angry and exhausted, but tried to be polite. He kept repeating, in English, "I just want a chance to see my daughter. This is a nightmare. Please, let me see my daughter. I know she is innocent." Police finally pulled everybody out of and off the vehicle, literally kicking them out of the way, and the taxi, with a security officer seated alongside the driver, pulled away from the crowds.

As the taxi left the airport, Mark turned around to look for the taxi with Tom and Ramsey, but what he saw following him was a caravan of cars, vans, and camera trucks with bright lights. The taxi was going more than sixty miles an hour when a press vehicle caught up and cut it off. The taxi was forced to stop, brakes screeching, while reporters yelled out questions and tried to take more pictures. The driver spun around and took a small, dark side street. Mark said he thought his life might be about to end, but he was too numb to worry about it.

Finally, the taxi arrived at the Sheraton Hotel, in downtown Lima. The press caravan was still in hot pursuit, and there were another fifty or so journalists and cameramen waiting at the hotel entrance. Ramsey and Tom, each in separate taxis, arrived about ten minutes later. Mark said it was after 1 a.m. when, exhausted and sweating, he went to his room. He tried to make this sound like an adventure, but his voice told me it was an extremely harrowing experience. He promised to phone again after he saw Lori.

On Thursday, the home campaign continued while I anxiously awaited Mark's call. In the afternoon a TV crew from Peru's Channel 5 rang my intercom wanting to interview me. Even though I had spent the morning in interviews with local newspapers, this was different, and I decided against it. I had not yet done a TV interview, and the Peruvian crew only spoke Spanish, a language I barely understood. I recalled Mark's experience of the previous night, and so I wasn't surprised that this crew would not take no for an answer. They stopped ringing the intercom only after a neighbor confronted them and threatened to call the police.

Meanwhile, the wire service Agence France-Presse had reported that the Peruvian police claimed that Lori had been posing as a journalist, using false press credentials to gain intelligence for a planned attack on the Peruvian Congress.

First of all, I knew that Lori could never be involved in "a planned attack on the Peruvian Congress." And also I knew that Lori had legitimate press credentials for two magazines. I immediately called *Modern Times* and *Third World Viewpoint*. The editors of both publications sent letters verifying that Lori was writing articles for them, and I faxed these to Mark.

Mark finally called in midafternoon. He had seen Lori and she was okay. The visit was in the DINCOTE office of the secretary to Colonel Juan Gonzales Sandoval. Sandoval, nick-named "The Jackal," was the police officer in charge of the investigation. Lori, escorted by guards, entered smiling, look-ing paler and thinner since her visit to New York in Septem-ber. She did not look abused. They sat side by side on a sofa, while two guards sat across the room. They talked in syllables and whispers, knowing that the room was most assuredly bugged, for about forty-five minutes, during which time Lori tried to convince Mark not to worry, and Mark tried to con-vince Lori not to worry. Lori asked about Kathy and me and how we were dealing with all this, and also expressed concern that Mark looked so tired. She said she was being interrogated day and night and had been accused of "everything under the sun." She kept repeating that she was innocent, that she could never be involved with terrorism. But Lori was more knowl-edgeable than we about Peruvian justice and knew that al-though she was innocent and the charges against her were preposterous, she might very well be convicted of something. There were hundreds of innocent people in Peruvian prisons. The conversation was interspersed with hugs, but whenever tears welled up, Lori reminded him that they should not cry. The guards would see that as a weakness, and interrogators could use any weakness to force a false confession. Mark told her he would be going to the embassy to meet various lawyers. He assured her he would hire the best one he could find.

Mark, Ramsey, and Tom had met that morning at the U.S. embassy with Jim Mack, who was in charge while the ambas-sador, Alvin Adams, was out of the country. Mack had bad news. Ramsey's request to meet with President Fujimori had been denied. He said President Fujimori was a very strong-willed, difficult man and the U.S. had very little influence with him, which was hard to believe given the amount of financial aid Peru received from the United States. He added that, unfortunately, Lori's arrest came at a time when Peru was angry with the United States over the impending sale of some military jets to Ecuador. Mack believed there was no chance that Lori would be simply expelled from Peru, the solution that Mark, Ramsey, and Tom had been looking for.

Mark called again that night to tell me about his afternoon and evening, which he spent with Ramsey and Tom interviewing lawyers at the embassy. Mark couldn't remember all of those interviewed, but a few of them stood out, and he described them to me.

Ronald Gamarra of the Peruvian Legal Defense Institute had written a leading text on terrorism-related cases in Peru. Tom Holladay translated as Gamarra eagerly provided information about the legal process. He was later joined by an energetic and enthusiastic colleague, Ernesto de la Jara. They both seemed interested in the case, but would not commit themselves to taking it. Neither had ever represented a foreigner accused of terrorism, a situation that seemed to Ramsey and Tom to present special issues. And they had seemed concerned for their own security, particularly if they took the case of a foreigner.

Several of the lawyers who came were elderly former congressmen from opposition parties who were eager to represent Lori but had no experience in criminal law or terrorism cases. Ramsey and Tom thought their lack of appropriate experience and their affiliation with political parties that opposed President Fujimori made them poor choices.

Vivid in Mark's mind was Jose Ugas, who spoke excellent English, was very articulate, and very confident. Ugas had been successful earlier that year in securing the release of an Italian woman who had been sentenced in Peru for terrorism. Ramsey and Tom explained that Lori needed a lawyer in order to make her official statement. She had been interrogated now for a whole week. The twenty or so codefendants had already made their official statements. Ugas replied that he would be out of the country and would not be able to see Lori for a few weeks. But he insisted his absence wouldn't matter because regardless of who was her lawyer, regardless of whether she was innocent or guilty, she would be convicted. He suggested the best approach was to have her convicted as quickly as possible, without putting up a fight. Then in the appeals process he could turn things around. He described how on appeal the Italian woman pled guilty and was expelled from Peru. This made no sense to Mark, Ramsey, or Tom. Ugas seemed to be an insider, a negotiator, and not a real counsel. Lori was innocent, and they were looking for a lawyer who would argue she was innocent and fight for her acquittal.

One of the lawyers we tried to contact before Mark left the United States was a man named Aramburu, who had been instrumental in helping an American photojournalist arrested in Peru years before. Mr. Aramburu had called the U.S. embassy and recommended the services of Grimaldo Achahui Loaiza, who came for an interview late in the day. He was an experienced criminal lawyer from Cuzco, now living in Lima. He was an Incan descendant and had the courage to take on difficult cases, and had already defended a Chilean citizen accused of terrorism. He was totally familiar with DINCOTE, their officers, and the situation, and had dealt before with Colonel Gonzales, whom he described as a "very hard man." He knew some of the other lawyers involved in the defense of Lori's codefendants and had learned what the case was about from them. Based on what he heard, read, and read between the lines, Mr. Achahui believed Lori was innocent and wanted to defend her. All were impressed and, as Mark pointed out to me, Mr. Achahui was also the only lawyer interviewed that day who actually *wanted* to defend Lori. So Ramsey and Tom recommended that Mark see Lori the next day and give her a choice: Grimaldo Achahui or the team of Gamarra and de la Jara. Although this team had not yet agreed to represent her, Ramsey and Tom thought they could be convinced to take the case after they met Lori and confirmed her innocence for themselves.

Before Mark said goodnight, he told me about his ride from the embassy to the hotel at about midnight. He was in the embassy van, and whenever it stopped at red lights, beggars would come alongside, hands outstretched. Some were old or lame, and some were very young children, children who should have been tucked in bed, children who had no future. At one busy intersection, a child in rags, perhaps six or seven years old, carrying an infant on her back, came up to the van, begging for money. Mark said he looked at her and at the baby, thought of Lori, and understood why she was in Peru. How could anyone see these sad faces with their big brown pleading eyes and not want to decry the system that keeps them hungry?

On Friday evening at 6 p.m., Kathy and I were eating dinner—the homemade lentil soup that my neighbor had just delivered. It was hard to imagine that this evening marked only one week since I first heard the news of Lori's arrest. In one week my whole world had turned upside down. During this week I hadn't once thought about classroom lectures or grading papers. Instead of researching physical properties of crystalline materials, I was researching the Peruvian justice system, or, as I saw it, the Peruvian system of injustice. Instead of learning dance technique, I was learning how to speak in sound bites. I had just finished my first TV interview, with NY1, a local news cable station. Kathy watched the filming of the interview and said I was fine, but I had been so nervous that immediately afterward, sitting and eating my soup, I had no recollection of what they asked or how I had answered.

Mark called and told me he was allowed another visit with Lori, a shorter one this time. He had described the lawyer interviews to Lori, and she decided that Mark should hire Grimaldo Achahui. Later in the day, Mr. Achahui tried to see Lori at DINCOTE, but was refused permission. Lori's formal deposition was scheduled for 9 a.m. Saturday, and he could meet with her then, but not before.

Mark sounded so very tired. He admitted to me that he'd had a lot of trouble sleeping, and that he had nightmares whenever he started to doze. Mark had reached the point where he wasn't sure he could think clearly. But he thought Saturday would be a really important day. After one week, Lori had still not been formally accused of anything. Mark thought that once Lori gave her deposition, the police would release her.

He wanted me to spend Saturday watching the news on TV, particularly the Spanish-language stations in case there was an announcement about Lori. He also suggested I invite Kathy and Judy and Ken to spend Saturday with me so I wouldn't be alone.

I had no doubt about Lori's innocence. I was telling everyone we were hoping the case wouldn't even go to trial, but everything I had heard the past week indicated otherwise. I was also troubled that Mr. Achahui had not been permitted to meet with Lori. Every day things seemed to get worse, and my utterances of hope were belied by the knots in my stomach. On the other hand, Mark, perhaps because his extreme fatigue compromised his judgment, really believed that there was a good chance she would be released and come home with him. But no one else did.

I turned on NY1. I had been told the story would be repeated every hour all night. But Michael Jackson, who was performing in New York, fainted while on stage, and his story replaced mine. My television debut was postponed.

Kathy, Ken, and Judy came to keep me company. We watched TV and waited. And waited. We were expecting something to happen, but we were not sure what. We couldn't do anything but stare at the TV, wait for a news report, and hope that Mark would call. The day progressed very slowly until Mark finally called at 11 p.m. His day was also one of waiting, in DINCOTE headquarters, with Ramsey and Tom. Lori's interrogation started at 10:40 a.m. and, except for a short lunch break, it continued uninterrupted until past 7 p.m. Mr. Achahui had a chance to explain the process during the lunch break, and Tom and Ramsey translated for Mark. Mark said that all he could remember was that although Mr. Achahui was introduced to Lori and was allowed to sit in the interrogation room, he was not permitted to speak with her.

At 7 p.m. Mr. Achahui returned to say the interrogation was over for the day. Lori had done a good job answering. But Mr. Achahui thought that some answers could be made clearer, and Colonel Gonzales agreed that this could be done on Sunday morning. Next, the statement, page by page, had to be typed, reviewed, signed or retyped and then signed. This process lasted another three and a half hours. At about 10:30 p.m., Lori's statement was signed and sealed, and it was agreed that the clarifications would be made at 9 a.m. on Sunday. After a whole day of extremely tense waiting, Ramsey, Tom, and Mark were exhausted. Mr. Achahui and Colonel Gonzales were also exhibiting signs of fatigue. But as they were ready to leave, Lori came out of the interrogation room, and, despite the grueling day, she smiled, waved, and seemed very confident.

We all jumped up when the phone finally rang. Mark apologized for keeping us waiting all day for an event that never happened. There was no public phone in DINCOTE, and he hadn't wanted to leave for fear of missing something. He promised to call again early the next day.

I knew what the day had been like for me, in my own home, amid close family, sitting and waiting for news, maybe news that Lori would be released. But I couldn't imagine what it must have been like for Mark, sitting all day in DINCOTE headquarters, just down the hall from Lori but unable to be with her or even know what was happening to her, much less help. Fortunately, he had the company of Ramsey, Tom, and Tom Holladay. The day was now over, but we really didn't know much more about Lori's fate than when it started. And I couldn't imagine what the day was like for Lori, facing The Jackal and his questions for nine hours, learning that the lawyer she had begged for when she called us five days earlier was not permitted to speak with her or give her advice until all formal proceedings were completed.

Mark called around noon on Sunday to say that Colonel Gonzales had changed his mind, and that Lori would not be allowed to clarify her statement. Lori was still not charged. Mr. Achahui explained that according to Peruvian law, the police could take up to fifteen days before charging a suspect in treason/terrorism cases. Mark suggested that I come to Peru so I could see Lori before those fifteen days were up, since it was unclear if we'd be allowed to visit Lori once she was formally charged.

We agreed that I would leave for Peru Monday morning, and then Mark would return to New York on Tuesday morning. This would allow time for him to fill me in on details Monday night and would get him to New York for his Tuesday night class. He had already missed a whole week of classes, and final exams were approaching. In spite of his exhaustion and his preoccupation with Lori, he still had obligations to his students. Ramsey had left Peru that morning, but Tom would be able to stay with me until December 15—the fifteenth day.

I was anxious to get to Peru. I needed to see Lori, and I wanted to know what was happening firsthand. I was glad Mark was coming home. He needed to rest. It was unfortunate that Ramsey had to leave—his political insights were invaluable—but I was very relieved to know that Tom would be there to help with legal questions and with Spanish.

I purchased airline tickets, called a colleague to arrange for further class coverage, asked Kathy to stay in the apartment while both Mark and I were away, and packed for the trip to Peru.

▪ Monday, December 11 to Friday, December 15

I left for Peru on Monday morning. I was scheduled to change planes in Miami and arrive in Lima at around 11 p.m. As luck would have it, my flight from New York to Miami was cancelled at the last minute, and although I caught the next possible flight, it did not reach Miami in time for my connection to Peru. Instead I spent five hours in the Miami airport waiting for the midnight flight. I called Mark and arranged to meet him the next morning at the Lima airport, where we could spend an hour together before he boarded his flight home.

I spent the entire day waiting in airports. I stared much of the time at the airport TV screens, thinking there might be news about Lori. I considered buying a mystery or adventure novel, but I knew I wouldn't be able to concentrate. For the past ten days I had been too busy to think beyond what I was doing at the moment. But there I was, finally alone with my thoughts; no phones were ringing, there were no faxes to send, and there was no one with me to joke about movie offers. My stomach was churning and my head was throbbing. It was at the airport that I started imagining the worst, that I would finally get to see Lori and she would be ill, or injured, or distraught, or that I would travel all the way to Peru and not be allowed to see her at all.

I have been to Peru many times since this first trip, and each time I have had the same fears, the same knotted stomach, and the same throbbing head, from the moment I leave for the airport until I actually see Lori.

The only reading material I had brought was a report by Human Rights Watch: Americas entitled "Peru, The Two Faces of Justice." Bob Schwartz, a colleague of Ramsey Clark, had given it to me. He was concerned that Mark and I, in spite of all we may have heard, still had an unrealistic view of Peruvian justice. He told me that this report would be upsetting but that I had to read it. While I waited in Miami, I followed his advice.

Bob was right. The report certainly didn't alleviate my anxiety about Lori's immediate safety, and it added to the more deep-seated fear for Lori's future. It was filled with accounts of secret trials, disappearances, long sentences, and torture. It had statistics and descriptions of legal issues and a discussion of the "repentance law," which allowed *arrepentidos,* those who repent, to receive reduced or suspended sentences for themselves or their relatives if they would implicate others. Hundreds, if not thousands, of innocent people were in prison because someone pointed a finger, often at someone they didn't even know.

The most heartrending parts were the accounts of selected cases. The one that remains in my mind is that of a mentally retarded woman who worked as a live-in maid. She did not know, nor could she comprehend, that she was employed by a high-ranking member of the Shining Path, a Peruvian guerrilla group. She was arrested along with her employer. She pleaded that she knew nothing about the Shining Path, and her employer testified that she was hired specifically because she was mentally retarded and would not understand anything about his activities. Nevertheless, she was sentenced to life in prison as a Shining Path leader. The report pointed out that she remains in prison, although prison guards have confirmed she is clearly mentally retarded.

When I finished reading, I found that my fear was now mixed with tremendous anger. I was angry that such a system existed and that, as far as I knew, aside from human rights activists, few Americans were even aware of it. Before reading the report I had some general idea that Peruvian justice left much to be desired, but I had no idea of the extent of the injustice or the cruelty. Reading the report made me want to scream.

The plane landed in Lima at about 5:30 a.m., and I met Mark in the airport coffee shop. I have never seen him look so exhausted or so distraught. To add to his misery, he had the flu. We spoke of his final visit with Lori on Monday, which would be his last one for a while. They had both tried to be cheerful for each other. They joked and talked and hugged. I could see the tears well up in his eyes as he told me how he traced the features of her face with his index finger—her forehead, eyebrows, nose, mouth, and chin—so he could remember her more precisely. As I hugged Mark and said good-bye, I promised I'd call at every opportunity. He said he would meet me at the airport when I came home, and was hoping that Lori would be with me.

Tom Nooter had accompanied Mark to the airport, and he went back with me to the Sheraton. Although there had been no journalists at the airport, they were already congregating outside the hotel when we arrived at about eight. They were also in front of the embassy when I went to meet Julie Grant and Tom Holladay, and they positively swarmed around Julie, Tom, and me when we arrived at DINCOTE for an afternoon visit with Lori.

I was so anxious to see Lori and so enormously relieved when I finally saw her. She greeted me with a big smile, a big hug and a big "hi, Mom!" She was wearing black slacks, a white shirt, and a maroon cotton blazer, the same clothes she wore in the newspaper photos. Her brown hair fell with a slight wave below her shoulders, almost to the middle of her back. We were sitting in someone's office, and police were coming and going in the room, but Lori and I tried to ignore them. We sat close together and talked in a whisper. Lori knew that her conversations with her lawyer had been monitored, and we were always concerned that someone was listening to us also—not just that day but on subsequent days in DINCOTE, and later years at prison visits. We had nothing criminal to hide, but it was so difficult to speak as mother and daughter with strangers listening in.

Lori wanted to know about everyone at home—Kathy, my father, Judy, and Ken and her cousins Jon and Matt. She asked about my cats, Muffin and Bon Bon. Lori referred to them as her little sisters, and wanted to hear about their latest adventures. We talked about all the people that were calling from across the country.

She discussed the prison. The food was not terrible. It was in fact the same as the food served in the DINCOTE cafeteria. Mr. Achahui had brought her fresh fruit. She joked that he was skilled at choosing fruit, but that she'd feel more confident in his skills as a lawyer if she knew he had at least once won a case. Mr. Achahui had told Mark he previously had defended those accused of terrorism. But he hadn't said, and embassy officials didn't tell us, that he had defended Victor Polay, founder and leader of the MRTA. After a spectacle of an arrest and a secret military tribunal, Mr. Polay had been sentenced to life in prison. Mr. Achahui was similarly unsuccessful with others accused of treason. But Lori knew—and I was learning—that there was not much a lawyer could do to affect the decision in these cases. At any rate, I was glad to see that Lori could still joke about her situation. It probably sounds strange to joke about such a serious matter, but Lori and I tended to do that, in conversations and letters, to try to find humor even in the serious, and especially in the bizarre.

I, in turn, joked that I had warned her that anthropology is a dangerous field of study. She should have stuck with mathematics. She replied that it wasn't anthropology that got her into this mess, it was music. Then she became more serious and said she had been thinking about her life and what had drawn her to Latin America and finally Peru. Her life's goals had changed when she was fourteen years old and a member of the junior high school chorus. The group had made a radio/TV commercial for the organization CARE. While the rest of the chorus sang, Lori did the voiceover about starving children throughout the world. Now, twelve years later, she told me that thoughts of starving children still haunted her.

I told Lori about the movie offers, and we entertained ourselves by deciding who should play whom. She said she had heard that the Peruvian newspapers were filled with stories of her supposed love affairs, and that if a movie were made, she'd insist that at least one of her lovers be played by Antonio Banderas. She promised to cast the other lovers by my visit the next day. Of course, this was all in fun, since we assumed no movie would actually be made. The last thing Lori would want was a movie made about her.

That evening Tom and I walked around downtown Lima while he filled me in on what he had learned during the week. I asked if he had spoken to Lori, and he said that although he and Ramsey were told by embassy officials that they had permission to see Lori, Colonel Gonzales refused to allow them to do so because they were not accredited as lawyers in Peru. However, he had spoken several times with Mr. Achahui and was starting to understand some of the Peruvian procedures. An important issue was still whether Lori was to be charged with terrorism, which would mean a civilian trial, or treason, which would mean a military tribunal. Colonel Gonzales had originally told embassy officials that a civilian trial was likely. However, in recent days, he indicated that he expected that Lori, and those arrested following the La Molina shoot-out, would be brought before a military tribunal. If that were the case, there wouldn't be a trial. A military judge, who didn't even have to be a lawyer, would look at the statements made by Lori and all the others, along with any evidence provided by the police, and make a decision of guilt or innocence. If guilty, he would impose a sentence. Lori still had not officially been charged with anything. But Peruvian law said police had fifteen days from arrest to do so, and in cases of treason that could be extended to thirty days. I asked Tom how Lori, a U.S. citizen, could be charged with treason in Peru. I was under the impression that you could only be treasonous against your own country. Tom said that Peru had its own definition of treason. Anyone accused of taking up arms against Peru or anyone considered a leader of what Peru deemed to be a terrorist group was charged with treason. Peru had already used this definition to convict several foreigners, but as yet no U.S. citizens, of treason. This was still perplexing to me. No one had said anything about Lori "taking up arms," and no one could possibly believe she was a leader of a terrorist group.

As we walked, we passed many newspaper kiosks, each surrounded by people reading the front pages hanging on the walls. Lori's photo was everywhere. Tom said it had been like that since he arrived. Although the raid in La Molina had resulted in the capture of some important members of the MRTA, it was Lori who made the headlines. The newspapers and TV reports were filled with all sorts of accusations: She rented the La Molina safe house where the shoot-out took place; she had false press credentials in order to enter the Peruvian Congress; she was a terrorist sympathizer; even that she was an international arms dealer. Every day presented a new sensational version of Lori's alleged activities. As each fantastic report faded, another, even more outrageous, would appear. All of these activities were said to have aided the MRTA in a future plan to kidnap members of the Peruvian Congress. It was all insane. Lori may have sympathized with the plight of the poor, she may have been critical of the Peruvian government—but arms dealer? Kidnap members of Congress?

Colonel Gonzales had told Tom and Ramsey about the rental of the La Molina house, but when asked if they could see the lease, the Colonel demurred. Lori did not sign the lease. She did not rent the house after all. Lori lived in an apartment in San Borja, nowhere near La Molina. Tom said he saw Lori's doorman on TV, telling reporters that Lori was a model tenant, saying that he witnessed the police search of her apartment and they hadn't found arms, attack plans, subversive literature, or pamphlets—just clothes and books.

We already knew that Lori's press credentials were authentic and had been issued by the appropriate Peruvian agencies, and didn't understand why the police insisted on saying they were false. And as for the accusation of arms dealer, this seemed to be based on the fact that Lori knew Pacífico Castrellón, a Panamanian citizen who also had been arrested on November 30 and accused of transporting weapons to Peru for the MRTA. Castrellón was seen on Peruvian TV literally on his knees, begging forgiveness and pleading for mercy. Castrellón "repented" and pointed to Lori, saying she was an international organizer. I suggested to Tom that in court it would be Lori's word against his, and I was sure that Lori's word would prevail. But Tom reminded me that if the case was to be heard by a military tribunal, there would be no courtroom and no opportunity for Lori or Mr. Achahui to cross-examine Castrellón, or for Lori to explain anything at all. That's why we had to hope for a civilian trial, where evidence would be subject to inspection, witnesses would be subject to cross-examination, and Lori would be able to testify. But again, I was painfully aware of how many cases there were of innocent people who had been wrongly convicted of terrorism by civilian courts that also had hooded, unidentifiable judges.

The next three days were a round of trips to and from the embassy, to and from DINCOTE, to and from Mr. Achahui's office. There was little time to rest or eat. Sometimes meals were limited to the M&M peanuts in the hotel room mini-fridge. We spent a lot of time sitting in traffic and waiting at DINCOTE. In the evenings, Tom and I were interviewed by Peruvian press and TV journalists.

All of my visits with Lori took place on the thirteenth floor of DINCOTE, sometimes in an office, sometimes in the hallway. It was not usual for so many detainees to be held at this facility, or for them to have visitors, and unlike most prisons there was no special room to accommodate visits. Sometimes some of Lori's codefendants were also on the thirteenth floor visiting with their family members or meeting their lawyers. There were always police coming and going, typing, filing, talking, listening, and sewing. The official statements of all twenty-one detainees and all records of evidence were actually hand-sewn into one very thick volume.

At one visit Lori introduced me to Nancy Gilvonio. I had read about Nancy in the early press reports, where she was identified as a Bolivian named Rosa. She was working as a photojournalist, and Lori knew her by her Bolivian identity. She did not know that Nancy was married to Nestor Cerpa, a leader of the MRTA. Rosa (Nancy) was also in the Congress on November 30, and she too was arrested and taken off the bus in downtown Lima early that evening.

As Lori and I sat huddled, whispering, she described her arrest and its aftermath.

She had gone to the Congress on November 30, as she had several other times, to gather material for the articles she was writing—to observe the debates and to see how individuals

voted and argued. But on that day the discussion centered on
a recently exposed scandal involving the appropriation of the
homes of arrested drug traffickers by high-level officials in the
Peruvian National Police, and after a while, Lori decided that
the debate was not of interest for what she was writing. She
preferred to go home and listen to the outcome on the TV
news. Nancy also decided to leave, and at about 7 p.m. they
boarded a bus for their respective trips home.

After a few blocks, several men got onto the bus and
dragged Lori and Nancy out, separately, to waiting cars. Lori
thought she was being kidnapped, kidnapping being common
in Lima. She yelled and tried to get away but could not. She
was driven to DINCOTE headquarters, where she was asked her
address, occupation, etc., and her personal possessions, including her money, credit card, and watch, were taken.

I had already pieced together that information from newspaper and embassy reports. But I had assumed that Lori spent
that night, like all succeeding nights, in DINCOTE. I had no
idea that she was driven to the house in La Molina at about 8
p.m., and was held there in the car until well after daylight the
next morning—hours during which all hell seemed to break
out around her.

When she first arrived all was quiet, but she could see
what appeared to be police in civilian clothing holding weapons while sitting in unmarked cars. And then the shooting
started. Lori was thrown facedown on the floor of the car, and
when a grenade landed very close by, the car was driven down
the street. Later, after gunfire broke out right behind her and
the police threw themselves to the ground or behind trees and
cars, Lori was moved two blocks further away. But she still
could hear the shooting. At times she was permitted to sit;
other times she was pushed again to the floor. It was absolutely harrowing. For hours she listened to the intensified gun
battles, not knowing what was happening at the house or

its surroundings, and not knowing what would happen to her. She was frightened for herself, for those in the targeted house, and for the families in nearby homes. In the morning, the shooting had ended, and before she was returned to DINCOTE, Lori was moved closer to the scene of the fighting. She saw a multitude of military vehicles. The fronts of all the houses in the area were riddled with bullet holes. It wasn't until much later, in DINCOTE, that she learned what went on that night.

As I listened to Lori's account of that evening, I became more and more horrified. But we were sitting in DINCOTE trying not to show any emotions, not wanting to let the police know how we felt. I was just so, so thankful that Lori wasn't harmed. I wondered why she, but not Nancy, was taken to La Molina. Maybe the police thought that such a harrowing experience would convince Lori to "repent."

During another visit Lori pointed out Pacífico Castrellón. Lori told me that she had met him in an art gallery in Panama on her way to Peru in November 1994. He was an architect and an artist. She had remained friendly with him, had met his friends and often borrowed his van when she needed a car. Despite reports in the Peruvian press, he and Lori were not romantically involved, although Lori hinted that fifty-two-year-old, married Castrellón, might have preferred that they were.

Castrellón's name was on the lease to the house in La Molina. It was a large house, one that could accommodate many visitors and Lori sometimes stayed in a room there when she was not traveling elsewhere in Peru or other South American countries. After a while, a portion of the house was sublet and then Lori decided to rent the apartment in San Borja in order to have more privacy. Lori told me, as she had told Mark and as she had told Colonel Gonzales on many occasions, she knew absolutely nothing about weapons hidden in false ceilings in the house. She had never even visited the sublet portion of the house, had absolutely no knowledge that members of the MRTA were living there, and certainly knew nothing of any plans to kidnap members of the Peruvian Congress.

Lori had met with many people, at many places, while in Peru. If some were members of the MRTA they would not have identified themselves as such or revealed their real names or their positions in the organization. And speaking with them did not make her a member of the group. She told the police repeatedly that she was not a member of the MRTA, had never worked for them and knew nothing of their plans.

I told Lori that Castrellón had "repented" and made accusations against her. As it turned out, the police had already told her that he had accused her of all sorts of crazy things. Lori said that some of the women detainees had been threatened with torture, and it was possible that Castrellón was threatened also. DINCOTE has a long history of torturing detainees, even those who have absolutely no useful information. She added that Castrellón had a family in Panama, and he probably would have said anything to minimize his sentence. Maybe he was even hoping his testimony would lead to his release.

Lori had been asked if she wanted to repent. Of course she could not predict what she might or might not agree to do if she were subjected to torture. But otherwise, she would never apologize for something she had never done, would never say she was guilty when she was innocent, and would never, ever look for favors by pointing a finger at someone else. And I certainly would not ask her to do so.

Before I left for Peru, friends in the States suggested that I should be pragmatic, encourage Lori to "cooperate," convince the authorities she was psychologically unstable, or do whatever it takes to get her home. I was aware that while some people naturally "connected" to Lori, others just did not understand her. A brief biography—dates, places, hobbies, people she knew—didn't help explain her. Yes, she likes music and movies and has favorite movie stars. She succeeded academically, can solve mathematical equations, and plays the guitar. But none of that explains why she was in Peru, or why she wouldn't cry, confess, or repent.

Lori has written, "I have done most everything I've done, and certainly all important things I've done, because it was my moral obligation to do so." And as I sat with her in DINCOTE, she reminded me once again that it was her moral obligation not to be silent, that to be silent in the face of social injustice and abuse is to be an accomplice to evil. She was not a saint and did not wish to be a martyr. She simply strongly held to her principles. She certainly was different from the members of her generation who focused solely on the comfort of themselves and their families and friends. And she also differed from people like myself who were deeply angered by injustice but made little effort to effect change. As I listened to Lori, as much as I wanted her to come home, I could not ask her to forget her sense of moral obligation and be pragmatic. Relinquishing her principles would have meant total defeat. I also sensed that I would no longer be a silent accomplice.

On my visits to DINCOTE I had several opportunities to meet with Colonel Gonzales. He was always extremely polite. Our conversations were always with an interpreter, but he was soft-spoken with a kind smile, even when he told me it was too bad that my daughter was a terrorist who would spend a long time in prison. At one visit I asked if he could return the books taken from Lori's apartment, textbooks on women's rights and feminist issues, and the tape of Lori singing Afro-Peruvian music that she had made for Mark's birthday. I pointed out that none of these personal items were relevant to the case. But, smiling once again, he said they were now and would remain police property. I asked him if Lori's eye-glasses and her money, which still had not been returned to her, were also to remain police property. He didn't respond.

Colonel Gonzales always made a point of reminding me that he was not pleased with our choice of lawyer. He claimed that Mr. Achahui was a member of the MRTA. After all, why else would he have defended so many of them! I knew that when Ramsey and Tom learned that Mr. Achahui had defended Victor Polay, they had agonized over whether or not to change attorneys. But the fact remained that he was still the only attorney with the appropriate experience who was also committed to helping Lori. I recalled that Mr. Achahui had told us he no longer owned a car because he was afraid it would be bombed, and that he—like others who defended those accused of terrorism—risked being accused and convicted himself. So, although the Colonel was trying to convince me to change lawyers, his accusations only succeeded in explaining why there were so few lawyers willing to defend those accused of terror-ism. It was easy to understand why most Peruvians accused of terrorism were defended by "faceless" DINCOTE-assigned pub-lic defense attorneys, lawyers who, like the judge and prosecu-tors, wore hoods when they met with their clients so nobody would know their identity.

On Wednesday morning Tom and I were contacted by a man who said he had "connections," and could arrange for Lori's release. Although he wasn't specific, the general idea was that his connections and $300,000 put into the right pockets would do the job. On one hand, several people had suggested that there should be a way to buy Lori's freedom. On the other hand, we had been warned to beware of seemingly sincere people who would take our money and run. Tom decided to test the usefulness of this particular gentleman's connections. Tom explained that he had not been permitted to meet with Lori, and proposed that this gentleman demonstrate his abilities by arranging for him to consult with her. The gentleman said it was as good as done. When we arrived at DINCOTE that afternoon, it would be arranged. It sounded good, but it never came to pass. The embassy made inquiries and discovered that a lawyer mentioned by this gentleman did indeed have a reputation for being able to "buy people out" of prison. But, apparently, Lori's was not a case that could be bought off. It was President Fujimori who, for whatever reasons, held up Lori's passport on television claiming she was a terrorist, and he was watching procedures very carefully.

On Friday morning, December 15, we went to DINCOTE to see Lori. This was the fifteenth day, the day when Lori and the others were to be charged. Although there was still some hope that the foreigners, Lori and Castrellón, would not be accused of treason and would be given civilian trials, Colonel Gonzales had said that this was unlikely. He then told all the families that we could return again that night at 6 p.m. for a final visit.

Tom and I were leaving that night for New York, but fortunately our flight wasn't until midnight. We checked out of the hotel, went to the embassy to say good-bye to Tom Holladay, and then to Mr. Achahui's office to say good-bye there. At 6 p.m., I went with Tom and Julie Grant to see Lori one last time. The thirteenth floor was crowded with visitors waiting to see detainees. The police were racing around with papers, and the atmosphere was chaotic. After a few minutes Colonel Gonzales appeared and announced that plans had changed, that all the detainees would be held for another fifteen days at DINCOTE before they would be formally charged. The prosecutor and police needed more time for their investigations. I recalled that Peruvian law allowed the investigation to extend to thirty days in cases of treason. The good news was that I could continue seeing Lori. The bad news was that they chose to treat this as a treason case and it would be heard by a military tribunal. And military tribunals almost always convicted.

.

▪ Saturday, December 16 to Thursday, December 21

Tom had to return to obligations in New York. But I couldn't leave Peru knowing I would be forfeiting chances to see Lori. I checked back into the Sheraton and called Mark to update him. Kathy was with him at the time. She wanted to join me. She wanted to see Lori. We arranged for her to arrive Monday morning.

Saturday and Sunday were very quiet. I went to see Lori both days, but the visits were very brief, about ten minutes, because DINCOTE was short-staffed on the weekends. I finally got some rest and was able to focus on writing a final exam for my physics class. The exam was scheduled for Tuesday, and I once again imposed upon my colleagues to administer it. But it was my responsibility to write the exam, grade it, and assign final grades. So on Sunday I handwrote the exam, and on Monday faxed it to Nassau Community College. That part of my life seemed so far away. I was reminded that there was a time, not so long ago, when I encountered problems that had logical answers. I missed the logic. I missed being in the classroom. I wanted my old life back.

Kathy's arrival provided a big boost to Lori's spirits, and mine too. Although invariably conversation during our visits with Lori turned to details of her case, most of the time we reminisced, joked, and just talked about whatever came to mind. Kathy had brought along photos of her cats. Cats are always a big source of entertainment in our family. We discussed movies we had seen recently and books we were reading. Kathy talked about her research for her thesis and how she was progressing on the furnishing of her new apartment. Lori had been at the apartment in September when the first new item of furniture, a sofa, had arrived, and Kathy brought her up to date on her later acquisitions. Each day, back in the hotel, Kathy and I planned what we would do the next day to keep things cheerful. We also visited the supermarket and bought some of Lori's favorite foods and toiletries. DINCOTE encouraged visitors to bring food to supplement what they provided, and things like soap, toothpaste, and toothbrushes that they didn't supply at all.

We visited for an hour or so each day, and we knew that was the only break Lori had from her prison cell, not counting her nightly interrogations by Colonel Gonzales. It seemed that every night, at about 2 or 3 a.m., Lori was awakened and brought to Gonzales's office. One night there was a gun on his desk, and he asked Lori to pick it up. She, of course, refused. Another night he showed her a magazine photo of a female MRTA soldier holding a rifle. Gonzales said that he thought it was Lori. Lori told us that aside from the woman having long dark hair, the photo looked nothing like her. Nevertheless, the photo appeared the next day in the Peruvian papers.

The DINCOTE police gave whatever information they wanted to the Peruvian press who then printed it as "the truth." In fact, although the three of us talked in whispers with occasional outbursts of laughter, the newspapers reported "sources" detailing violent arguments as Lori's mother and sister screamed at her to confess. After all, if the police, through the media, could convince the Peruvian public that "even her family knows she's guilty," certainly no one would clamor that she needed a trial.

Like the previous week, our visits were sometimes in an office and sometimes in the hallway. Kathy and I often waited for Lori in a large corner room with wraparound picture windows looking out over downtown Lima. The remaining walls were filled with bookcases, one of which held a set of books edited by Lenin. I assume they were confiscated from previously arrested "leftists." It was amusing to imagine Colonel Gonzales reading books by Lenin, a thought that was complemented by the TV report that the Marxist members of the MRTA were playing Monopoly when the shoot-out started at the La Molina house.

On Wednesday, the newspapers highlighted the "press presentation" of Miguel Rincón and Jaime Ramirez, two of the men arrested at the La Molina house. Rincon was alleged to be the second in command of the MRTA, and Ramirez was said to be a high-ranking leader of the group. The two men were paraded before journalists in striped prison garb and allowed to say a few words. This practice dated back to 1992, when the police started parading nearly everyone detained on terrorism charges in these striped "jailbird" suits. The rules were changed around 1994, so that now police could present a detainee to the press only if there were evidence that he or she was a terrorist leader. Mr. Achahui, the press, and embassy officials speculated that police did not think Lori was a terrorist leader because she was not presented. I asked Lori about this. She said that Colonel Gonzales told her several times that she wouldn't be presented, but he did not say why.

Meanwhile, we were learning more about military tribunals. Embassy officials had asked for permission to attend Lori's trial, only to learn there would be no trial to attend. There was only the case file, the hand-stitched compilation that would include information about Lori and the other defendants. It would contain the defendants' statements, a review of the evidence presented by the police, and the conclusions of the prosecutor as to the degree of participation of each defendant. When the file was deemed complete, Mr. Achahui would be informed that he could review it. He and the twenty other attorneys in this case would each have a portion of the twelve hours allocated for reviewing the one copy of the file that would probably be well over two thousand pages. At best he could give a cursory reading to some parts and hope that the parts he did not have time to glance at were not important for Lori's defense. After that, he would present a written defense to the judge, or possibly, if permitted, a short oral defense. Sentencing would take place twenty-four to forty-eight hours later. So each day we checked with Mr. Achahui to see if he had been notified about his access to the case file. As the week wore on it became clear that, despite rumors to the contrary, nothing would happen before Christmas. This did not stop newspapers from printing headlines, on several occasions reading LORI BERENSON TO BE SENTENCED TODAY. But I had long since learned that the Peruvian newspapers were not a good source of information.

As Christmas approached, Kathy and I had to decide how long we would stay in Peru. The embassy was already short-staffed and would have only a skeleton crew during the Christmas–New Year period. And DINCOTE officials indicated that they too would be short of personnel and visits would be very brief or not permitted at all. It didn't make sense to stay if we couldn't visit Lori. And then, I had to return to New York, at least temporarily, to grade exams and submit final grades. Although I wanted to be in Peru when the judge issued his verdict, I knew that I would not be allowed to be with Lori when the verdict was announced. I would only hear about it on the news.

We were told that after the verdict, Lori would be moved to the maximum-security prison in Chorrillos, Lima, regardless of whether she was found guilty or innocent. According to Peruvian law, even if the judge declared Lori innocent, the police have an automatic appeal, and Lori would remain in prison during the appeals process. If Lori were found guilty, she could appeal while remaining incarcerated. We expected the verdict would come just after the new year. So Kathy and

I decided to leave on the evening of December 21. Then I would return to Lima to visit Lori in Chorrillos, in early January.

Before we left, we brought Lori some things that she might need in Chorrillos, including a Bible. We were told that in some maximum-security prisons that was the only reading permitted. Lori gave us some personal items to hold for her in New York, because she was told that when prisoners moved from one prison to another, personal belongings often got left behind. Once again, we all tried to smile for each other, but this parting was very difficult. I tried not to think about Lori being alone for ten or more days in that horrible place. I would not be able to see her or speak with her, and with the embassy short-staffed, I might not get regular reports about her. But even if I stayed, I wouldn't see her. I had to go.

As Kathy and I prepared to leave DINCOTE, we couldn't help but notice the cheerful Christmas decorations. I wondered if they also decorated the rooms that they used to torture detainees. As we waited for the elevator, we noticed the police dragging four-foot-tall bags, each with a large Santa Claus face on it. The bags were filled with bullets and other ammunition they had taken from the house in La Molina. A surreal end to a surreal visit to Peru.

▪ Christmas to New Year's Day

I returned to New York and completed the end-of-semester paperwork. From the last week of December until the middle of January, Mark and I were free from all teaching duties. In addition to the holidays, December 24 is our wedding anniversary, December 29 is Mark's birthday, and the first week in January had, in recent years, been spent on vacation—away from work and away from the cold.

As soon as I returned we cancelled our vacation plans. But we decided to try as best we could to keep up some other traditions. For the past twenty or so years we celebrated our anniversary at a performance of the Alvin Ailey Dance Theater. Mark and I very much enjoy modern dance, and the Ailey Company, one of our favorites, is always in New York in December. So on December 24 we set out to celebrate thirty-two years of marriage with an evening at the ballet. But at the first intermission, we left. Neither of us could enjoy the performance.

Invariably, everything, then and every minute since Lori's arrest, reminded us of her. That night we were reminded of the times she and Kathy had come with us to see the Ailey Company. Although neither of them ever became fans of ballet, they both enjoyed the Ailey signature piece, "Revelations," performed with a live gospel chorus.

We left the theater and walked along Fifth Avenue, toward Rockefeller Center with its big tree and Christmas angels. And Lori was everywhere. Across from Rockefeller Center we saw Saks Fifth Avenue, where Lori sang Christmas carols in 1982 and 1983 as part of her junior high school chorus. And on the next corner there was St. Patrick's Cathedral, where Lori sang carols with her high school chamber chorus in 1986.

Musical reminders of Lori are inescapable. Music has always been so much part of her life. Wherever she traveled, she had a guitar. One of her greatest pleasures was learning and singing new music. The first thing she did when she came home was to pick up the guitar and sing for us. Between visits, she would send us tapes. We have tapes filled with old folk songs, classical choral pieces, and the music of Central and South America. Some tapes had a theme, like romantic melodies, old favorites, or Peruvian folk songs. Others have titles to remind us of the place or time when they were made, like "Lori in El Salvador" or—one of our favorites—"Lori with Mononucleosis."

So, on December 24 we went home early and we played a tape Lori had made for us in 1993. It opened with the message, "The next song I'm going to dedicate to my mother and father for their thirtieth wedding anniversary. It's called "Amada Mia," and it would be sung from Dad to Mom." It was one of the most beautiful songs she sang. But on our thirty-second anniversary it only made us miss her more. Mark's birthday on the 29th was also sad. The family had a tradition of giving each other handmade birthday cards and, often, homemade gifts. This year, there was no card from Lori, and the tape of Afro-Peruvian music she had made especially for Mark's fifty-fourth birthday now belonged to Colonel Gonzales.

On December 26, Gerry Fuller, the consular officer on duty for the holidays, called to say that he had visited Lori at DINCOTE. Lori asked him to tell us that she was fine. She also thought I might be amused by the latest "2 a.m. incident." On Christmas Eve at about 2 a.m., she and three other prisoners were "invited" by the Colonel and members of the DINCOTE staff to participate in a holiday toast, a toast to the demise of the MRTA.

▪ Wednesday, January 3 to Thursday, January 11

On January 3, Mr. Achahui was called to read the case file. He was allotted one hour and forty minutes to look through the more than two thousand pages that constituted the file on all twenty-one codefendants. He formally requested that the judge allow him one half hour for an oral defense, in addition to the written defense.

On January 4, Gerry Fuller informed us that Lori had been transferred from the DINCOTE building to a small jail across the street. He said that conditions there were rather dismal. The cell was only six feet by six feet with a low ceiling, just about Lori's height, and she was sharing it with a codefendant who had received five bullet wounds during the shootout in La Molina. They slept on mattresses on the floor. The mattresses filled the cell. The entire facility was filthy and rat-infested. Lori told Mr. Fuller that although she wasn't being mistreated, her cellmate was receiving inadequate medical treatment. She had been operated on for her wounds, but it appeared that she was released too quickly from the hospital. She asked Mr. Fuller to inform us of the problem so that we could inform the International Red Cross.

With the help of Tom Nooter, we contacted the chief of the Red Cross delegation in Lima, who said that they were well aware of the wounded cellmate's situation; the doctors had tried to visit her at the prison but were denied access. It was hard to imagine the cruelty of it. Depriving a detainee of needed medical treatment was surely a form of torture. And I knew that Lori must have been overwhelmed with frustration, wanting to get help for this unfortunate woman.

On the same day, the prosecuting attorney met with the judge. Neither Lori nor Mr. Achahui was permitted to attend this meeting, and we still do not know what specific charges the prosecutor made against Lori. All we learned was that the prosecutor asked that Lori be found guilty of treason and sentenced to thirty years in prison. Thirty years! We couldn't believe it. I wanted to cry but I was numb. All our hopes now rested with the judge.

Mr. Achahui went before the judge on the morning of January 8, and he was allowed to present a twenty-minute oral argument. He argued that Lori was innocent and that nothing he saw in the file warranted a charge of treason, and further that the case should be moved to a civilian court.

That afternoon, we received calls from Reuters and Associated Press correspondents in Lima. They told us that Lori had been presented to the press. She was in civilian clothes, not the striped prison garb, and she spoke, actually shouted, for about a minute. Both reporters had taped her speech and said they would send us a transcript. They suggested we might be able to see it on a Spanish-language news broadcast in New York.

We watched the news and were frightened beyond belief by what we saw. Lori hardly looked like the same person I had seen eighteen days earlier. She was screaming, her face distorted as she yelled. She was disheveled. Her eyes looked like they belonged to someone else. I knew Lori's eyes and these weren't her eyes. At first I thought she had been drugged. She looked so angry. Then I remembered Lori's wounded cellmate, and I thought, of course Lori was angry. I guessed that she had not slept for days. The smiling, confident, calm Lori was gone. What had they done to her?

She had started speaking as she walked up the stairs to the stage and then stood, hands at her sides, flanked by two female guards in sunglasses and miniskirts. Some members of the audience were shouting, *"Traison a la Patria,"* "Treason against the Fatherland." Other journalists shouted questions at her. But this was not a real press conference with questions and answers. The news broadcast only showed snippets, and the TV reporter spoke over Lori's voice, so I never heard what she said. The scene then jumped to tables displaying all sorts of weapons. And lastly, I saw an interview with Colonel Gonzales, who declared that Lori had just admitted her guilt, that she was a member of the MRTA.

We were almost paralyzed with fright and overwhelmed with questions. Why was she presented when Colonel Gonzales said she wouldn't be? Did they surround her with weapons to make it look like she was an arms dealer? Did they set her up to look guilty? The answers to those questions weren't difficult to surmise. But there were other questions for which I had no answers. What had they done to Lori? Was she tortured? Was she okay now? I was sure that whatever happened to her would not have happened if I hadn't left Peru. Maybe if I had stayed they might not have put her in the cell with the wounded woman. Or maybe I could have helped Lori's cellmate get the medical attention she needed. Or if I had been able to visit Lori, they couldn't have mistreated her or her cellmate. It went on and on. I never should have left Peru. Now, more than four years later, at quiet moments these thoughts painfully return.

Some small relief came with the transcripts and then a translation of what she said. In spite of pronouncements by Colonel Gonzales, she never admitted any kind of guilt, and she never said she was a member of the MRTA. More importantly, the words, if not the facial expressions, were from the Lori we knew—words of compassion and commitment.

> I am to be condemned for my concern about the conditions of hunger and misery that exists in this country. Here nobody can deny that in Peru there is much injustice. There is an institutionalized violence that has killed the people's finest sons and has condemned children to die of hunger. If it is a crime to worry about the subhuman conditions in which the majority of this population lives, then I will accept my pun-

ishment. But this is not a love of violence. This is not
to be a criminal terrorist because in the MRTA there are
no criminal terrorists. It is a revolutionary movement.

I love this people. I love this people and although
this love is going to make—cost—me years in prison,
I will never stop loving, and never will lose the hope
and confidence that there will be a new day of justice
in Peru.

Whatever had happened to make her shout these words,
whatever had happened to distort her face, whatever had happened to make her so angry, nothing could stop her from expressing her concern for those suffering conditions of hunger
and misery. She still carried the message of the CARE commercial she made twelve years before. She was still haunted by the
thought of starving children, and if that was a crime, then she
would accept her punishment.

We spoke to Julie Grant after she visited Lori and talked
with her about this press presentation. She explained to Lori
that the television commentary made it difficult to hear her
words, and that the press had focused on her defiant tone,
ignoring the words. When she told Lori that the press reported
that she had admitted to being a militant, or member of the
MRTA, Lori immediately protested, saying that she had admitted no such thing. Yes, she did say that the MRTA did not have
"delinquent terrorists." She explained that she made a distinction between "revolutionary" and "terrorist" organizations, and
in her distinction the MRTA was revolutionary. Then Lori
quickly and emphatically added that she was not a terrorist
and was incapable of participating in terrorist activities.

On January 9, all the newspapers, in Peru and the United
States, carried a photo of Lori, mouth wide open and distorted,
eyes wild. Neither TV nor print media included Lori's words,
only the image. A woman with a distorted face, screaming, is

not very sympathetic. And what we recognized as anger was seen as defiance or militancy. People across Peru saw this picture and combined it in their minds with the picture of the weapons and the words of Colonel Gonzales. Everyone declared her to be guilty. No one ever heard what she said. No one cared what she said. And no one knew the whole story.

On January 11, specifically citing the press presentation as proof of Lori's involvement, a hooded, anonymous judge found Lori guilty of treason and sentenced her to life in prison with no possibility of parole.

PART TWO

HOW DID

THIS

HAPPEN?

■ Reflections

We could not accept the possibility of thirty years, and now it was "life with no possibility of parole." How? Why? Mark and I had spent our professional lives immersed in the fields of mathematics and physics, disciplines based on logic, and we could not make sense of the Kafka-like military tribunals and so-called justice in Peru.

There was much speculation in the United States and Peru, by the media and ordinary citizens, about why Lori was arrested, why the Peruvian government decided to keep her in the headlines, and why she was singled out for such harsh treatment. I heard more than once that the raid on the house in La Molina was a hastily conceived attack designed to make headlines, replacing the late November coverage of an embarrassing government scandal involving high-ranking military police officers who had taken personal possession of real estate confiscated from drug dealers. The raid and arrests at La Molina rapidly diverted attention. But the question remained: "Why Lori?"

Lori's visits to the Peruvian Congress had clearly put her in the wrong place at the wrong time. But the Peruvian government decided to a focus on Lori, not on Pacífico Castrellón, a Panamanian, or Nancy Gilvonio, believed at that time to be Bolivian. In his televised address the day after the arrests, it was Lori's passport President Fujimori waved, it was Lori whom he called a *"gringa terrorista."* In addition to being tough on terrorism, Fujimori was also now seen by his public as standing up to the United States.

Lori was arrested in a country where the president controls both the legislature and the judiciary, so that a presidential pronouncement of *"gringa terrorista"* is an instant conviction. No one could imagine Mr. Fujimori returning to television to admit that he made a mistake, to say there was no evidence that Lori Berenson was associated with terrorism. And what judge would risk defying authority?

President Fujimori used Lori to send a message—to human rights activists, freelance journalists, and others who work on behalf of the poor—to stay out of Peru. And maybe he planned to use Lori as a bargaining chip. The Peruvian government was angered that Israel was planning to sell military aircraft to Ecuador, Peru's border enemy. Because the planes had U.S. parts, the United States had to approve the sale, and there was speculation that the U.S. decision on the planes would determine Lori's fate. Then, as the United States approved the sale, Peru sentenced Lori.

While I was speculating on the motives of Fujimori and the Peruvian government, others were asking about Lori. Who is she really? What was she doing in Peru?

▪ Looking Back

Lori spent most of her childhood in Manhattan. A week after Lori's fifth birthday we moved to East Midtown Plaza, a complex of buildings between First and Second Avenues, between 23rd and 25th Streets, that was built specifically to accommodate middle-income families. Most of our present neighbors moved in with us over twenty-five years ago, attracted as we were by the reasonable cost, the wide-open plaza with children's playgrounds, and the good local public schools. Lori attended Public School 40 on 20th Street and then Junior High School 104. Lori's life was filled with friends, after-school activities, and sleepovers, just like all the other girls in the neighborhood. She was always a serious student with a particular talent for mathematics and science. And then there was music.

We no longer have the tiny violin she learned to play when she was eight, but I remember how the two of us went skipping down Second Avenue, violin case swinging, on the way to music school. I don't know why we started skipping, but it became one of the fun things we did every Friday. When Lori traded the violin for a clarinet, the skipping stopped but not the wonderful hours I spent listening to her practice. While at J.H.S. 104, she realized her musical strength was her voice. She sang in the school madrigal chorus and in the school productions of Broadway musicals, including the title role in *Jesus Christ, Superstar*. When it came time for high school, Lori passed the exams for Stuyvesant High School and the Bronx High School of Science, both known for their emphasis on science and math. But she was also accepted at the LaGuardia High School of Music and Art and Performing Arts, and she decided it offered the best possibility of combining a good academic education while continuing to study music. She was right. A similar decision was made when she chose to attend the Massachusetts Institute of Technology, M.I.T., in fall 1987.

Although M.I.T. is known for its engineering and science departments, it also has well-respected programs in liberals arts. So while Lori was studying physics and calculus, she also sang in the chamber chorus and took several courses in anthropology and political science. It was then that she developed a strong interest in the people and culture of Latin America. She worked as a research assistant for Martin Diskin, a professor of anthropology and well-known authority on agrarian economics in Central America. Lori helped analyze land and wealth distribution in El Salvador and assisted in a project studying Salvadoran immigration patterns and requests for political asylum. Martin Diskin remained Lori's mentor and friend long after she left M.I.T., until his sad and untimely death in 1997.

When Lori came home on school breaks she talked about her studies and encouraged me to read some of what she had been reading. She reminded me that several years earlier we had watched a movie, *Choices of the Heart,* about four American women, three nuns and a lay worker, who on December 2, 1980, were raped and killed by right-wing death squads in El Salvador. I borrowed a copy of *Murdered in Central America,* which recounts this incident and the U.S. government's attempts to "minimize—and even at times justify" the execution of Ita, Maura, Dorothy, and Jean. Similarly, there were books about Archbishop Oscar Romero, who had been savagely gunned down in San Salvador, the capital, on March 24, 1980, while saying Mass, a day after he pleaded with the Salvadoran National Guard, police, and military, "in the name of God stop the repression."

I found I was following newspaper stories about El Salvador more closely. In the 1980s, a civil war raged between the right-wing Salvadoran government, and supporters of the FMLN (Farabundo Martí National Liberation Front). The United States strongly supported the government with arms, money, and advice, despite reports that they were aiding death squads and other human rights violators.

The more Lori learned about El Salvador, the more she needed to know. And she wanted to learn the contemporary history and culture of that country directly from the people living it. She took intensive courses in Spanish, and in March 1988, while still a freshman at M.I.T., she spent her two-week spring break visiting El Salvador. She traveled with a group of Quaker women, visited villages on the outskirts of San Salvador, and met many Salvadorans, taking note of their lives and their reaction to the war and the U.S. involvement. One afternoon she observed in horror—fortunately from a safe distance—as helicopters strafed a village. It was a village she had visited only hours earlier, a village filled with civilians, women, and children struggling for survival. The helicopters were almost surely donated by the United States.

The two weeks that Lori spent in El Salvador were certainly harrowing for me. Although I knew she was traveling with a group of mature women, who would take every necessary precaution, we were not in daily contact and I could not help but worry. People often ask how I could let her go. After all, she was so young, only eighteen. I never felt I had a choice, and anyone who knows Lori understands that. Mark and I always encouraged Lori to be independent and to have the courage of her convictions. We knew that Lori couldn't sit by and do nothing while she knew others were suffering. And I quickly realized when she returned from that trip, I knew from her face and voice when she told me what she had seen and heard, that she would be going back.

In January 1989, Lori participated in a student-exchange program at the University of El Salvador. The exchange included morning Spanish-language instruction and afternoon meetings to learn about contemporary El Salvador. She met with representatives of community organizations, women's groups, and youth centers. She visited poor neighborhoods and health clinics to view firsthand the obstacles to meeting human needs in a time of war. During this visit it was difficult for Lori to ignore the high price of war. In a letter home, she wrote that she felt so guilty for having so much when she saw such poverty, misery, and hopelessness among war-torn families.

Lori and the other exchange students initially roomed at a boardinghouse. But later, they relocated to the homes of students they met at the University of El Salvador. Lori had made the acquaintance of Mario Flores, an economics student and she moved in with him, his wife, Doris, and their two small children.

On February 2, 1989, Lori's M.I.T. mentor, Martin Diskin, was visiting El Salvador along with Massachusetts congressman Jim McGovern. At that time, Mr. McGovern was an aide to Congressman Joe Moakley. They met for lunch that afternoon in the Camino Real, an upscale hotel in San Salvador, with Lori, human rights worker Jennifer Casolo, and Ruben Zamora, the founder of one of El Salvador's main political parties, the Democratic Convergence. Mr. Zamora's brother had been assassinated while serving as El Salvador's attorney general, and Ruben Zamora devoted all his efforts toward seeking peace in his country.

When Lori returned that evening to the Flores's home, she found the house in shambles. Doris Flores was huddled on the floor, holding her young children close to her. Hysterical, she told Lori that the National Guard had taken Mario away. Lori immediately called Martin Diskin, and he and Jim McGovern, in spite of the obvious dangers, spent the entire night visiting all the National Guard branches in San Salvador in an effort to locate Mario Flores. They could not find him. The next day his mutilated body was discovered on the side of a road. He had been horribly tortured. All his vertebrae were crushed, and he had been strangled and shot in the head.

Lori wondered whether she was somehow to blame. If she had not gone to the luncheon, would her presence in the house have kept the National Guard away? Perhaps, but not for long. During the twelve-year civil war in El Salvador, tens of thousands of civilians "disappeared" or were killed by the military, the National Guard, and right-wing death squads.

This experience had a profound effect on Lori. When she returned to Boston in April 1989, she took a leave of absence from school in order to do whatever possible to bring attention to what she had seen, to do whatever possible to help the Salvadoran people in their efforts to find peace and prosperity. She worked on educational projects for the Central America Network, including preparations for an even larger student exchange that July. She also helped to organize student and community visits to congressional offices in Massachusetts, seeking to share with U.S. representatives the reality of U.S. policy in the region. Later, she worked with CISPES (Committee In Solidarity for the People of El Salvador) in their Boston, New York, and Washington offices, often working more than fourteen hours a day.

Lori's decision to take an extended leave of absence from M.I.T. left Mark and me with strongly mixed feelings. Our household was one where we always read the newspapers and sometimes discussed politics. We could be classified as liberals, but we weren't activists. Except for joining most of our generation in protesting the war in Viet Nam, we rarely participated in rallies or even signed petitions. But Lori brought us into the active struggle for justice in El Salvador. At a rally memorializing those killed by death squads, Mark carried the cross commemorating the death of Mario Flores. But even though we had become more activist and we understood Lori's need to leave school and work full-time at what she believed in, we had also spent our lives wedded to the notion that education, formal education, is of primary importance. After all,

Mark and I were academics. But the decision was Lori's, and in 1990 she chose to return to Central America.

By that time the fighting in El Salvador had intensified to the point that a visit there would prove much too dangerous. Nicaragua, however, was peaceful and housed a large Salvadoran refugee community, including members of the political wing of the FMLN, the Salvadoran leftist rebels. While the military wing of the FMLN was engaged in battles, the political wing was widely accepted around the world (although not by the United States) as an important Salvadoran voice, with diplomatic representatives attending meetings and engaging in peace negotiations. Lori moved to Nicaragua and worked with these displaced Salvadoran refugees, joining a Jesuit project to identify displaced and "disappeared" persons. She also worked as a secretary for representatives of the FMLN, translating U.S. news articles into Spanish and FMLN news releases into English. She wrote home frequently about her life in Nicaragua and also about the ensuing prospects for peace in El Salvador. Lori served as a secretary and translator during the peace process that was brokered at the United Nations in December 1991, and signed in January 1992.

In these few years, Lori's work as a secretary, translator, and human rights activist had enabled her to contribute, at least in a small way, to the peace process and the end of a twelve-year civil war. She was barely twenty-two years old.

Following the peace accord, Lori moved to El Salvador and continued to work for the FMLN, which was now an official political party. She served as an observer in the elections of 1994, writing us to say that elections seemed to go more smoothly than anticipated, especially considering that rural villagers had to wait up to sixteen hours before voting. In that election the FMLN won 25 percent of the seats in the Salvadoran Congress. Their popularity continued to increase, and in March 2000, they increased this to about 40 percent and won seventy-eight mayoral positions, including in San Salvador, the capital.

During the years she lived in Latin America, Lori came home often, usually timing her visits to coincide with family occasions—birthdays, weddings, etc. And between visits we always kept close by mail and by phone. I still have all of her letters—hundreds of them—and I enjoy rereading them. I learned all about her new friends, including her sixty-five-year-old "other grandmother," who complained about the way she dressed and reminded her to not stay out too late, but whom Lori obviously adored. I followed the antics of her friends' children and watched them grow through her anecdotes, silly drawings, and photos. There was the six-year-old who "was fascinated with animals and had all these animal books. He learned how to read midway through [my stay at his home] and was very excited to read to everyone *'Mamá me ama. Amo a Mamá'* Very cute." And there was Misa, about whom she wrote, "He is presently playing push the chair. He also talks— in what language, we don't yet know. Everyone says that he must be speaking English because no one understands him. I suggested that perhaps it's German or Japanese, because I don't understand him either. He just looks at you directly and starts saying 'Lay Ya Gla Ya Ya EEEE… Nay Yay' etc. and you just have to answer *'Asi'* or *'De veras'* (Oh, really!)"

She described everything—the streets in Managua and San Salvador, the beaches and the volcanoes, and every insect she met. There were the ones that do nothing except "fly around like crazy and make noises but are big, like this [⎯⎯⎯⎯⎯⎯⎯⎯⎯⎯⎯⎯⎯⎯⎯⎯⎯⎯⎯]," and the mosquitoes and fleas that seemed to feast on her.

Often we read the same books and exchanged letters discussing them. Particular favorites were Tony Hillerman mysteries. There were so many letters pondering the love life of Hillerman's Lt. Chee, that an uninformed reader might have

thought Chee was a friend of ours. We also read the works of
Gabriel Garcia Marquez. Lori was fortunate in being able to
read them both in English and Spanish, and she would let me
know if I missed out on anything in the translation. In one of
her last letters she said she was translating a novel by a Uru-
guayan author which was not yet available in English, but
which she thought Kathy and I would want to read.

Lori continued to read about human rights, and economic
and social issues in Latin America, including books about Peru.
In September 1994, on her visit to New York, she talked a lot
about Peru—its culture, its long, rich history, and its politics—and told us of her plans to travel there. We reminded
her that when Mark had an opportunity to speak at a health-
care convention in Lima in 1991, she had advised him not to
go. She had warned him that the Shining Path, a Maoist guerrilla group, was wreaking terror in Peru, and given the ran-
dom nature of their violence, no one in Peru was safe, including
North Americans. The Shining Path were often likened to the
Cambodian Khmer Rouge because of the level and horror of
their violence. The targets of that violence were ordinary citizens and, often, the poor peasants for whom they were supposedly fighting. But in 1994, Lori said that the Shining Path
was no longer a threat; their leader, Abimael Guzman, had
been arrested and imprisoned in September 1992, and although
there were occasional flareups in the Peruvian jungle, Peru was
essentially a safe place. I had read quite a bit about the Shining
Path and was still a little concerned. On the other hand, Peru,
particularly Lima and the Inca ruins in Macchu Picchu, had
once again become popular tourist attractions for Americans,
so I assumed it was probably safe.

Much less was known about the MRTA, a smaller revolutionary group. Their goal was to become a legitimate part of
the government. But they too were known in Peru for acts of
violence, although they were far less violent than the Shining

Path. The MRTA came to international attention one year after Lori's arrest, in December 1996, when they overtook the Japanese ambassador's residence in Lima with the hope of exchanging hostages for political prisoners.

Lori went to Peru in November 1994 with plans to travel for a while, in South America in general and Peru in particular. She still had money in the trust fund that had been set up to cover college expenses and would be using some of it to see a bit of that part of the world. She went for the same reason she had gone to El Salvador. She went because she had to see for herself, to learn about the people and the politics by living there.

Lori's letters from South America are filled with her observations about the culture, language, music, and politics of Peru and its neighbors, along with comparisons with what she knew about Central America. And, there was always the weather. Lima lies in a desert on the ocean. The humidity is incredibly high all year, making it cool and damp in the winter and hot and even damper in the summer, although rain is rare. Soon after Lori arrived in Lima, she wrote about walking along the running path, at the edge of a cliff, about eight hundred feet up, overlooking the ocean below. She said it was "neat to walk there in the morning, although the mornings are almost always gray, even, sometimes with a sort of misty drizzle, but not enough to get me really wet." In fact, the sky is usually gray in Lima, and Lori lamented that she hardly saw the sun and hadn't seen nighttime stars since leaving New York. In January 1995, when the Peruvian summer set in, Lori decided to travel to cooler climes, visiting Chile, Argentina, and Bolivia, and the Southern Andes of Peru. We have letters regaling the wonders of Tiahuanaco, a pre-Incan ruin in Bolivia's high plains, the beauty of Lake Titicaca, the enormous highland lake on the Peru–Bolivia border, and, of course, Machu Picchu and the Incan city of Cusco. Lori also visited Buenos

Aires, Argentina, and Santiago, Chile, big cities that reminded her more of New York than of Latin America.

Wherever Lori traveled, we learned about the local music. When she had been in Central America, not only did we get tapes of her singing and playing guitar, but also pages and pages of lyrics, in the original Spanish along with Lori's translation to English. Now we learned that some of her favorite music was by a Bolivian group named Kjarkas. She lamented that it was hard to find their music in Lima. She used to call the Bolivian airlines hoping to be put "on hold," because they played music by Kjarkas for those who waited. She also wrote about Huayno music, which, she explained, was indigenous Peruvian music that varies from region to region, and said she was learning to recognize the regions based on the instruments and type of song.

As usual there were discussions of food. The Peruvian national dish is *ceviche,* fish or shellfish cooked briefly in lemon juice. Historically it was an inexpensive dish, but now the price of fish was too high and she had learned to make a less expensive national dish called *cau cau.* This is made of *mondongo* ("cow innards"), potato, onion, garlic, a little tomato, and cumin. And even less expensive, with no meat at all, is a vegetarian dish from the highlands called *locro,* made of squash, potatoes, corn, chili, and cheese.

And as to the politics . . . April 1995 was the national election, and Lori had several months to watch the campaign and report on the "circus." She recounted stories of President Alberto Fujimori publicly feuding with his wife, Susana, who at one point decided to run for president herself. She described some of the smaller political parties, one of which campaigned with dancing women in scanty clothes, another that campaigned with a puma, and a woman campaigning for Congress exhibiting a large red number thirteen, the number assigned by her party, drawn on her right buttock. Lori thought that former U.N. secretary general Javier Pérez de Cuéllar, who was a presidential candidate, had good ideas but little charisma, and she supplied us with anecdotes about several other presidential candidates who had diverse views and constituencies.

When it was over, Alberto Fujimori was elected for a second five-year term. And "number thirteen" was elected to Congress.

In July 1995, Lori wrote suggesting that we visit Peru. She said it was safe for tourists, and there was a lot to see. In addition to visiting her in Lima, we could all go to Macchu Picchu and Cusco and also Paracas, an area known for its seals. Lori and I are both animal lovers, and although she had not yet been to Paracas, she knew that from what she heard, I would want to go there. We could also see the Nazca lines in the south or the ruins in Ancash, north of Lima, or Colca Canyon near Arequipa, or, maybe, Lake Titicaca on the Bolivian border. It sounded wonderful, but when we checked our calendar, we couldn't schedule a long enough vacation to make the trip worthwhile. It made more sense for Lori to come to New York for her Uncle Ken's fiftieth birthday in September. We would then plan a trip to Peru at a later time.

When Lori came home, she could tell us much more. In New York, she talked about the poverty in Peru that overwhelms more than half the population. She described the slums of Lima and the children begging in the streets, while "neo-liberal economics" helped the rich get richer.

Lori had been reading books on women's issues and was making connections between what she was reading and what she was seeing. She wanted to write about human rights and, in particular, the effects of poverty on women in Peru, and she contacted two small magazines to see if they would be interested. Although she did not have a degree in journalism, she had experience writing news releases in El Salvador. She was not looking for a salary, but for additional experience that possibly could lead to a future career. And, more importantly, she wanted to recount what she saw in Peru.

She met with editors at *Modern Times,* from Columbia University and *Third World Viewpoint,* a quarterly based in Brooklyn, both of which were interested in articles. They wrote letters testifying to their interest, and when Lori returned to Peru she received press credentials from the Peruvian Association of Journalists. For one of her first reports she met with several officials. We have the original transcriptions of the interviews Lori had with three members of the Peruvian Congress—Dennis Vargas Marin, Maria Jesus Espinosa, and Anel Townsend—and with Rocio Palomino, the head of a women's rights organization.

Lori also observed plenary sessions of Congress, particularly when relevant bills, such as those concerned with human rights, women's issues, poverty, or decentralization, were discussed. She wanted to see if there were conflicts between what members of Congress told her in interviews and the way they spoke or voted. She wanted to observe who filibustered when the discussion turned to human rights or women's issues.

Congress was one of the few places in Peru where the political opposition could voice their ideas. But she also knew that to write about Peru, she needed to hear the views of diverse sectors beyond the government, including those who might support revolutionary movements. By the end of November Lori had much of the material she needed. And then she was arrested. Colonel Gonzales has her computer with the drafts of the articles she was writing.

Lori's arrest and the hours in the car in the midst of the La Molina shoot-out were just the beginning of six weeks of incarceration by the brutal antiterrorism police. A few years later, in a letter to me, Lori wrote a brief account of those weeks. It was written in Spanish and, to my amazement, was approved and stamped by the prison censors.

While imprisoned by DINCOTE, I was interrogated day and night and was held in isolation. But I was aware that because I was a U.S. citizen and my situation was being followed by the U.S. Embassy and the media, I was spared the treatment others usually receive. The usual routine included torture, maltreatment and humiliations in order to make prisoners 'talk,' even when they have no information to offer. Human rights reports are filled with accounts of such torture.

In my case, I witnessed how officers in DINCOTE treated a codefendant [Nancy Gilvonio.] They found among her personal possessions a photo of her two children, two boys aged one and six. They threatened to find the children and bring them, along with her, to military quarters where they would torture her, rape her, and then torture her children in front of her in order to see if they could make her 'talk.' Fortunately, she was able to alert her brother, who was also her lawyer. Her children were quickly sent out of the country and the threat was never carried out.

When I was moved to a new jail on December 28, another codefendant was already in the cell. She had been seriously wounded when she was arrested in the shoot-out on November 30, and then further mistreated. I found her very thin, without clothes, without anything. She had been literally thrown there within ten days after a serious operation, forced out of the hospital by a doctor from the Peruvian National Police. She had bullet wounds in her four extremities, one that fractured her arm, and another that was still in her and was apparently pressing on the nerve of her right leg, near her knee, because she couldn't control its movement and had no sensation. The bone of her left leg was fractured and another bullet had cut through her bladder and intestine. She was unable to eat, because she couldn't get up to reach the food that was brought to the cell. Much less could she clean herself or her open wounds. She was lying on a dirty mattress without medical attention in a jail where rats ran freely. She had fresh scars in her intestinal region, a colostomy bag, and a catheter. She was immobile and alone. I saw how she was able to face her situation with such courage, despite her pain and despite the unhealthy conditions and the inadequate care.

The mistreatment of this woman alone was enough to infuriate me and rouse my indignation. And I also knew that a codefendant, Castrellón, had spoken half-truths and outright lies about me in order to clear himself. I already knew that the judicial system was not independent and that the supposed 'freedom of expression' was not really a freedom. I knew that thousands and thousands of prisoners had been convicted in summary trials by the faceless military tribunals, that cruel tortures were applied equally to the innocent and the guilty, to men, women and children, without respect for human dignity.

But perhaps the strongest feeling I had came from knowing the impunity with which all this occurred, from knowing that political life in Peru denied people the right to oppose the status quo, to propose change. I was well aware of these realities, not to mention the type of trial that was awaiting me. All of this roused my indignation and anger. And when on January 8 I was told I would be presented to the press, I decided to address these evils. I knew it would be the last chance I might have until who knew when, maybe my last chance ever. I knew that the prosecutor was already asking for thirty years or life imprisonment, and that in military tribunals, the judge is unlikely to disagree with the prosecutor's request. I thought I had little to lose by speaking out.

When they took me to the room where the journalists were waiting, they told me that there was no microphone, that the room was pretty full and that I would have to raise my voice if I wanted to be heard. That was not difficult for me, since I studied voice in school and I know how to use breathing to speak or sing loudly. I knew I would be given only a brief time and had to speak quickly.

I have been told that my expressions, my movements showed anger, rage. I imagine so, because I was angry. I was enraged. I honestly believe I had more than enough reasons to feel that way. I had been deprived of all my rights and my dignity for forty days. I knew that I was going to be tried and condemned without any evidence, without anyone showing that I was guilty, that I would be condemned largely based on statements of a codefendant who had tried to save himself. I was angry because I knew that the method most often used for interrogation of prisoners was torture, because I saw how children are threatened with torture, and because I saw how a seriously wounded woman was made to suffer more than a stray dog. I was angry because I saw acts that should never be permitted by civil society, acts that clearly would rouse indignation and anger in anyone, even more so when one knows she is impotent to do anything in the face of this monstrous injustice. Similarly, I felt indignation at the misery and hunger in which the large majority of the Peruvian people and people in the Third World live, the institutionalized violence and injustice that has become the norm in these people's lives. I knew that January 8, 1996, was the last time I would be able to speak out about this reality.

I do not regret having spoken. Under other circumstances perhaps it would not have been necessary to do so, or to do so in such a way as I did. But given the situation, I believe it was good that I spoke out. I have been here almost four years feeling completely impotent in the face of so much injustice, but at least I did what I could when I had the chance.

PART THREE

1996

■

NO

VISITS

ALLOWED

▪ The Sentencing

On January 11, specifically citing the January 8 press presentation as proof of Lori's guilt, a hooded, anonymous judge sentenced her to life in prison with no possibility of parole. While the sentence was read, a hooded soldier stood behind Lori with a loaded gun pointed at her head. Lori was not able to speak on her own behalf—to proclaim that she was innocent. There never had been a trial.

Nancy Gilvonio, Miguel Rincon, and Jaime Ramirez were also given life sentences. Pacífico Castrellón was sentenced to thirty years, which to a fifty-two-year-old man is equivalent to life. Repenting didn't count for much in this case.

On January 12, Consular Officer Julie Grant visited Lori, who had been moved to the maximum-security prison in Chorrillos. She called to tell us that Lori was "physically fine but still in shock." Lori wasn't guilty and couldn't fathom why the judge declared her a "national" leader of the MRTA. He never gave specific reasons or described why she was guilty of anything, much less treason. When Lori was told that the Peruvian press had claimed that she was an international arms trafficker, she shook her head and said, "The whole thing is absurd."

After the sentencing, Glyn Davies, acting spokesman for the U.S. Department of State, had read the following press release:

> The United States deeply regrets that Ms. Berenson was not tried in an open civilian court with full rights of legal defense, in accordance with international juridical norms.
>
> Ms. Berenson may appeal her conviction in stages to two higher levels of the military appeals tribunals, and we understand that her attorney is filing such an

appeal. It is not clear whether a final appeal might be made to the Peruvian Supreme Court, a civilian body.

The United States remains concerned that Ms. Berenson receive due process. We have repeatedly expressed these concerns to the government of Peru. We call upon the appeals process to accord Ms. Berenson an open judicial proceeding in a civilian court. The United States will continue to follow this case closely.

This was the first of several press releases. The others followed the two so-called "appeals" that still did not require an fair open judicial proceeding before civilian judges and indeed were nothing more than a rubber-stamp confirmation of the January 11 decision. The civilian Supreme Court refused to hear the case, claiming it did not have jurisdiction. Expressions like "regrets," "concerns," "follow this case," and later, "hope" and "monitor" were common in these press releases. We never saw "condemns," "urges," "requests," or anything that a government truly concerned about its citizens would say. Such pallid statements in light of the gross violations of Lori's rights gave us little hope that our own government would stand up for her. Nonetheless, the Peruvian press, across the political spectrum, was highly critical of these statements, which were interpreted as a challenge to Peru's sovereignty.

Mark and I learned of the sentence in the same way that we learned of much of what's happening in Peru; from members of the press, who always reached us before the embassy. We immediately made plans to go to Lima. We had been told that prisoners found guilty of treason could not have any visitors for the first year of incarceration. But Mr. Achahui had filed for a review, the so-called "appeal," and he believed that we would be able to visit until all reviews were exhausted. Julie Grant had told us that at her last visit, Lori repeatedly expressed concern for all of us, wondering how we were coping with the verdict and the sentence. We were anxious to see Lori, to tell her, "We're okay," and to remind her of how much we love her. We wanted to assure her that we would never rest until she was free.

▪ Trip to Peru, January 1996

We arrived in Lima late in the evening on January 17, along with Tom Nooter and members of the ABC television show *Primetime Live*. The next morning we met with embassy officials, who confirmed that Lori was at the Chorrillos Prison. But when we went there, the prison director told us she had been moved the day before to the southern Andes, to Yanamayo Prison in Puno.

I was suddenly filled with anger and fear. The U.S. government, particularly the embassy, had assured us they would "follow this case closely." But they were not even aware of Lori's whereabouts, let alone her needs. If we hadn't come to Peru, how long would it have taken for the embassy to learn she was transferred, and how much longer before they brought her the basic necessities for survival high in the Andes? In Puno the temperature dipped well below freezing each night and it did not warm up much inside the unheated prison during the day. And Lori had been sent there without any warm clothes. In fact, she only had the clothes she was wearing, minus the jacket she had worn since her arrest. It had been taken away because the maroon color was "kind of red," and red, along with black and green, was a forbidden "revolutionary" color. I was anxious to get to Puno, not only to see Lori but to bring her warm clothing and blankets, basic necessities such as toothpaste, a toothbrush, and soap, and fresh fruits and vegetables to supplement the meager prison diet.

We returned to the embassy and, controlling our anger as much as possible while expressing our deep concern, explained that they were misinformed about Lori's whereabouts, and asked them to arrange for us to visit her in Puno. They conferred with Doctora Carmen Ranilla, the Director of Prisons for Puno, and she assured embassy officials that we could visit and bring warm clothing and supplies. She would inform the Yanamayo Prison director of our plans.

On January 20, we caught the 6 a.m. flight from Lima to the city of Juliaca, over five hundred miles to the southeast. Once the flight headed inland over the Andes, leaving behind the fog that usually engulfs Lima and the coast, the view was quite breathtaking. I've made this trip many times since, and I'm always amazed at the sight of tiny villages sprinkled among barren mountains, seemingly isolated from each other and the rest of the world.

The two-hour flight, including a brief stop in Arequipa, was followed by a one-hour, thirty-mile van ride from Juliaca to Yanamayo Prison in Puno. As soon as we deplaned in Juliaca, I knew we were in another world. Immediately, Mark and the crew from *Primetime* were affected by the altitude. The prison is at a height of 12,700 feet, and Juliaca airport is just slightly lower. The airport offers *mate,* coca leaf tea, the local prescription for the dizziness and headache that comes upon those not used to the altitude. There is also a medical room as soon as one enters the terminal, so that those who feel faint can lie down. Fortunately, I never felt anything more than a slight headache, nothing like the extreme headaches or faintness suffered by Mark on his first few trips. Only later that day, when walking up stairs, did I really notice the altitude. After climbing one flight, my calves felt as though I had done ten. And carrying heavy packages was an exhausting proposition.

The last uphill half-mile of the ride to the prison was over a road deliberately studded with deep holes, boulders, and logs. The van was forced to go very slowly, weaving snakelike, in and out and around obstructions. From a distance we could see machine-gun stations at each corner of the prison and, as we neared the entrance, we were stopped by soldiers armed with automatic rifles.

John Quinones of *Primetime Live* served as our translator, and he, Mark, and I were led inside to meet the prison director, Comandante Teddy Bartra. The comandante told us that we could leave the supplies, but we could not see Lori. Doctora Ranilla and the Bureau of Prisons did not have jurisdiction over prisons such as Yanamayo and, therefore, did not have the authority to grant permission for a visit. Citing the one-year period of no visitation, he could only allow us to see Lori if authorization was in writing and signed by the Minister of Justice, the Minister of the Interior, or President Fujimori. Imagine—we would have needed permission of the president of the country or a specific member of his cabinet in order to visit Lori!

The director volunteered to call Lima so we could speak with U.S. officials. Since it was Saturday, this meant speaking with the marine guards at the embassy, requesting that they contact Julie Grant or Tom Holladay and ask one of them to call us at the prison.

We had come so far. Lori was so near. We longed to see her.

Comandante Bartra told us he was very glad we brought warm clothing and blankets. He said the prison had only enough blankets to allow one per prisoner, and he was very concerned because Lori had arrived with only sweatpants and a lightweight shirt—not nearly sufficient for the climate. He explained that the prison had no heat. The cells faced a corridor, and the opposite wall of the corridor was lined with windows, high windows near the ceiling. The windows had no glass—only horizontal wooden slats that allowed some light to slant in during the afternoon, but let the cold wind whip through all day and night. Prisoners slept with multiple blankets or sleeping bags. As he spoke, I noticed that he and all his staff were wearing down jackets, gloves, and hats. And this was indoors, in the afternoon, in January, the height of summer in Peru. I had only been there a few minutes, wearing a winter coat, and already I was cold.

While we waited for the embassy officials to return our call, two prison guards checked through the supplies I had brought, and I started to learn the ever-changing rules about what is and isn't permitted. I told the guards that I already knew that red, black, and green were not allowed, only to learn that Comandante Bartra did not really care about color rules. I learned that toothpaste in a metal tube (almost all toothpaste comes in metal tubes) was not allowed. The guards squeezed the paste into a plastic bag. I learned that the cardboard tube had to be removed from inside the rolls of toilet paper, to prevent us from sending secret messages. I had brought some fancy Peruvian chocolates, but each was wrapped in foil, and the guards said I had to unwrap them all and put them in a bag. Not all of our fruits and vegetables were accepted either. We had brought broccoli, but the guards insisted that since Lori had no cooking facilities, she could not receive broccoli. I could not convince them that broccoli could be eaten raw. Fortunately, unlike later visits to Yanamayo, I did not have to peel the fruit.

I had brought Lori knitting supplies, and she was permitted to have the yarn and plastic needles. I was told she could have books in addition to a Bible, as long as they were in Spanish, and not political. Comandante Bartra suggested that I buy them in Lima and send them to the prison. Newspapers and magazines were not permitted. We discussed mail. Letters to Lori had to be in Spanish so the censors could read them. According to Peruvian law, prisoners were allowed to receive any number of letters. However, the law did not say prisoners had a right to send letters. Thus, letter writing was a privilege, subject to the discretion of the prison director. For example, as a punishment for some infraction of regulations, that particular month, January 1996, Yanamayo prisoners were not permitted to send out letters. The comandante went on to explain that he believed that prisoners should be allowed books and craftwork and even musical instruments. He said that several prisoners had guitars, and that Lori could also have one. But we had to be aware that the next prison director could change the rules.

After an hour, we still hadn't heard from Lima. We decided to call the embassy from the hotel, and if permission were granted, we would visit on Sunday. We were very cold. I couldn't imagine how Lori or anyone else could survive in an all-concrete cell in that cold, cold place, with only one half-hour each day outside in the warm sun.

We stayed that night at the government-run Isla Verde Hotel on Lake Titicaca. The views of the lake, and the sunrise, were spectacular. Under other circumstances, we would have loved to tour the lake, the largest lake in South America, and one of the highest navigable lakes in the world. Legend has it that Manco Capac and Mama Ocllo, founders of the Incan empire, emerged from the lake. A popular tour is to the *Uros,* the floating islands made of woven *totora* reed that were built centuries ago yet continue to evolve. We didn't tour the lake on that trip or any of the many other trips we took to that region, even though Lori encouraged us to do so. We were always too busy, and I preferred to walk around the city of Puno, home to the Quechua and Aymara descendants of the great Indian empires of Peru and Bolivia.

And then there was the sky. As Lori wrote later to Lea Wood of Vermont,

> The sky of Puno is an intense blue, very beautiful as it is in all of the Altiplano. But what is most beautiful about this sky is that it doesn't belong to anyone, yet at the same time it belongs to everyone, the whole nation, the whole continent, the whole planet, and so also does peace, dignity, and liberty.

▪ Return to Peru

We never did get permission to visit Lori on Sunday but we stopped by the prison anyway, bringing some woolen leggings and other warm clothes we had bought locally. The comandante wasn't there, but we had a long conversation through our translator with the guard who checked the supplies. He said he had studied engineering, and I told him I taught physics to engineers, and we discussed different courses and different ideas. He also said he had read a bit about General George Armstrong Custer and he wanted to know if we could find a book about the general suitable for his ten-year-old son. He said his son wanted to become a doctor, but he wanted his son to become a soldier, and he hoped that the life of General Custer would inspire him. The guard was clearly a Peruvian Indian, and I couldn't but wonder if he knew that Custer's forte was killing Indians and that finally, in turn, he was killed by them. We did find a book and sent it to him.

We returned to Lima on Sunday evening and spent the next two days meeting with the press and shopping for items that consular officers would bring to Yanamayo. Because Peru was signatory to the Vienna Convention, consular visits could not be denied, even though family visits were not permitted for a year. The embassy planned to send someone once each month. They suggested that we send packages and letters to them, and they would bring everything to Lori.

While in Lima, we had many interviews with journalists. We told them Lori's side of the story, and they told us what they had learned from Colonel Gonzales and others at DINCOTE. Although Lori had already been sentenced, Peruvian officials had never told Lori, her lawyer, the embassy, or us the specific charges against her. In fact, not informing Lori of the charges was in violation of Peru's own laws. Officials did, however, discuss their ever-changing, preposterous accusations with the media.

We first heard about Lori's bank account from Gabriel Escobar, a reporter for the *Washington Post*. But we heard the same story from John H. Richardson of *New York* magazine and Terry Wrong of *Primetime Live*. Each was told that there was "strong evidence" that Lori was guilty of arms trafficking and that the proof was Lori's New York bank account, which had a balance of about $50,000. DINCOTE believed, or at least wanted the media to believe, that the money came from the MRTA to be spent on arms. In fact, a DINCOTE official, in a conversation with John Richardson, implied that since her parents were "of modest means," they couldn't have provided these funds and, therefore, the money *must* have come from the MRTA. The reporters were all shown the bank account, and Terry Wrong was even given a copy that he showed me. Incredibly, although this was a joint account, my name was gone. These funds, which came from royalties on textbooks Mark had written, had been in a joint account bearing both Lori's and my names for over ten years, but apparently DINCOTE didn't check on their origin. They didn't care about the facts. If this was deliberately shown to reporters as an example of "strong evidence," it was clear that they didn't have any credible evidence at all.

John Richardson described this and other so-called evidence in his February 19, 1996, article in *New York* magazine. On par with the bank account story was the Quito story. Richardson met with someone identified only as Comandante G. at DINCOTE. He was told that Lori had been seen with Castrellón at a meeting with MRTA leader Nestor Cerpa in Quito, Ecuador, and that Interpol (the International Police Organization) had confirmed it. Richardson spoke to someone at Interpol, who "explained that such information would have come from the Ecuadoran police, since all Interpol does is hook up local police across national borders." Richardson contacted Deputy Chief of Mission Gonzalo Salvador at the

Ecuadoran Embassy. He was told, "When we saw this reported in the *New York Times,* we informed our authorities. They did not know about this meeting—otherwise our police would have apprehended them. I think that information came from Peru."

The information came from Peru? What happened to confirmation by Interpol? I guess DINCOTE never dreamed that Richardson wouldn't just take their word for it, that he might actually call Interpol to check. And of course Interpol and the Ecuadoran police said there was no information about a meeting—there was no meeting.

And as for the charges that Lori was posing as a journalist, Richardson cited the letters supporting her accreditation from *Third World Viewpoint* and *Modern Times.* He even learned that she submitted a copy of *Third World Viewpoint* to the Peruvian journalists' association, not hiding its leftist slant. Richardson had called both publications and was assured that Lori was writing articles for them; he learned that she had phoned them a few weeks before her arrest to discuss deadlines.

I thought Richardson best summarized it when he wrote, ". . . the DINCOTE's evidence would be laughed out of any civilized court."

In spite of all that went wrong on that visit to Peru, the exhausting travel to and from Puno, the profound disappointment of not being allowed to see Lori, and, in particular, my ever-growing concerns for her condition, I have rather fond memories of my last evening there. Mark and I were joined in our hotel room by Tom Nooter, Grimaldo Achahui, and John Richardson, all guitarists. Tom and Mr. Achahui brought along the guitar they had purchased for Lori earlier that day, and John Richardson brought the Peruvian *charango* he had bought as a remembrance of his trip. He had spent the previous night learning to play this tiny Peruvian mandolin, which has a bowl-

shaped resonance box and five pairs of strings. He had practiced two songs, both of which he dedicated to Lori—Leonard
Cohen's "Bird on a Wire," with its refrain of "I've tried in my
way to be free," and Bob Dylan's "I Shall Be Released." That
was the start of a singalong. Mr. Achahui played and sang
Quechuan songs from Cusco, his hometown. Tom, looking
and sounding every bit the folksinger, played some music by
Phish. I played "The Gypsy Rover," a song I used to sing every
Monday afternoon when I brought my guitar to play for Lori's
first-grade class. Mark added harmony. It would have been a
perfect evening if only Lori had been there singing and playing along with us.

▪ Our New Lives

And so we returned to New York. We returned to our home, to our friends, to our jobs, but not to the lives we once knew. I would not be able to visit with Lori for almost a year, but aside from my hours in the classroom or grading papers, my every waking moment, and many of my dreams, were filled with Lori. I met people who I would never have imagined would play a part in my life: members of Congress, ambassadors, assistant secretaries of state, and well-known TV newscasters. And I learned new skills: how to lobby Congress, write op-ed pieces and letters to the editor, design brochures, speak in sound bites, and fight misinformation

I was overwhelmed by many emotions, the strongest of which was anxiety, not knowing at any given moment whether or not Lori was okay. But there was also anger, not only directed at the Peruvian government, but also at State Department officials who made no effort to secure Lori's freedom and did their best to discourage anyone else from trying to do so. We were on a constant roller coaster as events, or just rumors, gave us hope or led us almost to despair. I knew we had to stay on an even keel and not be drawn into the ups and downs. I knew it was unproductive—in fact, counterproductive—to dwell on my anxieties and anger. I needed to take the tremendous energy building within me and turn it into action. I also had to reserve some of that energy for what might very well become a long-term struggle.

Each month we sent a package to the embassy filled with clothes, books, gifts sent from around the country, and letters from around the world. Consular officers would then bring everything to Lori along with fresh fruits and vegetables. We sent a sleeping bag, a down jacket, vitamins, and medicines. Mark's Aunt Sally, eighty-eight years young, sent slippers that she had knitted, and they were so well liked that she sent additional ones for Lori's small community—her cellmate and three other women with whom she spent her thirty minutes in the yard.

And then I eagerly awaited the phone call describing the visit. The embassy reports were the closest I could come to being with Lori—speaking to someone who had just spoken to her, had just seen her. Letters from Lori were several weeks old when I read them. The embassy reports were up-to-date.

I got my first glimpse of what Lori's life was like in March, after Tom Holladay's visit. His report, which in its written version was long and detailed, painted a vivid picture of Lori and Yanamayo.

12 March 1996: 2nd Consular visit to Lori Berenson at Yanamayo Prison

1. Consul General (Congen) visited Lori Berenson at Yanamayo Prison on the evening of 7 March for an hour and fifteen minutes. The visit took place in a private office with only Berenson and the Congen present. Three boxes containing mail, food, sleeping bag, clothing (parka jacket, boots, socks, jeans, and tights) miscellaneous toiletries, handicraft items, writing supplies, and a guitar were delivered after close review by prison personnel.

2. Ms. Berenson appeared to be in good health. She has not lost her vitality or her sense of humor and says she is adapting to the rigorous conditions. Other than an episode where mail was denied all prisoners after her attorney was quoted in the Lima press as stating she had complained about the food and a water shortage, she had no complaints. The Congen reviewed major United States and world news developments (no TV, radio, or periodicals are allowed in Yanamayo). Berenson says she tries to spend the

day active and without sleeping so she can sleep at night after lights go out at 10. She says she still gets too much sleep and often wakes up before the sun comes up. She says she has not been dreaming. She reads, writes, exercises, and does handiwork to pass the time between the half-hour daily yard time. She is interested in things to do: crafts, correspondence courses, reading and writing material, religious education, anything. She had not yet received the eyeglasses we had handed to the ICRC [International Committee of the Red Cross] representative in Lima for delivery earlier in the week. The Congen confirmed with the director that glasses had not been delivered and followed up on 11 March with ICRC Lima. They said the Puno office had not delivered the glasses as planned but promised they would be delivered. Berenson does not need glasses for close vision. She says it is very noisy in the prison during the day with the prisoners, particularly the Sendero Luminoso [Shining Path] members, yelling constantly. Congen met briefly with the prison director before and after conversation with Berenson and the next day met with XII Regional Police Commander, Peruvian Nation Police (PNP), General Luis Alberto Coquis Coz, who appears to have taken a personal interest in Berenson's welfare. The prison is run by PNP personnel. The perimeter is secured by the army.

3. Health: Ms. Berenson still suffers from an altitude-related circulation to the extremities problem, which is being treated. Her hands and (she says) her feet are afflicted with purple blotches under the surface, which itch. Constant scratching has caused two fingers to crack open but these are not infected.

Berenson is satisfied with the medical treatment she is getting for this condition in the prison and is convinced her condition is improving. She understands this is a common problem of adaptation to the high altitude and the cold. We will check this out with post medical personnel.

4. Food: Prison director told Congen his per capita daily budget for prisoner food is s/1.50. (Current exchange rate is $1.00 = s/2.35 [or 2.35 Peruvian Soles]) He says inflation is rapidly eating away his budget. A bag of rice, for example, has increased in Puno in the last three months from s/40 to s/75, he said. He says prisoners can and do supplement diet from food brought in by family visitors and do share what they get with other prisoners. He added, however, that most prisoners are never visited. Only about seventy of the three hundred ever get visited either because their families are old, too poor, or live too far away. Berenson has not complained about the food and says it is adequate if monotonous. She has requested supplements, which we are providing her with funds from her parents. Cooked and dry foods are allowed. Packaged items must be unwrapped and put in clear plastic bags. Food requiring cooking is not allowed.

She gets three meals a day: Morning—bread and warm water-based liquid (coffee, tea); Midday—stew, rice, soup heavy on starch; Evening—soup with sweet drink (sugar and water).

Director told Congen that after three years, prisoners at Yanamayo start having stomach problems caused by the combination of the high starch diet and the effect of high altitude on the metabolism. Congen observed that if the policy of keeping these people for a very long time holds, prisons will soon have a serious medical/geriatric caseload.

5. Water: The director admits he has had a serious water problem. The water for the facility is drawn from a water course up the hill. This is adequate in the rainy season. There is a cistern up there, but the pipes broke and there was no water for six days. In dry season, the water is trucked in. Berenson was quick to point out that drinking water, which she prepares with chlorine tablets, is always available. Water for bathing, laundry, and flushing toilet is hauled to cells and stored in buckets. Bathing is with cold water. Berenson tries to bathe daily when water is available.

6. Sanitation: The water problem also impacts on living conditions in the 1.80 meter by 2.00 meter cell fitted with a basin and a toilet hole. Berenson says, however, that the cold keeps the smell down and that there are no flies in the prison. One of the two occupants of the cell sleeps on a mattress on the floor and the other on a built-in concrete bunk about a meter off the floor.

7. Special Visits Suggested: The director suggested to Congen that the embassy seek exception to allow Berenson's relatives to visit her before the first year is out. Director said this suggestion is supported by his immediate supervisor, the regional police commander. It was not clear whether his suggestion is meant only to benefit Berenson or is part of a larger effort to influence a loosening of the regime. The director has implied that he thinks the regime is too tight. We will nevertheless take him up on his suggestion and advocate an exceptional visit by Lori's

parents next June–August, the halfway point in her one-year isolation.

8. Needs: Ms. Berenson had the following requests which department should pass on to her parents. We will then work out which we buy from OCS trust funds provided by parents and which parents send. Fruit, cheese, hard candy, dried fruit, one hundred Peruvian soles, thermal underwear, cheap watch, eyeglasses, knitting needles [wooden or plastic], writing and reading material, correspondence course, English-Spanish dictionary, old magazines (over five years old).

I envied Mr. Holladay. He could see Lori, enjoy her sense of humor, ask about her day and about her dreams—and I couldn't. I, her mother, had to hear this all secondhand and then wait anxiously for the next secondhand report.

By the end of March, Lori finally received the eyeglasses we sent to replace the ones taken and lost by DINCOTE after her arrest on November 30. Over the next months, along with other supplies, we sent several cheap watches, each of which mysteriously disappeared between the time the embassy delivered the supplies and the time Lori received them. Workbooks for Lori to teach her cellmate "English as a Second Language" similarly disappeared. Lori's need for clothing diminished as people across the country read about Lori's plight and sent warm sweaters, gloves, scarves, and hats. At one point Lori wrote asking that we not send any more sweaters, because she had no more room, reminding us that the cells were designed for one person but occupied by two.

Future reports were not as detailed but always discussed Lori's health. And although the March report indicated that she was satisfied with the medical treatment and was convinced her condition was improving, her altitude-related circulation problems worsened. At a later visit, Tom Holladay became concerned and asked us to obtain whatever information we could about this condition, which he was told was Raynaud's syndrome. After consulting with several doctors, I learned that this syndrome is precipitated by cold, and is due to a combination of neurological and circulatory factors that result in reduced circulation in hands and feet. But Lori's symptoms also suggested secondary polycythemia, which results when one's body attempts to compensate for an oxygen deficiency by manufacturing more hemoglobin and more red blood cells. These cells then clog small veins and capillaries. Because this hemoglobin is low in oxygen, the skin takes on a bluish hue.

Whatever the cause, Lori's condition became particularly severe during the Peruvian winters, when nighttime temperatures in Puno dropped well below freezing and even daytime temperatures inside the prison rarely reached 40 degrees. Consular reports described her hands as completely swollen and purple, cracked and bleeding, but doctors assured me that the condition would not cause permanent injury. The recommended "cure" is a move to a lower altitude and warmer climate, but even after Lori was transferred in October 1998 to a prison in the city of Arequipa, at an altitude of 7,600 feet, a mile lower than Puno, the condition persisted, although not as severely. U.S. doctors now speculate that nutrition and, in particular, vitamin deficiencies may be the problem.

Other health problems became a concern at Yanamayo. In 1996, the prison in the nearby city of Juliaca was undergoing repairs, and a portion of Yanamayo was reserved for "common prisoners." Tuberculosis spread among them and took several lives, but, fortunately, did not reach the sector with political prisoners. Lori also was spared the typhoid epidemic. But the flu sent everyone, including Lori, to the infirmary. As time went on, Lori was afflicted by the gastric disorders that Comandante Bartra had described to Tom Holladay and also by repeated bouts with strep throat and laryngitis. By the time I saw Lori in December 1996, she could not speak above a whisper. Worst of all for Lori, she could not sing.

Although in March Comandante Bartra had suggested the embassy seek permission for us to visit Lori after six months, and Tom Holladay wrote he would "advocate an exceptional visit," we never heard further about this. In May, Comandante Bartra was replaced by Victor J. Ordinola Ruiz, a man who unlike Comandante Bartra showed no inclination toward "a loosening of the regime." He was much more "to the book" than Bartra—forbidding the wearing of green, red, and black colors, limiting mail, and defying the Vienna Convention by limiting the time for the consular visits.

▪ Communicating with Lori

Each month we got a new list of what Lori needed, and we then forwarded the items to the embassy. Mostly we sent things to occupy her time—books and craft materials. Knitting is one of my favorite pastimes, and Lori had learned to knit as a child. As a teenager she often had knit scarves and shawls as gifts for friends and relatives. But, as I learned on my later trips to Puno as I watched the local women knit in the market, our skills paled compared to those of these Indian women. Lori's cellmate taught her new knitting techniques and also how to make dolls and stuffed animals, and I sent her loads of yarn and fabric for these projects. I was able to send her photos of my latest knitting efforts, and she sent descriptions and drawings of hers, including baby dresses that she and her fellow prisoners made to be sold in Lima. Knitting seemed to relax and please Lori, and she wrote, "My baby sweater is *sooooo* cute, so if I'm to have any nieces or nephews I can make them stuffies [stuffed animals] and teeny weeny sweaters."

I tried to imagine Lori's day. Except for meals and thirty minutes out in the yard, she structured her own time. If I were in her position I might not have bothered getting out of bed, preferring to stay under the warm blankets. I could not contemplate washing myself and my clothing with ice-cold water while standing in an ice-cold cell, and I might have given up on knitting, writing, or playing the guitar in favor of keeping my hands in warm gloves. But Lori was always an incredibly busy person, often doing several things at once. So I knew that in spite of the cold, her swollen fingers, and the poor lighting, she would stay awake and productive. And whenever I found time to knit or read, I liked to think that Lori was knitting or reading too. We continued our practice of "reading together," books like *Of Love and Other Demons* by Garcia Marquez and *Paula* by Isabel Allende, and discussed them in our letters. *Paula* was a particular favorite of Lori's and the four women in her "community." Mark wrote of this to Ms. Allende, and she graciously sent each woman a book with a personal message. In Lori's she wrote, "Love and hope to you dear friend . . . To Lori Berenson in celebration of the invincible spirit."

What Lori and I couldn't do "together" was take the long leisurely walks we loved. I remember one summer when Lori worked evenings. I would meet her after work so we could walk the three miles home and talk about our day. But now she was confined to a six-foot-by-seven-foot cell for twenty-three and a half hours a day, where the only walking she could do was in small circles, and the lack of oxygen made even that difficult.

We communicated as well as possible by letter, a process complicated by my very limited fluency in Spanish, the only language permitted. And then we had to phrase our thoughts to satisfy the censors. I was always so excited when a letter from Lori came but then had to wait for the translation. I would pore over the letter and look for Lori in it. And although much of her personality was buried by the translation, I could always find it somewhere, particularly in the humor. Every letter, no matter how serious, always had some comment that was followed by "ha, ha" or a smile face or a frown face. And I wanted her to find the real me in my letters, so I always included silly drawings like the one of my cats that had accompanied letters to Lori ever since she spent a summer away from home at age twelve. In earlier years, the cats were Toulouse and Heidi, Lori and Kathy's childhood pets. Now it was Muffin and Bon Bon who added their "meows" to my love at the end of the letters.

We invested in computer software to help translate the letters. The first thing I entered was *"Hola mama y papa,"* which, because I forgot to put in the accents, translated as "Hello sucks potatoes." In general, even when I included the accents, I couldn't make much sense of the translations from Spanish to English, and I doubted it was any better in the other direction. The key was to write in simple sentences, whenever possible avoiding words with multiple meanings. If not, the translator invariably chose the wrong word so that "spring is here" became a sentence about mattress springs, and any reference to "book" referred to "booking a reservation." Lori got used to the simple sentences that made my letters sound like a grade-school composition, and she found many of the translations quite humorous. But because she knew both languages she usually could decipher the meaning. Friends, relatives, and total strangers started writing to Lori, many using computer translators. Lori received letters asking her to *"Guarde sus alcohol para arriba,"* which brought a smile as she realized the writer was encouraging her to keep up her spirits, not to raise her alcohol, and she assumed that the young man expressing "hot desires" was simply sending "warm wishes."

In spite of everything, it was clear from Lori's letters and the consular reports that Lori remained psychologically strong and true to herself. Tom Holladay puzzled over why she minimized personal complaints and focused on general problems. Given what we were hearing about deteriorating conditions and Lori's health, there were times I wished she would emphasize her own problems. But then again, that would not be like Lori.

In letters she wrote of the major health problems of the other prisoners in her wing, describing cases of severe bleeding ulcers, poorly healed broken bones, and ailments resulting from torture. She asked us to relay information to Amnesty International and to supply medicine. Her concern for the well-being of other prisoners caused Peruvian authorities to claim, "See, she's one of them. She's a terrorist." Once, when questioned about conditions by a Peruvian official, Lori first recounted the difficulties of another prisoner and then discussed her own problems. The official replied that only a member of a terrorist group would talk first about others and then about herself. Can you imagine? To put others before yourself is to be a terrorist? By that criterion, every compassionate, caring person I know is a terrorist.

A reporter once asked me if I wished that I had brought up Lori differently. I thought this the most bizarre question, and immediately answered, "No!" But later I gave some thought to what, if anything, in her "upbringing" had shaped her into such a caring person. I remembered an incident when Lori was eight, in the third grade. She came home one afternoon very upset about a situation in which the teacher unfairly favored one of her "pets" over another pupil. The two girls had collided accidentally in the schoolyard, and the teacher ran over to her pet, who was not hurt, leaving the other little girl bleeding and crying. Lori was greatly upset by the unfairness of it, upset by the system of favored and unfavored, even though she herself was a favored pet. I cannot remember what I said, but I know I would *not* have said, "Forget about it. As long as you're the pet it's okay." On the other hand, I probably did not recommend that eight-year-old Lori confront the teacher. I don't even know if Lori remembers this incident. But from then on I noticed she sympathized with the "have-nots." As she grew older, after the CARE commercial, her sympathy included starving children. And in later years, sympathy changed to action as she used her voice not just to speak for those who were not otherwise heard but to enable them to speak for themselves.

▪ The Campaign

In our efforts to turn anger into action, our apartment became campaign headquarters. Brochures, computer printouts, letters, and newspaper clippings were strewn about our two offices and also covered tables and filled boxes in the kitchen and living room. Our phone rang constantly, and our mailbox was always stuffed. There were a few phone calls and letters expressing the hope that Lori rot in hell, but they were the exceptions, and we learned to ignore them. And there were those who insisted we could buy her out and those who promised their fellow militia members would storm the prison and free her if we provided them with the lay of the land. But mostly we heard from people who had read newspaper articles about Lori and tracked down our phone number or address and asked what they could do to help. And those who joined our efforts told their friends, who also joined. Our network grew, providing contacts with so many wonderful people. We designed and reproduced brochures. We sent out updates of Lori's situation by e-mail and regular mail. We organized letter-writing campaigns, rallies, and conferences.

We continued to be the creatures of habit we had always been, only the habits changed. Mark's day started before 5 a.m., when he turned on his e-mail and responded to the messages that had arrived since he turned it off at 10 p.m. the previous night. Each day we received dozens of messages reminding us that there were people thinking of Lori and us, praying, writing letters, organizing locally—messages of encouragement and hope. And we responded to all of them. Mark next checked the news on the Internet, particularly the Peruvian press, downloading relevant articles. Following routine, I came to breakfast at 7 a.m., and with the help of an English-Spanish dictionary, we worked together to understand events. Lori's situation was political, and in our efforts to resolve it, we needed a better understanding of both U.S. and Peruvian politics.

Ramsey Clark was our chief strategist. We spoke to him nearly every day, and we sent him every important letter or document we drafted, asking for his suggestions. Whether it was experience, innate ability, or a combination of the two, he could foresee how subtle changes in wording could greatly alter the perception of a message. We would not meet with important officials without him, because although we could hear what was said, he could hear what was meant. He advised whom we should contact, and when. He kept us focused on the big picture rather than expending energies on the lesser problems. He was our guiding light, and in spite of his incredibly busy schedule, he was always there when we needed him, whether for advice or simply for reassurance. He often referred to himself as an incurable optimist. But he wasn't a dreamer—more an optimistic realist. And quite often we needed his positive thoughts to keep us going.

Our overall strategy, laid out by Ramsey in early 1996, never changed. We needed to convince President Clinton that he or a high official representing him must tell the Peruvian government in no uncertain terms that Lori Berenson should be released, and that failure to release her would result in severely deteriorated relations between the two countries. Unfortunately, although President Clinton and the State Department publicly regretted the lack of due process in Lori's case, they would not take a strong, effective stand for her release unless pressed hard. We therefore turned to members of Congress, asking them to consider withholding military assistance to Peru and to pressure President Clinton. And we knew the way to reach members of Congress is through their constituents. That meant we had to organize a nationwide grassroots campaign. And in the process, we had to fight the State Department.

▪ The State Department

From the moment of my first conversation with embassy officials, on December 1, 1995, I sensed that they intended to do
as little as necessary to help Lori. Their initial stance was that
Mark and I should locate a Peruvian lawyer, but we should
not come to Peru to do so. Lori was being held at DINCOTE
headquarters, infamous for torture and mistreatment of prisoners, and all they had done was left a calling card. It wasn't
until members of Congress started making inquiries that embassy officials agreed that we should come to Peru, that they
would help us find a lawyer, and that they would visit Lori
often and arrange for us to visit her. But that very same week,
there was also a devastating decision to treat her case on the
consular rather than the political level. That meant the consular officers would ensure she had enough blankets, but there
would be no serious efforts on the part of the ambassador or
political officers at the embassy to obtain her release. And this
decision was made before Lori had made any statement, before she had even hired a lawyer.

Several of the consular officers were quite empathetic and
went out of their way to see that Lori was as comfortable as
was possible, and we were grateful. But that was not enough.
We wanted embassy officials to tell the Peruvian government
in no uncertain terms that U.S.-Peruvian relations would suffer
unless Lori received justice.

We heard repeatedly about an Italian woman who was sentenced by a Peruvian military tribunal in 1994 for her involvement with the MRTA, and we were told that after a vociferous
response from the Italian government, she was returned to Italy
and set free. In 1996, when a Japanese citizen was arrested for
involvement with the Shining Path, rather than facing a hooded
military tribunal in Peru, she was quickly returned to Japan.
We met foreign diplomats, members of Congress, the press,
and ordinary citizens who could not understand why the U.S.

government did not act immediately to have Lori expelled and returned to the United States.

Some have opined that the State Department would certainly not go out of its way for someone like Lori, who was "on the other side" in El Salvador and who was known to have leftist views. Others say the U.S. government, just like the Peruvian government, wanted her to serve as an example to discourage human rights workers and freelance journalists from traveling to foreign shores and "meddling." Or, perhaps the government believed the Peruvian accusations in spite of Lori's refutations. And then again, maybe the embassy staff suffered from "clientitis," identifying more with Peru than the United States, and didn't want to rock the boat. Or maybe it was because Peru was an ally, and it's always easier for the United States to get tough with an enemy like Cuba or Iraq than with an ally. I think all of the above are factors. But mostly I believe the State Department simply won't go out of its way to help anyone if it means a detour from "business as usual." And "business as usual" focuses on business and investment, not on protecting human rights, even of its own citizens.

State Department officials had given us two pieces of advice.

First: Maintain a low profile, do not make any "noise" for two years, and after two years maybe Mr. Fujimori might be more amenable to dialogue. Sure. The State Department would have loved that! In two years all the staff would be rotated to other positions, so that when we revived our efforts, Lori would be somebody else's problem. In the meantime, for two years Mr. Fujimori would be given a message that no one cared about international norms of due process, human rights, or Lori Berenson, and he could continue to act with impunity. After all, this was the man who was elected to the presidency in 1990, and then in 1992 shut down Congress and rewrote the Constitution so that he could consolidate power in the presidency, control the new Congress and judiciary, and ensure that he could run again, and then again. No way would we be quiet for two years.

The second piece of advice: Lori should use the bilateral transfer treaty between Peru and the United States that would allow her to serve her term in a U.S. prison. This suggestion was also ideal for both Peru and the State Department. Lori would be out of Peru, out of Fujimori's hair, and out of the embassy's jurisdiction. She would no longer be an issue in U.S.-Peruvian relations, and the State Department could continue with "business as usual." Meanwhile Lori would spend her life in prison, albeit a U.S. prison, under the jurisdiction of a different government agency, the Justice Department.

"Transfer" sounds good until you learn the details. Lori's sentence would be based solely on the crimes the Peruvian government claims she committed, she could never challenge the legality of her conviction, and the United States could not retry her. She could never demonstrate her innocence in a U.S. court. And in spite of everyone's belief that after transfer "someone" would arrange for her release, the treaty clearly states that no U.S. official could pardon her.

The United States Department of Justice "Fact Sheet" on the treaty specifically states:

> [Peru] retains exclusive jurisdiction over the sentence and the authority to pardon or grant amnesty to the offender. For this reason, a transferred prisoner cannot challenge his or her conviction in a new judicial proceeding in the courts of the [United States] on the grounds the trial in [Peru] was somehow unfair or that he or she did not commit the crime. Suits in United States courts seeking this result have been dismissed, citing terms of the treaty. Thus, once a transfer occurs, the prisoner forfeits the right to "collateral attack" on the sending state's conviction.

We had lawyers, Justice Department officials, the State Department, and persons close to President Clinton make inquiries about transfer, and the bottom line was always the same. Lori would be in prison with no way out. The office of the Special Assistant to the President and Senior Director for Multilateral and Humanitarian Affairs carefully considered the provisions of this treaty. In a letter, they wrote, "Should Lori agree to seek a transfer . . . under the terms of the transfer treaty, transfer constitutes an acceptance of the foreign conviction and sentence."

Of course, there are prisoners who accept their sentence and prefer to serve it in a prison that has heat, running water, reasonable food, other amenities and comforts, and is closer to home. That's the purpose of such treaties—to provide better conditions for those who are guilty. But Lori is innocent. Why would she agree to accept her conviction and sentence? Why would she waive her fundamental human rights and agree to spend the rest of her life in a U.S. prison? Certainly not for heat and hot water. Transferring meant giving up. And while she was still physically and mentally able, Lori was not giving up. Mark and I were not giving up either.

Many people, including some of our closest supporters, relatives, and best friends did not understand why Lori would not transfer. No matter what we said, deep down they believed if she came to a U.S. prison, somehow she would be released. But their deep-down beliefs were nothing but wishful thinking. Latin Americans understood. A Nicaraguan friend agreed Lori should never transfer because "in the United States the law is the law and forever is forever, but in Latin America the law always changes and nothing is forever."

When the State Department realized that we weren't going to take either of their suggestions, they embarked on their own campaign, a campaign of misinformation and misleading information. The pattern had already begun in January

1996, when John Richardson interviewed "senior embassy officials" for his *New York* magazine article. He reported, "They said they couldn't get too specific about the facts of Lori's case, because Lori had insisted on her right to privacy; then they proceeded to repeat a lot of rumors, leaving the impression that they thought she was at least partly guilty. But when I asked whether they had confirmed any of the allegations independently, they said no, that wasn't their job." So, what *was* "their job"? Well, apparently at least part of their job was to leave John Richardson and anyone else who inquired about Lori with "the impression that they thought she was at least partly guilty."

One of the most damaging State Department strategies was to claim Lori did not want help. Lori had said that any campaign should always indicate that she is just one of the many who were wrongly imprisoned in Peru, that the campaign should go beyond "Save Lori." This was used by the State Department to tell members of Congress, the religious community, and human rights groups, "Lori wants no help." This clever tactic was extremely successful, as prospective supporters shrugged their shoulders, saying, "if she doesn't want our help, there is nothing we can do!" We were appalled.

With the help of Tom Holladay, we were able to get a letter from Lori in June 1996 that was addressed to members of the Senate and House of Representatives. In it Lori emphasized that she wanted, and greatly appreciated, congressional help. But, either because the State Department continued providing misinformation or because their initial statements had made such lasting impressions, for years we continued to hear "but she wants no help"—despite Lori's own words to the contrary.

Letters from the State Department, while critical of the lack of due process in the military tribunals, left the public impression that Lori had had a trial and a series of appeals.

Mr. Achahui had filed for a review by the Superior Military Court, and on January 29, 1996, this three-member hooded tribunal adopted one point of Mr. Achahui's argument. They found that the prosecutor in the original proceeding was at fault for failing to prepare a list of charges against Lori, and they imposed a "sanction" on him. But, unbelievably, in spite of this "sanction," Lori still was not told the charges against her or given a chance to defend herself against them, and her sentence was upheld.

The next appeal was to the Supreme Military Council, a five-member tribunal. Their decision to uphold the sentence was announced on March 15. However, on February 27, Peruvian newspapers and TV quoted the Peruvian minister of justice as saying, "The Berenson case is closed. The sentence is irreversible." This was more than two weeks before the decision. In fact, as a U.S. embassy internal report pointed out, it was "indeed, before the prosecutor has even officially notified the Peruvian defense attorney that the prosecutor has taken up the case—and seems to circumscribe if not preclude the Council's authority to modify the lower tribunal's sentence." In other words, the appeal was denied even before it was filed. But publicly the State Department continued to tell members of Congress that, "the court found her guilty as charged" and "the Supreme Military Council confirmed the sentence," as if there had actually been a real trial and an authentic appeal.

Much of the misleading information promoted by the State Department was sent to members of Congress and, later, ordinary citizens, in carefully crafted letters. We would have expected U.S. officials to consider Lori innocent until *proven* guilty. But every letter stated, "The United States Government has taken no position regarding Ms. Berenson's guilt or innocence." The letters then proceeded to hint at her guilt and link her name with terrorism: "She and others were accused of planning to storm the Peruvian Congress and take hostages"; "the MRTA, with which Peruvian authorities say Ms. Berenson was associated, has mounted hundreds of terrorist attacks . . ."; "the charges against Ms. Berenson are very serious." Even Colonel Gonzales had assured us nobody believed Lori was planning to storm the Peruvian Congress. So why was the United States making that accusation? And why were attacks by the MRTA relevant to Lori's guilt or innocence?

But nowhere in these early letters was there any indication that Lori claimed she was innocent. It took two years, *two years,* for us to convince the State Department, in particular Assistant Secretary of State Jeffrey Davidow, how outrageous that omission was. Later letters read, "Ms. Berenson continues to maintain that she is innocent. She has stated that she has never promoted, planned or participated in violent acts, nor has she been a member of any organization that promotes or participates in violence." But these new letters continued to include the old insinuations of guilt.

I have met with many members of the State Department: secretaries, consular officers, ambassadors, and assistant secretaries of state. While there are certainly many caring individuals, I tend not to think of the State Department as a group of people, but as a "thing," something that travels down a predetermined road, running over anything in its path, not stopping or detouring for anyone. The State Department had, and has, a long-term political plan vis-à-vis Peru, and down the road there were cutbacks in the coca crop and, of course, increased investment by U.S. companies. Fighting for democratic principles and human rights for the Peruvian people was off the main route, and fighting for Lori Berenson's rights seemed not to be on the map at all.

I was reminded of something I once read about horror stories. The gist was that the scariest stories were like those of Ira Levin, where in, say, *Rosemary's Baby* or *The Stepford Wives,* the heroine turns to the one she loves and realizes he is "one of them." I thought we were fighting the horror of the Peruvian government and turned to officials of the State Department for help, only to find they were, taken as a group, "one of them."

■ Lobbying Congress

Soon after Lori's arrest, many people sent off letters to Secretary of State Warren Christopher. As far as we know, none of those letters were answered. Letters to nonelected officials were a wasted effort. We encouraged everyone to concentrate instead on Congress. Although the State Department is responsible for carrying out foreign policy, Congress controls the foreign-operations budget, deciding how much money gets allotted to support State Department efforts. And members of Congress often are responsive to their constituents.

Members of the House of Representatives commonly inform their colleagues about particular issues and elicit their support by circulating "Dear Colleague" letters. Senators also do the same, but House and Senate members do not send joint letters. In February 1996, Congresswoman Constance Morella from Maryland joined our Congresswoman Carolyn Maloney in sponsoring a Dear Colleague letter, asking House members to sign a letter to President Fujimori. They reminded him that "the Peruvian government has made numerous promises to the international community to reform its antiterrorist and treason courts to bring them in line with the international covenants which Peru has signed," and urged him to let Lori have a chance to tell her side of the story. This letter was signed by twenty-four members of the House of Representatives.

Mark and I knew that there were many more than twenty-four congressional representatives who, if they heard Lori's story, would sign letters on her behalf. In March we asked Carolyn Maloney to circulate a new letter, and we convinced our New York senators, Democrat Daniel Patrick Moynihan and Republican Alfonse D'Amato, to do likewise. Unfortunately, Dear Colleague letters are easily lost among all the other papers circulating in Congress, and members or their aides have to be reminded to read them and prodded to sign. So we embarked on our new careers as lobbyists, meeting with members of Congress, or, most often, their aides, and telling Lori's story.

On March 19 we went to Washington with appointments in several offices, including that of New Mexico congressman Bill Richardson. Due to a scheduling conflict, I went to Richardson's office without Mark, not knowing if I'd meet with the congressman or his aide.

I met the congressman. And instead of offering to sign a letter on Lori's behalf, he volunteered to go to Peru and negotiate Lori's release. I am sure whatever I said at that point was incoherent. I was stunned. I knew that some of his constituents had already corresponded with him about Lori, and I had been told he would be sympathetic. But I did not know that he was a famous "rescuer," that he had been instrumental in securing the release of U.S. citizens held prisoner in North Korea, Iraq, and Cuba. He described some of this to me and said he credited his success to his ability to work behind the scenes, unconnected to the State Department, their normal diplomatic channels, or their "business as usual" mentality. Wherever he traveled it was known that he was very close to Bill Clinton, and was unofficially the President's Special Envoy for Human Rights.

I left his office, walked outdoors, and gave a cheer that Lori probably heard from her cell in Yanamayo. The congressman had cautioned that some releases had needed long periods of negotiation, and it might be more difficult to negotiate with an ally than with an enemy. But Mark and I were convinced that in spite of daily ups and downs, if we could just hang on, Bill Richardson would bring Lori home.

Ramsey Clark and Tom Nooter joined us in a meeting at the congressman's office in early April. We all agreed that for the next several months he would "call all the shots." He had already cleared this with Carolyn Maloney and other members of Congress who were actively working on Lori's behalf.

He planned to go to Peru sometime that summer after making arrangements through the Peruvian ambassador to the United States, Ricardo Luna, who he believed was anxious to have this issue resolved. To us the summer seemed so far away. We wanted him to go immediately. But prior commitments prevented his going before mid-August. In the meantime, we were to get as many signatures as possible on the new House and Senate Dear Colleague letters to President Fujimori, and have them reach Peru about two weeks before the congressman's arrival. And we were to continue making noise, the more noise the better, until the beginning of August. But then he wanted the Peruvians to have two quiet weeks to contemplate their need to resolve Lori's case.

▪ Making Noise

So we set about making as much noise as possible. We spent two days in Boston and Cambridge speaking at several college campuses, Cambridge City Hall, and at meetings of local human rights and social action groups. These appearances were all arranged by James Williamson, a human rights advocate and Massachusetts supporter of Lori. This was the first time we took our campaign "on the road," and we were pleased with the events and the media coverage.

We strengthened our contacts with human rights groups, meeting with Coletta Youngers of the Washington Office on Latin America, Anne Manuel of Human Rights Watch: Americas, Joy Olson of the Latin American Working Group, Carlos Salinas of Amnesty International, and Joe Eldridge of the Lawyers Committee for Human Rights. They saw Lori's situation as a means of focusing the attention of the U.S. public on Peru, informing the public about the hundreds, maybe thousands, of innocent Peruvians wrongfully imprisoned. We knew Lori would be pleased with this approach. She had emphatically asked that we always point out that she was only one of many. In fact, she had concluded her June 1996 letter to Congress by writing, "I have confidence that this help from you will benefit not only me but will improve the judicial system to better defend the basic rights of man in Peru."

We spoke at a congressional colloquy on human rights in Peru sponsored by Maurice Paprin, cochairman of The Fund for New Priorities, an organization that fights for social justice. More than seventy people, including many congressional aides, heard human rights activists, legal experts, and members of Congress discuss the general situation in Peru and Lori's case in particular.

We organized a letter campaign to the U.S. representatives to the World Bank in an attempt to affect a loan to Peru. U.S. law requires executive directors to international banks to oppose assistance to any government that engages in a pattern of gross violations of internationally recognized human rights. But when we met with representatives of the State Department and the World Bank, we were told that they never declared anyone a "gross violator," and they had no intention of doing so in this case. Business as usual.

On May 20, President Fujimori visited Washington. Following Congressman Richardson's advice, we did not demonstrate there, but instead held a vigil in front of the Peruvian consulate in New York. In support, former president Jimmy Carter issued a press release on behalf of the Carter Center for Human Rights, which we read to the one hundred fifty or so people who came out in 96-degree heat to rally for Lori. In his statement, President Carter decried the lack of due process in the secret military court that tried Lori and urged the Peruvian government to retry her in a civilian court

While we were protesting in New York, President Fujimori was speaking with President Clinton and members of the NSC (National Security Council) in Washington. We learned of this twenty-minute meeting from Deputy National Security Advisor Nancy Soderberg. Due process for Lori was one of four issues President Clinton raised, and Ms. Soderberg vividly remembered that at the mention of Lori's name, President Fujimori proceeded to rant and yell for several minutes, leaving the rest of the room aghast at his undiplomatic behavior and stupefied into silence.

We also received a letter from President Clinton in which he recounted this meeting and his hope, expressed to President Fujimori, that Lori's case be transferred to civilian courts. But, as he politely phrased it, Mr. Fujimori's response "did not indicate a disposition on his part to intervene in the process." President Clinton closed by assuring us he would continue to closely monitor Lori's case. Unfortunately, "monitoring" sounded very passive, and Lori needed action.

▪ Back to Congress

We started lobbying in earnest. We wanted the House and Senate letters to tell Mr. Fujimori it would be wise to listen to Congressman Richardson. The question was how best to reach as many as possible of the four hundred thirty-five representatives and one hundred senators. On our first lobbying trip we had appointments at eight offices. That would not do. So, while whenever possible we called ahead for appointments, we also went door-to-door without prior arrangements, asking to meet with the legislative assistant for foreign affairs or human rights. Sometimes we met with the aide. Other times we only got the name of the aide. We left packets, always with an eye-catching photo of Lori. We kept careful records of whom we saw and where we visited. We followed up with phone calls to the offices where we had left information. We spoke to the aide, or, more often, the aide's voicemail. We updated our information packets with the names of all those who recently signed. We returned to Washington, revisited offices of those who had not yet signed, visited new offices, returned to New York and made followup calls and repeated this process again and again and again.

We weren't the usual lobbyists. We were parents with a unique stake in obtaining support. We caught the ear, and often the heart, of aides in a way that professional lobbyists could not. Mark's passion and pain were felt by all who listened. But we could not have done it without our ever-growing nationwide network. As time went on, we found that more and more aides were well informed about Lori, usually because they were hearing from constituents. Congressmen tend not to go out of their way to help nonconstituents. It was a combination of grassroots action, knocking on doors, and persistent followup that led to ever-increasing support.

On August 5, the House of Representatives forwarded a letter with eighty-seven signatures to President Fujimori asking him to set aside Lori's conviction "now" and "afford her a fair public trial or set her free." Twenty senators signed a similar letter that was sent the next day. Even though we were congratulated on our ability to gather so many signatures, we were still disappointed. We thought, ideally, everyone should sign the letter, and certainly we thought with more time we could at least double the number. But Congressman Richardson was leaving for Peru in a few weeks, and there was no more time.

Bill Richardson went to Peru and met for forty minutes with Foreign Minister Francisco Tudela and forty-five minutes with President Fujimori. He conveyed his message: Lori was "a thorn in the side of both countries." Mr. Fujimori indicated that Foreign Minister Tudela would be the one doing the negotiations. Mr. Tudela suggested that Lori utilize the bilateral treaty to transfer to a U.S. prison. Although he knew that a long sentence in a U.S. prison was not acceptable and more work was necessary, Congressman Richardson was optimistic, noting that the Peruvians seemed anxious to resolve this issue and had left doors open for negotiations. Mr. Tudela said he would get back to Mr. Richardson in a week or two and would possibly meet with him when he visited the United States in October.

On September 9, Congressman Richardson joined Tom, Ramsey, Mark, and me for dinner in our apartment. He told us of his visit to the embassy confirming that we had no friends there, a situation made worse by the lack of an ambassador. Alvin Adams had left some months before, and Ambassador Dennis Jett wouldn't arrive until October. Mr. Richardson emphasized how glad he was to be working outside the State Department, without worrying about whether or not he was "rocking the boat." Mark's notes from that meeting ended with, "We were unanimous in our belief that regardless how tough the negotiations might be, Bill Richardson would be in our corner."

▪ Meanwhile in Peru

While we were enduring the summer heat in New York, Lori experienced her first Andean winter. It was frigid and it was dry season, a time of severe water shortages. And with the arrival of the new prison director, Comandante Ordinola, mail was withheld, searches were frequent, and harassment increased.

In July, Lori wrote,

> The prison conditions for the five thousand or more accused of terrorism are extremely difficult, seeking the physical, psychological, moral destruction and annihilation of the prisoner . . . In this prison over the last few months the abuses and arbitrary policies have resulted in constant harassment of the prisoners. One would think that twenty-three and a half hours in a reduced space with lousy food would be enough. We spent two weeks with a severe water problem during which time we received only two to four quarts per person a day in which to bathe, wash clothing, plates, etc., and over the last few months there have been unusual and constant electrical problems . . . One can understand that the limited budget doesn't allow for excellent food, but on top of the reduced budget the corruption is such that the funds are even further diminished. Then we are condemned to eat only potatoes and rice every day, or some days only potatoes and sweet potatoes.

Lori commented that rather than fix problems, the authorities used situations of water shortages and frequent blackouts to "create tension."

In the fall, the embassy brought us relatively good news—that we would be able to visit Lori in December. At most two people could visit together for one half-hour. We immediately wrote to tell Lori we would be there on the 7th and she responded "[I] was very happy to know that you'll be visiting soon. I have literally spent two days singing, *viene mi mamá, viene mi mamá.*"

We were all so excited. Lori sent us lists of things she needed, half-jokingly requesting Mom's spaghetti or Dad's turkey. And she also reminded us, certainly unnecessarily, that November 13, her birthday, was approaching. She wrote,

> Could you bring the antibiotic that cures me of throat and other infections? As you must recall, as a "wee tot," I suffered from strep throat, a recurring bug that attacked me and penicillin didn't have much effect. Well, I have had chronic throat problems here that haven't been defeated, in spite of numerous antibiotic treatments, and I much prefer to take pills than to be injected. (I was injected six days ago for a throat infection and laryngitis with some antibiotic that smelled like Pinesol.) So, tell me the name of that antibiotic that finally cured my throat infection years ago, and again when I had bronchitis in 1986 and when I had my teeth pulled. If possible, bring sufficient dosage for a couple of throat infections, as I don't have any way to purchase or obtain prescription medicine aside from what is stocked here . . . Also bring throat lozenges that work.
>
> A helpful hint that I remembered because we're in the middle of a hefty electrical storm: Rainy season is from Oct./Nov. to Mar./Apr. although the sun is usually quite strong in the day. Use sunscreen and layers (and Dad should wear a hat). As Puno is one of the poorest areas in Peru, I wouldn't be too confident about anti-lightning systems. If there is an electrical storm,

remember that we're at 12,700 feet, no big buildings. I'd stay inside and watch it from the window. They look "neat." It also hails large pieces of hail every now and then, although supposedly the hail is much more dangerous in *ceja de selva* (eyebrow of the jungle) where the pieces of ice are quite big. I recommend layers because the temperature difference between sun and shade is significant, although that would be felt much more once you come in cold season (May, June, July) when the temperatures go well below freezing.

You should keep in mind that it is more likely than not that there will be a direct visit for Mother's Day. A direct visit may also be possible for Christmas but since that date is too soon, get reservations for the second Sunday in May. The church has been soliciting a group visit for children that day and it is likely the visit could be as long as three hours! It is also possible that the direct visit would only be with mothers and grandmothers, so, Mom should plan her visit in May, just in case we have any luck with direct visits. It's only six months away!

I am awaiting Dad's birthday card that I assume should have an unusual drawing this year. I'm in good humor, so anything is fine and remember this is my "three cube" (3^3) birthday. Very important.

It is a tradition in our family to give homemade birthday cards, and Mark always creates wonderful cards for Kathy and Lori. Lori in turn, like Mark, has a "thing" for numbers and enjoys describing the characteristics of the birthday—whether or not it's a prime number, multiples of her favorite numbers, etc. So twenty-seven was important because, as she pointed out when Kathy was twenty-seven, a person usually has at most four birthdays that are a "cube"—ages one, eight, twenty-seven, and sixty-four. Mark remembered that in several letters Lori had written that she was longing for chicken, and he designed a card featuring a big cake with twenty-nine chickens set on top instead of candles—twenty-seven chicken/candles for her age plus one "for next year" and another "for good luck."

November also brought the one-year anniversary of Lori's arrest, a sad anniversary for all of us filled with vivid memories for Lori. She wrote,

> One year gone by, today is Nov. 30. It's 7:50 p.m. and I can remember quite vividly the strange process that brought me to where I am now, a very long night spent listening to gunfire and explosions, witnessing the arrival of five hundred to a thousand members of the armed forces and police to "defeat" a small group of young Peruvians, about twenty of them.
>
> It has been an unusual year. In a certain sense time has passed quickly and what has been weird is that after being a rather private person, all of a sudden I'm quite public and I have connected once again to those I haven't seen in ages, which is really unusual. Ironically, I feel I'm in closer contact with my family than I've been in years.
>
> I assume that eventually we will all return to our normal states. I can return to being a private person, you guys can teach normally again, Kathy can study/ work normally again and all of our childhood friends and acquaintances might again become distant.

▪ The First Visit

We anxiously prepared for our first visit with Lori at Yanamayo. We wrote long letters, knowing that in a half-hour visit we would never be able to say all the things we wanted to say. We baked chocolate chip cookies and bought bagels from Lori's favorite shop. I froze a container of homemade sauce and a separate container of cooked pasta to bring in an insulated container. Lori would have to eat it cold, but she asked for Mom's spaghetti, and I was bringing Mom's spaghetti.

We arrived in Lima on Friday, December 6, and visited the embassy. We had put in a request for an "up-close" visit, one without screens between Lori and us, and Ambassador Dennis Jett told us he personally met with President Fujimori, who granted the request. The ambassador suggested that we not tell anyone of the arrangements and maintain a low profile during the trip, particularly avoiding the Peruvian press. We told him we planned to interview after the visit with United States and international press. In fact we had made arrangements with Calvin Sims of the *New York Times,* Lynn Monahan of Associated Press, and Saul Hudson of Reuters. But we had insisted that no one go with us to the prison or approach the prison at all, and that there be no interviews or photographs in public places. All year we had tried in vain to keep Lori's story alive in the media. Now, finally there was interest. There was news. And we couldn't miss the opportunity for coverage in the United States. But we were very willing to avoid the Peruvian press and remain out of the Peruvian public eye.

We arranged to meet Julie Grant the following morning to catch the 6 a.m. flight to Juliaca. Visiting was permitted from 10 a.m. to 4 p.m., and we wanted to be sure we arrived early. Julie was to accompany us and "show us the ropes." This would be her last trip for a while. State Department guidelines recommend monthly visits to prisoners awaiting trial and quarterly visits after sentencing. Consular officials had continued seeing Lori once a month while family was not permitted, but now that we would be visiting, they would go only once every three months.

We were so nervous about the visit that we hardly slept. How would she look? What would she say? We arrived at the airport at 5 a.m. only to learn that the 6 a.m. flight had been cancelled and we were rescheduled for the 10 a.m. flight. We finally departed at 1:30 p.m. It was rainy season in the Andes, and such delays weren't unusual. But all those hours in the hot, humid, crowded Lima airport, not knowing if or when the plane would leave, greatly intensified our distress.

We landed at Juliaca at 3:40 p.m., still an hour's drive from the prison, and were anguished at the possibility of not being able to visit Lori that day. After waiting almost a year I could not wait even one more day. Because we were traveling with Julie, the National Police drove us to the prison, and we stopped on the way to buy Lori a special gift—hot, barbecued chicken.

As luck would have it, by the time we reached Yanamayo we were in the midst of a heavy rainstorm. It was spectacular, just as Lori described in her letters. The lightning and thunder put on quite a show. But it also shut down all electrical power, so that when we arrived at the prison it was in total darkness.

Everything and everybody were thoroughly searched. The bagels were individually squeezed and smelled. The chocolate chip cookies were dumped on the table and put back in the container one by one. The books and cards were glanced at, with full inspection scheduled for later. The bottle of one hundred Keflex antibiotic capsules was to be sent to the medical office. The cardboard tubing of the toilet paper was removed. We were fingerprinted and "patted down."

It was well after the end of visiting hours when we met Comandante Ordinola. With Julie translating, he made it clear that he was not pleased with our late arrival or the request for a private visit. He pointed his finger at us and threatened that if anyone were to find out about the "special privileges," Lori would suffer and we would suffer. If anyone asked, we were to say the visit was in the *locutorio,* the usual visiting room. He took us there to see it so, if need be, we could describe it. It was too dark to see much except what looked like a long table with two screens about one foot apart, down the center, separating visitor from prisoner.

Finally, we were taken to see Lori. We met in an office and it was very dark. Her face seemed long and thin but we could not tell if she was pale or rosy. We could see that her hands were swollen but could not tell their color or if they were cut. She was dressed in so many layers, topped by the bulky sweater I had knitted for her birthday, so that even when we were permitted a hug, it was difficult to tell if she was unduly thin. We stood close together through the entire visit while three female guards hovered over us. We did not think they were fluent in English, but we spoke in whispers, worried that just a single wrong word could be picked up and somehow misused. Lori had no choice but to whisper. She had laryngitis.

We had each brought a list of things to say that we couldn't read in the dark. And a half-hour, actually twenty-six minutes, flew by before we could say much. Lori asked about family and friends and asked about her case. We told her about Congressman Richardson and she was guardedly excited about his efforts. She hoped he was as good a negotiator as we thought. She had little faith that President Fujimori would "do the right thing." We had wanted to tell her about all her supporters, about the vigils and colloquies. We had hoped we could give her a short break from the stresses of prison life, to joke, to talk about home, to provide comforting words. But we couldn't. There wasn't time. And it was dark. And Lori had so many questions. And the guards were hovering. And Lori was sure that the room was bugged. And she was worried that this private visit would be held against her. Time was up, we were allowed to hug and say good-bye, and we had barely said hello. And we hadn't relieved any stress. We may have added to it.

By the time we reached the Hotel Colon Inn in Puno, Mark was feeling really, really terrible. Although the altitude affected him immediately when we arrived at the Juliaca airport, he was so anxious to see Lori that he ignored the symptoms. But now in our hotel room he was nauseous and his head was throbbing. He drank some coca tea, took some aspirin, and taped a medicated patch across his nose. Reporters Sims, Hudson, and Monahan were at the hotel, also suffering from the altitude. Fortunately, I had only slight headaches that disappeared with aspirin.

We interviewed with the journalists in our hotel room. We discussed our visit and showed them the gifts Lori had given us, including a needlepoint picture of our cats that she designed from a photo we had sent. And, as always when we spoke to the press, we talked about Lori's innocence and the need for justice for Lori and so many others in Peru. When pressed for details, we described our visit in the *locutorio* with its double screens. We hated to lie, but Comandante Ordinola had really frightened us.

▪ After the Visit

We returned to New York and immediately made plans for Kathy and me to go to Peru in January. Regulations permitted one visit, for one half-hour, each month. Only immediate family members could visit, and for later trips, Mark, Kathy, and I would alternate. Although we would have preferred traveling in pairs, the expense precluded it.

The December visit generated sympathetic newspaper articles across the country, and we received many calls and letters offering to help. We were heard in radio interviews across the country and around the world, including the BBC, and Voice of America, as well as shows in Colombia and Venezuela. With all this notice, it was a good time to press Congressman Richardson to return to Peru. There were rumors that he would be nominated for U.S. ambassador to the United Nations, and although we thought he would be great for the job, we didn't want him to forget about Lori. We wanted him to go to Peru and push for a Christmas pardon.

We had arranged to meet with him on December 12. He had just returned from the Sudan, where he had negotiated the release of three Americans. He was disappointed that Peruvian foreign minister Tudela had not contacted him as promised, and had avoided him when he visited the United Nations in October. We told him that we knew that Mr. Tudela met with U.N. ambassador Madeleine Albright, but that, as far as we knew, neither he nor the ambassador mentioned Lori. But Congressman Richardson was undeterred and insisted that Lori was now his number-one priority. He said he would write to President Fujimori and ask for a Christmas pardon on humanitarian grounds. If Fujimori were to show any interest he would fly to Lima before Christmas. In the meantime we were to exert maximum public pressure on Peru, keep up the media coverage, and get letters from Congress suggesting a humanitarian pardon. As the meeting ended, he put an arm around

Mark's shoulder and said, "I promise I will bring her home." On December 13, Richardson's nomination for U.N. ambassador was announced, and in his interview with the *Washington Post,* he said that he still had to take care of some unfinished business, including securing justice for Lori Berenson.

■ The 2 A.M. Call

On December 18 at 2 a.m., the phone rang. In the thirty seconds or less that it took to get from my bed to the phone, my heart was pounding and I was shaking with fear. The call wasn't about Lori—well, not directly. It was a journalist asking if I knew that the previous evening the MRTA had taken hostages at the home of the Japanese ambassador in Lima. He wanted to know what impact I thought this might have on Lori's situation. The roller coaster had gone over the peak and was speeding toward the bottom. This time I couldn't stop it from dragging me along with it.

PART FOUR

DECEMBER 1996

TO DECEMBER 1998

■

CRISIS,

HOPE,

AND

DISAPPOINTMENT

■ The Hostage Crisis: December 17, 1996 to April 22, 1997

These were probably the worst months. We were totally immobilized. We were afraid for all those in the Japanese ambassador's residence, and we were afraid for Lori who was imprisoned in a country with a history of gunning down prisoners in their cells. All we could do was sit quietly and hope for a quick and peaceful resolution. This was not a time to rally Congress, seek attention, or hold demonstrations. In previous months we had been urging the U.S. embassy to consider Lori's case a political rather than a consular matter, and now we had to beg for even consular attention, to plead with them to insure her safety. And we turned to Congressman Richardson for help only to find that as U.N. ambassador he had "joined" the State Department. He was now "one of them." He wouldn't answer our calls.

On the evening of December 17, several members of the MRTA posed as waiters at a party celebrating the emperor of Japan's birthday at the home of the Japanese ambassador. Others, including MRTA leader Nestor Cerpa, dynamited a wall and entered the compound. Fourteen rebels took approximately five hundred guests hostage. U.S. ambassador Dennis Jett had left the party moments before the siege, but thirteen other embassy staff members were not as fortunate. By the next morning all the women and children, including President Fujimori's mother and sister, and eight U.S. citizens were released. On December 23, as a Christmas gesture, 225 additional hostages were freed, including all of the remaining U.S. citizens. Still held hostage were 140 men, including Foreign Minister Tudela, other Peruvian officials, several ambassadors, and leaders of the Japanese business community. As the days wore on, the MRTA continued to release others, and when the crisis ended, the number of hostages was reduced to 72.

The media was in a frenzy. Lori was the U.S. connection to this breaking story, and suddenly every network and every reporter wanted our comments. But the hostage situation was not about Lori, and we wouldn't give interviews. We issued a press release saying, "We are very distressed at the situation in Lima, and our hearts go out to all those in danger and to their families. We hope that this crisis is resolved expeditiously and peacefully. Until that time we won't make further comment." The phone kept ringing anyway. Reporters came to our door and milled around on the street outside. When I left for work I used an alternate exit to avoid them. On one occasion when I arrived at my class there was a reporter sitting amongst my students.

As the weeks and months dragged on, we were glued to CNN and frantic with worry. We continued our e-mail and snail mail correspondence with our support group, but we did not issue newsletters or updates or organize campaigns. For the first time since Lori's arrest we felt truly helpless and truly afraid for Lori's life. We were concerned for the lives of the hostages, but we also knew that there could be repercussions in Yanamayo, even if no hostages were harmed. In January, there were rumors that Lori and the others labeled as MRTA would be moved to Challapalea, a new prison at a height of over sixteen thousand feet, a very long car ride from Yanamayo. That would have meant unbearable, torturous, physical conditions, likely a death sentence for Lori and others unable to adjust to that altitude. What kind of people would even build a prison at such a height? The transfer was never made, but the threat alone was enough to frighten Lori and the others, not so much because of altitude or the conditions at the new prison, but because of the ride there. They feared that en route the government would kill them all and then claim they tried to escape. If you did not know Peruvian history, you might say this was a sign of paranoia. But Peru had a record of brutality against political prisoners. In 1986, the government massacred over three hundred men and women at three prisons. In 1992, under Fujimori's reign, forty were killed at the Canto Grande Prison in Lima.

Yanamayo Prison was totally closed to families, the Red Cross, and the Catholic Church, adding to our fears that prison officials could act with impunity. We begged embassy officials to go. We argued that since consular visits were guaranteed by international treaty, at a time when everyone else was forbidden to enter, the embassy surely should be sending someone weekly. But the last consular visit was a brief one by Julie Grant, when she accompanied us to Yanamayo on December 7, and embassy officials wanted to maintain their policy of quarterly visits. They claimed that it would be unwise for them to visit often, that frequent visits would further link Lori with the MRTA and do her more harm than good. This did not make the slightest bit of sense to me. How could consular visits harm her?

On February 26, two and a half months after the December visit by Julie and us, consular officer Gerry Fuller finally saw Lori. She described the atmosphere as extremely tense and asked that the embassy send supplies and visitors more often, noting that she and her fellow prisoners would feel much safer if prison authorities knew the embassy would be making frequent visits. But Lori's request was ignored, and no one returned until mid-April.

I knew that the State Department was more interested in supporting Mr. Fujimori than in securing justice for Lori or even insuring her well-being. And I was used to hearing their flimsy pretenses to the contrary. But when they insisted that they were helping Lori by not visiting her, they not only greatly increased my concern for Lori's safety, they insulted my intelligence.

The crisis had nothing to do with Lori and everything to do with Lori. She was in prison, far from the events in Lima, but because the hostage-takers were MRTA and she was accused of being MRTA, her name was drawn into the news and also into the negotiations. Although we avoided the press, reporters continued writing about Lori, speculating on the effect these events would have on her situation. And President Fujimori took every opportunity to link her to the events in Lima. And then too, MRTA leader Nestor Cerpa decided to include Lori in his demands.

When the crisis began, the rebels issued a communiqué demanding that the government commit itself to changes in its economic policies so as to improve the well-being of the majority of Peruvians. They also called for "the release of MRTA prisoners, as well as those prisoners falsely accused by the government of being MRTA militants." They wanted freedom for over four hundred prisoners, including Lori, whom they placed in the group of falsely accused. As time wore on and Fujimori pretended to negotiate, Cerpa began drawing up more limited lists, which became shorter and shorter and less and less controversial. By the end, there were twenty names, people that Cerpa thought would be acceptable to Fujimori, those prisoners Fujimori knew were not a threat. First on the list was Cerpa's wife, Nancy, who was imprisoned with Lori in Yanamayo. Archbishop Cipriani, a conservative supporter of President Fujimori who led negotiations seeking a peaceful resolution, argued for Nancy's release and later said, "[Peruvian] national security was not in danger from Nancy Gilvonio." Also on the list were foreigners, including Lori, the elderly, the very young, and the ailing. After the crisis, Reuters reported that an ex-hostage claimed that the rebels "called for [Lori's] release as a way of winning over American public opinion to the MRTA."

Cerpa apparently believed that Fujimori was engaged in serious dialogue, that he would keep his promise to the Japanese government to avoid bloodshed, and that his shorter list that did not include MRTA leadership would allow a negotiated settlement. We wanted to believe the same. We followed all the rumors, particularly those about release of prisoners. At one point there was speculation that the hostage-takers and some prisoners would go to Cuba. In early February, we watched in awe as newscasts showed Alberto Fujimori hugging Fidel Castro before they sat down to discuss this possibility. The media flocked to Havana to report on this meeting and await the possible arrival of Cerpa and the others. We waited to see if this bizarre turn of events would lead to Lori's freedom. But nothing happened. Negotiations dragged on. Nothing happened.

On Tuesday, April 22, at about 4 p.m., Mark and I were playing Scrabble and listening to the radio. When we heard a bulletin about Peru, we immediately turned on the TV to see a rerun of the massacre. We were overtaken by anguish as we watched a replay of commandos storming the Japanese ambassador's residence, thus ending the hostage crisis. We had hoped that the resolution would be quick and peaceful, but it was neither. Two soldiers were killed along with one hostage, a Supreme Court Justice who was shot in the leg and bled to death. Foreign Minister Tudela was shot in the foot. All the rebels were killed. President Fujimori proudly posed for photos while standing on the body of a dead rebel.

The freed hostages later filled in some details. The Peruvian agricultural minister told a television audience about a young rebel who surrendered but was gunned down. Newspapers reported that an intelligence agent who monitored the raid through listening devices heard two rebels being shot as they shouted, "We surrender! We surrender!" Some of the corpses were mutilated—one was left without head or arms.

Although the State Department declared that the United States gave no advice or training to the commandos, *USA Today* reported that a retired FBI agent claimed to have helped in

the training, stating, "We brought them to the United States."
Aviation Week reported that a CIA-operated spy plane was used
to track the movements of the rebels and hostages.

We were relieved that the crisis had ended but deeply,
deeply saddened by the loss of seventeen lives.

▪ Prison Visits Resume

Although the crisis was over, the prison remained closed to the church, the Red Cross, and families. We implored the State Department to secure a visit for Mother's Day, even if it wouldn't be the special three-hour, up-close visit that Lori had written about and been hoping for since November. But permission was denied. Finally, in mid-June, almost two months after the hostages were freed, Fujimori personally announced the resumption of family visits to political prisoners.

Whether it was a result of the hostage crisis and the attention the MRTA had brought to the extremely harsh conditions in Peruvian prisons or, as the Peruvian government claimed, changes had been "in the works" for a long time, there were revisions of the rules. Prisoners were now allowed out in the yard for one full hour each day, and families could visit for one full hour each week. Neither the prisoners, nor their families, nor the human rights community could applaud a system that confined prisoners to a freezing cell twenty-three hours a day. And we certainly could not visit weekly. But one hour in the sun was better than thirty minutes, and one-hour visits were better than half-hour ones. The new rules also allowed for two-hour visits for Christmas, Father's Day, Mother's Day, and prisoner birthdays.

Perhaps most significant for Yanamayo was the change of prison director. Comandante Pantaleon Valdivia Flores, unlike his predecessor, knew how to run a secure prison without harassing and abusing the inmates. Tom Holladay met with him after a visit to Lori in June and reported to us that the prison atmosphere was much improved. The comandante was concerned that the International Red Cross was still denied entry, particularly because the prison had run out of certain medicines. At the suggestion of Lori and the prison doctor, and with the comandante's approval, we were asked to bring medicated hand cream for Lori and, if possible, vitamins and various medications for other prisoners.

Kathy and I brought several hundred dollars' worth of medicines when we visited Yanamayo on June 28. Because of the medicines, or because we had missed the special Mother's Day visit, or for no particular reason, we were allowed to meet in the comandante's office. Lori was very much more relaxed than when I had seen her in December, although she still worried that the room was "bugged." This was the first time I got a good look at her hands, and they looked terrible. They were purple, swollen, and cut. Her face was very red and chapped, similar to what I had observed of many of the children in Puno. She still had a sore throat and laryngitis, and asked for more antibiotics. The cold, dry weather was making all her ailments worse. It was winter and Lori said it was so frigid at night that she slept under eight blankets. Kathy and I kept our winter coats on throughout the visit. Lori, more used to the cold, wore several sweaters.

As is typical of Lori, she spent part of the time expressing her concerns for fellow prisoners. She asked us to bring special medicine for a woman who had bleeding ulcers. She worried about another, who was still suffering from the effects of the torture inflicted by DINCOTE in 1993. She told us Nancy was grieving the death of her husband and lamenting her inability to be with and comfort her sons at such a crucial time. We learned about the arrest six years earlier of Lori's twenty-three-year-old cellmate. She had been injured in a crossfire between the police and the MRTA, and was accused of being one of the rebels, but her case had still not come to trial. It was so clear that she was innocent that a lawyer from the Catholic Church was defending her, and there was a good chance she would eventually be released. But meanwhile she had spent six years in prison and still suffered from serious injuries incurred at the time of her arrest. On top of that, her legs and hip had been broken in an auto accident while being transferred to Yanamayo in September 1994, and she still suffered from infections and pain from a pin in her hip.*

Lori's new society consisted of these four women, and they comprised her entire world. She shared yard time, books, and conversations with them. They sang together, and Lori said that on New Year's Eve they had danced together—in their separate cells. There were no workshops, so all crafts were done separately, but they shared raw materials and ideas. Church representatives brought their crafts for sale at local fairs. I remembered sending fake fur, plastic eyes, and the like for a teddy bear project and was rewarded with a gift—a three-foot-tall bear weighing over ten pounds. I was amazed with the finished product, as is everyone who sees it in its new home, seated on my living room couch, its paw casually thrown over the armrest.

The visit lasted longer than an hour, which was a great treat. Lori had so much to tell us and was also so thirsty for news. For six months she had had little or no correspondence with family or friends and wanted to know how everyone was, what she had missed. She knew the details of the hostage crisis and was well aware of the negative effect it had on her case. But now, two months after its bloody conclusion, everyone at the prison, even Nancy, was getting back to life as best they could. Lori expressed her thoughts in a letter that she asked me to send to her many, many pen pals.

* POSTSCRIPT: This young woman was declared innocent and released in April 1998, after seven years in prison, living under horrendous conditions.

22 June 1997

Dear Friend:

I am glad I am able to send you greetings after this long silence. I know that family visits are being permitted again and that I will be able to send this present note.

We have passed through a difficult and bleak time but I know that there will be a better day ahead, sooner or later.

We are returning to a series of projects and see the possibility of learning new types of arts and crafts, studying, and writing again to our families and friends.

We are in the midst of a moderate frost, waiting for winter to really appear, but we are happy, morally strong and uplifted by the warmth of friendship in this cold climate.

I would like you to know how much it means to me to receive your letters. I very much appreciate the help, uplifting words and the warmth that is sent to me. Your interest and concern help me to remember that I am not alone. For all of this, a thousand thanks!

I close this letter with all best wishes to you and your loved ones.

▪ The Campaign Resumes

Once the hostage crisis was over we geared up our campaign full force. We were so glad to be working again toward Lori's release. We gave newspaper interviews, I wrote an article for *Vogue,* and we appeared with John Hockenberry on MSNBC's *Edgewise* and with Deborah Norville on *Inside Edition.* We resumed our speaking engagements at churches, synagogues, human rights conferences, high schools, and universities. In May, we gave testimony at a congressional Human Rights Caucus hearing on prison conditions in Peru, summarizing our compilation of thirty-nine violations of the *United Nations Standard Minimum Rules for the Treatment of Prisoners,* conditions we had learned from Lori and from reports of other prisoners. Nobel Peace Prize recipient Archbishop Desmond Tutu wrote to President Fujimori asking him to give Lori a fair trial immediately or release her. Cardinal John O'Connor of the Archdiocese of New York wrote to the Peruvian president and also wrote to Lori. Our network grew. We sent out more newsletters and started a new congressional campaign. We again tried to contact Bill Richardson, now in New York as ambassador to the United Nations, but to no avail. After each attempted contact, Mark would repeat, "But he promised me, he promised . . ." After a while we gave up.

The hostage crisis had produced new misinformation for us to counter. President Fujimori told reporters in Washington that due process was not needed in Lori's case because she had admitted her membership in the MRTA at her press presentation. This made its way into various newspaper articles, not as "President Fujimori says that Lori admitted membership," which would have been bad enough, but simply as "Lori admitted membership. . . ." On May 19, a *Boston Globe* article stated, "She confessed her involvement with the group in a televised statement following her arrest." At our urging, the *Globe* checked into the statement and then issued a correction: "A story . . . incorrectly reported that Lori Berenson, a former M.I.T. student who is serving a life sentence in Peru for treason, had publicly confessed her involvement with Tupac Amaru rebels." We were gratified by the *Globe's* correction, but this was just one article in one newspaper. It was impossible to correct them all—although we tried.

And we still had our disagreements with the State Department. Consular officials continued their policy of visiting Lori once every three months. In letters to members of Congress and the public they described this as "visiting regularly," and when coupled with phrases like "we closely monitor her situation" and "we speak to her family often," members of Congress believed they visited at least monthly and kept us informed of Lori's condition. The truth was that *we* visited monthly—and in later years twice monthly—and *we* kept *them* informed of her condition.

By the fall of 1997, there had been a complete turnover of embassy personnel. Ambassador Alvin Adams had been replaced by Dennis Jett, and Jim Mack, Julie Grant, and Tom Holladay were also gone. Julie Grant's replacement, Mary Grandfield, brought a more human face to that position. She was always available to answer our questions, even if it meant us calling her at home. She shared books with Lori and tried to make her visits with her as pleasant and meaningful as possible. At our request she also arranged to call Lori occasionally, a request we could never convince Julie to act on. Of course, we would have preferred phone calls once a week, but at least we knew Mary would speak to Lori if there were particular problems or if she or we needed information.

We missed Tom Holladay, who as consul general had exhibited sincere concern for Lori's well-being. We did not interact much with his replacement, Annette Veler, or with Heather Hodges, who replaced Jim Mack. But like their predecessors, this new group kept the flow of misleading information. Together they took first prize in the contest for the worst letter about Lori, a letter to Senator Paul Coverdell of Georgia which was drafted by Mary Grandfield, signed by Annette Veler, cleared by Heather Hodges, and approved by Dennis Jett. It responded in two pages to the senator's inquiries about Lori. Almost one complete page was devoted to the MRTA, the hostage crisis, and the history of terrorism in Peru, none of which had anything to do with Lori.

In the last months of 1997, the hostage crisis was well behind us and our campaign was on an upswing. In October, Carolyn Maloney went to Peru to visit Lori. Lori was delighted with her visit, impressed that the congresswoman would travel so far to see her, and glad, as she told Ms. Maloney, that she had voted for her by absentee ballot from Yanamayo in the 1996 election. Afterward, Carolyn Maloney told the press that she found Lori in good spirits. "She's a very positive person even though she's in very severe conditions. When I walked in to see her, the commander of the base told me she liked the prison very much and never wanted to leave, and Lori said, 'He's got such a great sense of humor.'" But Ms. Maloney also expressed her concern about Lori's health, saying, "I held her swollen, red hands and they literally shook." While in Peru the congresswoman also met with Ambassador Jett and members of President Fujimori's cabinet, arguing for justice for Lori.

Carolyn Maloney was really terrific. In addition to sponsoring letters and attending vigils, she literally went the extra mile—indeed, the extra eight thousand round-trip miles— for her constituent. Without the support from Carolyn Maloney and other members of Congress, we would have had no hope. Many signed letters but others did even more. Senators Daniel Patrick Moynihan and Jim Jeffords organized Dear Colleague letters, Senators Christopher Dodd and Patrick Leahy spoke strongly on Lori's behalf on the Senate floor, and Senator Paul Wellstone wrote to Lori to express his support.

Congressman Jim McGovern, who had met Lori in El Salvador, spoke out at vigils, hearings, and press conferences. Representatives Connie Morella and Jim Leach always cosponsored the House Dear Colleague letters as did Ron Dellums before he retired. Representatives Clayton, Delahunt, Hinchey, McKinney, and Meek spoke up for Lori at hearings. And then there was Maxine Waters.

We met Congresswoman Waters that November at a ceremony sponsored by the Office of the Americas, a human rights and social justice organization headquartered in Los Angeles. She, Ramsey Clark, and Lori each received a Peace and Justice Award. Lori's award was for her "dedication to the suffering people of the Americas" and for "being one with the thousands of Prisoners of Conscience in Peru and throughout the world."

Congresswoman Waters received her award for her continued efforts in Congress on behalf of human rights and social justice. But she refused to accept the award—at least not then. She told the audience she would come back to accept it when Lori could accompany her. She vowed to help gain Lori's freedom—and she meant it. The following month she brought up Lori's case to the Congressional Black Caucus, spoke at vigils for Lori, and continued her efforts in later years by sponsoring an amendment to a funding bill, writing to President Clinton and discussing Lori's situation with the President's chief advisors. She brought renewed hope and new energy to our campaign.

And as the year drew to a close, the two-year anniversary of Lori's arrest was marked by vigils in cities across the country. The City Councils of Los Angeles and of Cambridge, Massachusetts, and the California State Assembly passed resolutions declaring Lori a Prisoner of Conscience and commending her work for human rights.

The House and Senate sent off letters on Lori's behalf, this time to Secretary of State Madeleine Albright, asking that she do "all within [her] power to impress upon the Peruvian government the importance of providing [Lori] an open and fair proceeding in a civilian court without further delay." We were now practiced lobbyists. We rallied our supporters, made an endless numbers of phone calls, and trekked from door to door in the corridors of Congress. Each new signature inspired us to seek more. We were obsessed with accumulating signatures, accumulating support. By December, one hundred seventy-five representatives and fifty-two senators signed their respective letters. A majority of the Senate! One hundred seventy-five representatives! Boy, were we proud of ourselves!

Unfortunately, the State Department, on behalf of the secretary, offered a feeble response. They sent the usual "Lori letter," replete with the subtle accusations and pats on their own backs for closely monitoring the situation, reiterating, "We have on many occasions urged . . . an open proceeding in a civilian court." I don't believe anyone, in or out of government, believed that "all within the State Department's power" was limited to occasional "urging." And I hoped others noticed, as I did, that Congress had asked for a "fair and open proceeding," while the response spoke only of an "open proceeding." What happened to "fair"? Perhaps they were hinting at something that became increasingly clear. A fair trial for Lori Berenson in Peru was not possible.

■ 1998 Begins

Once again we began a new year with a resolution that it would be the year of Lori's freedom. It wasn't. The year 1998 would end as it began, with Lori in prison, albeit a different prison. But it was a year in which our efforts started down new roads. Lori's case entered the international arena, Peruvian prime minister Javier Valle Riestra called for her pardon, we formed a national committee and, because it was now clear that a fair trial for Lori was impossible in Peru, we changed our focus to "Free Lori Berenson."

Each day there was more and more to do. In addition to our immediate campaigns, we sadly realized we had to develop long-term strategies. I could barely remember a life when I spent hours studying the physical properties of crystals, went to dance classes, took long walks, and went to movies. I no longer had time to cook, and often didn't have time to eat—at least not properly. Pizza became a dinner staple. Sleep? Well, I tried.

After thirty-two years of teaching statistics at Baruch College, Mark retired in order to devote full time to freeing Lori. Mark and I had always imagined we would die standing at blackboards with chalk in our hands. But now there was not enough time in the day for both of us to teach and do all that was necessary to help Lori. I was still teaching but no longer with the same effort as in the past. I wasn't revising my notes, devising new experiments, or creating new courses. I was unable to do what was necessary to keep my work fresh and exciting. Although I always tried to be available to help my students, I spent as little time on campus as possible. I didn't attend meetings, seminars, or campuswide activities. But I still enjoyed my time in the classroom, answering students' questions or watching those moments of "Eureka!" indicating a flash of understanding. And that classroom time, immersed in a discipline based on logic, was my escape from the unpredictable chaos that Lori's arrest had brought to my life. I decided not to retire—at least not yet.

In January, representatives from the Working Group on Arbitrary Detention of the U.N. High Commission on Human Rights visited Lori. My daughter Kathy had written to Boutros Boutros-Ghali, then U.N. secretary general, soon after Lori's arrest. Her letter was forwarded to the Commission on Human Rights in Geneva, and the Working Group began its investigation of the abuse of rights in Lori's case. After two years of gathering information from us and from Peru, they interviewed Lori. It took almost another year before they completed their report, which concluded, "The deprivation of Lori Berenson's liberty is arbitrary, as it contravenes Articles 8, 9, and 10 of the Universal Declaration of Human Rights and Articles 9 and 14 of the International Covenant on Civil and Political Rights." It added that Peru must adopt whatever means necessary to remedy the situation. But this was not binding. There was no penalty if Peru chose to ignore these findings. And the Peruvian government chose to ignore them.

They also ignored internationally recognized human rights groups such as Amnesty International, which in January 1998 stated, "Amnesty International considers Lori Berenson a political prisoner. Indeed, there is no way getting around that. Nor is there getting around the fact that she did not receive a fair trial. The circumstances of her arrest, trial and conviction raise troubling questions and make any decent human being feel a sense of deep repulsion against the unfairness of her treatment. It is sad but true however that hers is not an isolated incident of human cruelty."

Also in January, Lori's lawyers sent a petition on her behalf to the Inter-American Commission on Human Rights of the Organization of American States. The petition emphasized Lori's innocence, the horrendous prison conditions in Peru, and the numerous violations of international law, in particular, violations of the International Covenant on Civil and Political Rights and the Inter-American Convention on Human Rights, both of which Peru had signed. The petition ends: "Petitioner requests this Commission to recommend her immediate release from incarceration, together with all others similarly convicted, as she has been unjustly convicted of treason by an unconstitutional military tribunal which denied her the benefit of due process and a fair trial.

"Petitioner further requests this Commission to recommend her immediate release from incarceration, together with all others similarly convicted, on the grounds that the conditions of her confinement do not meet the minimal standards for the humane treatment of prisoners."

Unfortunately, submission of a petition was only the beginning of a long, multistep procedure. First the Commission would seek a response from the Peruvian government. Then it would hold a preliminary hearing to decide whether or not the petition would receive a full hearing. Assuming after the full hearing the Commission found in Lori's favor, Peru would have a period of time in which to implement corrective actions. If Peru refused to do so, then the Commission would take the case to the Inter-American Court. We were confident that the Commission and the Court would decide in Lori's favor, and since Peru had abided by decisions of this court in the past, we had hope that they would do so for Lori. But this could take years.

Lori's case at this commission was just one of many others against Peru. The most publicized were those of Baruch Ivcher and three judges of the Peruvian Constitutional Tribunal (the equivalent of the U.S. Supreme Court). Baruch Ivcher, an Israeli-born Peruvian citizen and owner of a TV station, had been persecuted in reprisal for broadcasting information on human rights violations and corruption implicating the SIN (National Intelligence Service) and Vladimiro Montesinos, its chief. Ivcher had revealed the use of torture within the SIN, as well as that organization's plans to spy on journalists, TV stations, and opposition politicians. Montesinos was a close ally of Fujimori, and a very powerful man. Ivcher was stripped of his Peruvian citizenship and his ownership of the station, and escaped the country. He was found guilty in absentia of "customs fraud" and was sentenced to twelve years. This was just one of many examples of the harassment of journalists, who were intimidated, jailed, or run out of the country for writing or broadcasting reports critical of the Peruvian government. And with no independent, impartial judicial system, any threats were not idle. Mr. Ivcher took his case to the Inter-American Commission, seeking the restoration of his citizenship and the return of his station.

The dangers of executive control of the judiciary were also evident in the case of the Constitutional Tribunal. When Fujimori was first elected in 1990, the Peruvian Constitution did not allow for successive reelection. In 1992, with the backing of the military and Mr. Montesinos, Fujimori instituted an *autogolpe,* or self-coup, disbanding Congress and the judiciary and rewriting the Constitution. This new Constitution permitted two consecutive five-year presidential terms, and he was elected for a second term in 1995. In 1996, the Congress, which had a majority from Fujimori's party and always followed his bidding, passed a law which interpreted the 1995 victory as his first under the new Constitution, allowing him to run again in 2000, even though it would be his third consecutive term. In 1997, the Constitutional Tribunal ruled that this interpretation was incorrect. Congress then removed the three judges who voted against reelection. The three judges appealed to the Inter-American Commission for reinstatement.

When Lori was first arrested, and for the next two years, our focus was on the lack of due process in the military tribunals and the need for a civilian trial. Even the Peruvian government admitted that there were hundreds of innocent people in prison who had been arrested under the antiterrorism laws, denied due process, and sentenced by hooded judges. To their credit, the Peruvian Congress appointed a three-member Indulto (Pardon) Commission that was to investigate cases and, if convinced of innocence, ask the president to grant a pardon. Human rights groups applauded the measure while arguing that those found innocent should simply be released and have their records cleared—"pardon" connotes "guilty but we forgive you," rather than innocence. But this was an important first step because it allowed for the release of those wrongly accused. It also was an important admission that mistakes had been made—in fact, that the system had allowed for a great many mistakes. Over a period of three years, four hundred eighty-nine prisoners were freed. The Commission found many others who were innocent but Mr. Fujimori refused to pardon them. Tom Nooter spoke with members of the Indulto Commission on Lori's behalf and was advised that she not apply to have her case investigated. Lori was too high-profile, and they would "shelve" her application rather than involve themselves in a controversial case. And applying to the Indulto Commission, or opening any other legal procedures in Peru, would have meant withdrawing the petition from the Inter-American Commission for Human Rights.

We applauded the work of the Indulto Commission and cheered whenever more innocents were released. The stories of their arrests, so-called trials, and years of imprisonment reminded all of the worst aspects of the antiterrorism laws in general and the judicial system in particular. The great majority of the wrongly imprisoned innocents had been tried in civil courts. Not only the military tribunals but the entire judicial system was incapable of providing fair trials in political cases.

Jose Miguel Vivanco, Executive Director of Human Rights Watch: Americas, in a report on Peru stated, "No government in the region—with the exception of Cuba—has more seriously interfered with the independence of the judiciary." Similarly, the *1998 United States State Department Report on Peru and Human Rights* points out, "Although the Constitution provides for an independent judiciary, in practice the judicial system is inefficient, often corrupt, and has appeared to be easily manipulated by the executive branch." And later, the 1999 report added, " Proceedings in the military courts—and those for terrorism in civilian courts—do not meet internationally accepted standards of openness, fairness, and due process."

Unfortunately, the same State Department that issued these reports continued to insist that the appropriate action to resolve Lori's situation would be to urge a new trial. This is just one of many instances when the State Department, in its narrow focus on its political goals, has ignored the advice of its own Bureau of Democracy, Human Rights and Labor.

But to us the message was clear. A fair trial had not been possible for Baruch Ivcher. A fair trial would not be possible for anyone that Fujimori or Montesinos wanted imprisoned. A fair trial would not be possible for Lori Berenson. We had to campaign for Lori's release.

▪ Visits to Yanamayo

Lori missed out on the daily ups and downs of the campaign to gain her freedom. At best we could give her a summary when we visited, which was every four or five weeks. Mark and I alternated, twice a year Kathy and I traveled together, and on rare occasions Mark and I went together.

I arranged my work schedule so that I had only late classes on Monday and no classes on Friday. That way I could leave for Peru Thursday night, return Monday morning, and not neglect my students. Continental Airlines instituted nonstop flights from Newark, New Jersey, to Lima, eliminating the worry of missing connections in Miami. Typically, on Thursday evening I took a taxi to the bus, the bus to Newark airport, and flew overnight, landing in Lima Friday morning. After many trips I felt like a commuter, tending to sit in the same airport seats, not noticing my surroundings, and dozing on the two-hour flight from Lima to Juliaca. Weather permitting, by early afternoon I was boarding a van heading south to Puno.

The van never left before it was completely full and, in fact, often managed to take on one or two more passengers than it was built for. But it provided a scenic though bumpy, crowded ride and only cost five soles, less than two dollars. It passed quickly through the city of Juliaca with its poorly paved roads that were flooded in rainy season and dusty in dry. After about fifty minutes of farmland, grazing animals, and an occasional factory, we would pass the turnoff to Yanamayo on our right and soon catch a glimpse of Lake Titicaca below on the left. Then came my favorite part of the ride, as suddenly, on the left, the entire city of Puno came into view—the center of the city, encircled by the many, many homes built into the mountainside, connected to the center by steep paths. As the van descended into the town it encountered increased traffic—other vans, taxis, bicycle-drawn carts, and pedestrians who

found it easier to walk in the road than on the narrow side-
walks.

I always stayed at the Colon Inn Hotel, introduced to us
by Julie Grant on our first visit in December 1996. It was rea-
sonably comfortable and was adjacent to the enormous market that covered much of the center of the city. Because the
altitude limited my ability to carry too much at once, I would
make several trips to shop, and it was very convenient to be in
a hotel so close to the market.

I brought a huge suitcase full of supplies that were only
available, or more conveniently located, in New York: clothing, powdered skim milk, vitamins, medicines, cookies, bagels, and books. And in Puno I would meander through the
market, shopping for fruit, vegetables, laundry supplies, toiletries, bread, cheese, gelatin, coffee, and tea. I bought enough
for four weeks, allowing for sharing. Peruvian prison officials
expected visitors to bring extra food to compensate somewhat
for the meager prison diet, and all brought some for sharing.
Because the prison was so cold, essentially a refrigerator, there
was no problem about spoilage—unless prison officials insisted
that the fruit be peeled.

Saturday morning at nine I'd leave for the prison, ten minutes away. I had a steady taxi driver, Zenon, who took me to
Yanamayo and then returned for me about four hours later.
The visit itself lasted only one hour, but there were three hours
of "check in" and waiting. Although visitors couldn't enter the
prison grounds until ten, a line formed long before. Even in
rainy season, there was bright sunshine early in the morning,
which even in the cold winter made the wait bearable.

All of us were loaded with bags of supplies and were anxious to see our loved ones. My conversations with the other
families were limited by my inability to speak Spanish. But I
could understand the language somewhat, and I found that
with a few key words and a lot of hand motion, I could com-

municate. Although I had traveled much further than the others, many visitors had taken bus rides from distant parts of the country and had been en route longer. And the expense was such that they could not come as often as I. In fact, many families could come only once a year, when the International Red Cross paid for the trip.

When the gates opened we proceeded one by one to the front entrance, where documents were inspected and supplies were glanced over. I then carried the bags of supplies about two hundred fifty yards uphill to the entrance of the main compound. This was physically the hardest part of the trip. I usually had well over fifty pounds of supplies, and carrying them uphill, even taking several trips, was not easy at an altitude of 12,700 feet. The other visitors had the same difficulty and sometimes the soldiers would help us. It all depended on the officer of the day, who had much leeway in deciding whether to help visitors or harass them. I found most of the prison personnel friendly and polite. They enjoyed practicing a few words of English and asked questions about New York. I would mail letters and packages to their relatives in the United States, and sometimes they gave us money to bring back medicines or clothes. Vitamins were very popular, especially those for children or the elderly. But if the orders were to harass, then harass they did.

There were at least two other stops at which identifying information was entered into notebooks. I was searched and fingerprinted and directed across a large courtyard, where tables were arranged for careful inspection of the supplies. In preparation, I had emptied all packaged items into clear plastic bags for easier viewing, and always followed the rules of no glass or metal containers. Books and the dozens of letters were set aside for approval by the censors. I held ready three copies of the required detailed inventory and waited patiently for my turn at a table.

Sometimes the inspection was quick and easy, and sometimes interminable and frustrating. Again it depended on the officer of the day. He decided which items were allowed and whether or not fruit need be peeled. I was told that prisoners can use fruit peels to make alcoholic beverages, but at Yanamayo this was not known to be a problem, and peeling fruit was just another form of harassment. I never knew if I should buy enough apples to last a month unpeeled or a few that, if peeled, would have to be eaten rather quickly. And similarly for pears, bananas, oranges, etc. After a while I stopped worrying about it, bought lots of fruit, if necessary argued that I should not have to peel, and, if I lost the argument, peeled a few and gave the rest to my taxi driver.

At one visit, a day that one guard termed "be tough on visitors day," the rules were really strange. Inspectors permitted a disposable razor but not its plastic cover, and removed all the plastic caps from the felt-tip pens. Although there had never before been a problem with Elmer's Glue, on this visit they wanted me to squeeze it into a plastic bag, rendering it totally useless. They permitted yards and yards of yarn, but they removed the shoelaces from a new pair of shoes, so Lori couldn't hang herself. Some visitors had brought plastic bottles of soda, which had to be poured into plastic bags. This reminded me of the time when Mark brought plastic bottles of water because there were cases of typhoid fever. When he was told to pour the water into some plastic bags that had been lying around, he caused a scene. He argued that according to rules, plastic bottles were allowed, and that to pour drinking water into dirty bags was unsanitary. They eventually allowed the bottles to pass.

In general, Mark and I argued for whatever we knew the government rules allowed. Sometimes, when the inspectors explained why a particular item was not acceptable, whether I understood them or not, I would simply repeat over and over,

"No comprendo, no comprendo," until they gave up and let the item pass.

The inspection was the last hurdle before seeing Lori, and when it finally ended, I was allowed into the building that housed the prisoners. To the right of the entrance is the first-floor *locutorio* and a metal spiral staircase leading up to the second floor. The second floor *locutorio* was where, except for a few special occasions, I met with Lori. Extending the length is a concrete slab, like a table, and rising up from the center of the slab to the ceiling were two wire mesh screens about a foot apart. The wires form a grid of one and a quarter inch squares. There are six immovable stools on either side. The entire room is encaged by vertical bars, leaving it open to view by the guards on the first floor. As I waited for Lori, I looked through the screens and beyond, through the bars that separated the *locutorio* from the adjacent corridor. I watched as guards walked by, and occasionally I saw the women prisoners as they were coming from or going to the yard. The women's cells were down this corridor to my right and around a corner. The men were off to the left, on the other side of the spiral staircase.

All this time, from the moment I had left for the airport on Thursday until Lori walked down that corridor and entered, my stomach had been churning and my head had been throbbing. I have visited Lori dozens of times, and my stomach and head do the same thing every single trip. I am always afraid that something has gone wrong since Mark or I last visited. The only way I am ever assured Lori is okay is when I actually see her. I need to see that smile and hear that "hi, Mom."

The *locutorio* was dimly lit, very noisy, and cold. Electric lights don't go on until 6 p.m. and the only available light comes through windows near the ceiling in the corridors. The windows have no glass, only horizontal wooden slats that limit the light but do nothing to stop the cold wind. The noise came from the prisoners. One group or another would bang on bars or chant, and the echoes off of the concrete and metal surfaces served to magnify the sound. I would sit for one hour, struggling to see Lori, struggling to hear her and struggling to keep warm. I wore a winter coat, gloves, and scarf, but after a short time my teeth would be chattering.

But I would have stayed for many hours, if they'd have allowed it. Although it was frustrating that I could not hug Lori or even touch her, it was wonderful to talk with her. We talked about family happenings, world events and Peruvian headlines. I updated her on our campaign, Congress, President Clinton, new supporters. She told me about prison happenings, projects she was working on, and books she had read. And we joked. In spite of the physical hardships, she was still the same Lori.

Sometimes the authorities permitted science magazines in English, so I would bring copies of *Discover* and *Natural History,* and if we had time we'd talk about them. Lori particularly liked articles on archaeology and anthropology, but she wanted to discuss everything: the sacrifices of pre-Colombian cultures, the effect of trauma on the brain, the properties of quarks, the age of the universe. If we didn't have time, she would write her thoughts and questions in a letter. But it was so much better to speak with her, to hear her voice—in English.

One hour goes by very quickly, and saying good-bye is always difficult. Lori always waited and watched as I descended the spiral staircase and then gave one more wave as the guard opened the door and I walked out into the courtyard.

I always spent Saturday afternoon shopping at the market. I'd have a list from Lori of what she needed, and I'd bring the supplies to Yanamayo on Sunday morning. It was another long process, as everything was again inspected and I had to wait until Lori received the packages and checked the inventory list to be assured she received everything.

Occasionally, depending on who was on duty, I saw Lori an hour on Sunday as well as Saturday. I was so happy to have that extra hour. Our lives had reached the point where one extra hour with Lori, even without the possibility of a hug, brought great happiness.

When I left the prison on Sunday I could finally relax. I had seen Lori and brought her what she needed. I had assured myself that her latest ailments were not life-threatening. And I had assured myself that even if prison had adversely affected her physical health, it could not affect her strong spirit.

I'd spend the few hours before leaving for the airport walking the streets of Puno. I would visit the main square, head to the lake, or browse the many bookstalls. I liked Puno. It wasn't too popular with tourists from the United States, but numbers of Europeans, Asians, and Australians, many with backpacks, came to see Lake Titicaca and the nearby Incan ruins at Sillustani, before or after visiting Bolivia, a bus ride away. There were various festivals, some celebrating Catholic feast days like the *Candelaria* in February and others commemorating more ancient times, like the November celebration of the birth of Manco Capac. But even without festivals, Puno was colorful and steeped in tradition. Many of the local women dressed as they had for centuries in multiple skirts and sweaters, with small black bowler hats seated atop their heads and long, thick black braids hanging down to their waist. They often had colorful cloths deftly folded to carry a baby, vegetables or whatever on their backs, and were likely to be conversing in Aymara. Although pop music tapes were available everywhere, Andean music, featuring *zampoñas* (panpipes) and flutes, was still popular. *"El CondorPasa,"* made famous in the United States by Simon and Garfunkel, an Andean anthem, was heard everywhere.

My memories of Puno may well be influenced by Lori. She had been there in 1995 and said it was her favorite place in Peru because of its rugged beauty and its history. Although all she could see from the prison yard was the sky, it inspired her and reminded her. In a letter to friends she wrote:

> The sky here is so blue and beautiful, as it must be in the countryside and over Lake Titicaca that I remember so clearly, but now I am unable to see. In precisely this region, el Collasuyo, the warriors of Manco Inca fought bloody battles in the war with the Spanish conquistadors in the 1500s. Although the Spanish won, the daring efforts of Manco Inca were not in vain. The Incas lost Copacabana then, lost their empire, and the Spanish gained a continent that they never knew how to care for. But from these Incas there remains a trail, a whole history for future generations to remember and admire and learn from.

▪ Father's Day

Mark was in Peru for a special Father's Day visit. Lori gave him a card she had made using a technique she learned from her fellow prisoners, whereby a design is sketched on the card and then colored threads are glued on in lieu of paint or ink. It pictured a father cat and two kittens. After the visit Mark flew to Lima and spent the evening at the airport, awaiting the plane to Newark. He didn't pay attention to the airport TV, where he could have seen the newly appointed Peruvian prime minister Javier Valle Riestra talking about Lori, saying, "I think we must look for a way to pardon her and expel her from Peru as an undesirable foreigner." Mark missed hearing him say that it was an error to charge her, a non-Peruvian, with treason, and that her secret military trial was flawed and was part of a "repressive" judicial system.

This was the beginning of a whirlwind week, with something new and exciting every day.

On Monday morning, reporters called from Lima to tell me of Mr. Valle Riestra's amazing declaration. For once reporters called with good news! The Peruvian prime minister told the world that Lori should be pardoned and sent home. I wanted to jump up and down for joy but was afraid to be overly optimistic. Lori's fate depended on President Fujimori, not his prime minister, even if Mr. Valle Riestra was an internationally recognized constitutional lawyer, and, ostensibly, Fujimori had appointed him because he wanted to improve Peru's human rights record. I hoped "this was it," but was prepared for it not to be. We anxiously awaited a response from Fujimori, and sure enough, on Tuesday, he announced that he would not pardon Lori. On Wednesday, having heard Fujimori's decision, Mr. Valle Riestra offered his resignation. He then agreed to stay on after much urging from the president, but vowed to continue lobbying for a pardon for Lori and improved human rights and democracy in Peru.

On Thursday President Fujimori was in New York to preside over a conference on microcredit at the Hilton Hotel. Our local support group was across the street, protesting his refusal to pardon Lori. A press conference that was slated to discuss Fujimori's economic policies was canceled after it was clear that the only questions reporters had were about Lori. And on Friday, when he spoke at the United Nations, members of the audience again brought up her name. Fujimori was visibly annoyed but stuck to his line that Lori had admitted her membership in MRTA, and he swore not to give her special treatment just because she is an American citizen. This prompted Ambassador Jett in Lima to express his disagreement. He told the press, "She . . . criticized the lack of justice in Peru, but never said she was a member of the rebel group." He also pointed out that Lori's nationality had worked against her, that "she had already received special treatment because of her nationality, as evidenced by the notoriety of her case and the harshness of her sentence."

We were very surprised by this rare public statement of support by the ambassador, particularly his direct refutation of Fujimori's remarks. We were more familiar with his efforts to turn off or limit support for Lori. After a meeting at the embassy, Blase Bonpane, director of the Office of the Americas, described Ambassador Jett as "blatantly adversarial." He said, "The Ambassador was most grateful to Fujimori for allowing the United States to establish a military base on the Peru/Colombia border and repaying Peru's debts to the World Bank. His concern for Lori seemed nonexistent." Lori had written to the ambassador, reiterating her innocence and asking him to visit her. But he declined, saying it would not be helpful to her situation, perhaps even harmful, if he were to visit—the usual incomprehensible embassy excuse. Perhaps he was afraid that if he met Lori face-to-face he would find it difficult to portray her as a terrorist.

At any rate, we could mark this as the time that Ambassador Jett stood up for Lori. It was also a time of extensive and positive media coverage. Not only were we interviewed, we were asked to schedule interviews for Lori after her release. The media really thought Lori was coming home and soon. We were a lot more skeptical. We could tell from Fujimori's statements and the coverage in the Peruvian press that we still had some time to go. But meanwhile this was a great opportunity to have Lori's story heard. I appeared as a guest on Fox News's *Cryer Report* and on Pacifica Radio's *Democracy Now.* There were editorials across the country supporting the prime minister's suggestion. An editorial in Thursday's *New York Times* concluded, "Mr. Fujimori should do more than just put up with Mr. Valle Riestra's criticisms. He should act on them, beginning with the cases of Ms. Berenson and others unfairly convicted by military courts."

We received phone calls from all over the country that week, including one very important one on Friday from General Donald Kerrick of the National Security Council. President Clinton and his National Security Advisor, Sandy Berger, had read the *New York Times* editorial while in China, and called to express their concern. General Kerrick said, "This nonsense has to stop." He said Sandy Berger wanted to meet with us. Ever since Lori's arrest, we had asked to meet with the president, or at least with Sandy Berger. Now, thanks to Prime Minister Valle Riestra, Mr. Berger was asking to meet with us. What an exciting week.

On August 7, Mr. Valle Riestra resigned, saying, "I am a democrat and here there is a totalitarian spirit." His departure was very unfortunate—for Lori and for all Peruvians. But overall his short tenure had a very positive effect. Our supporters, members of Congress, and President Clinton knew that a Peruvian prime minister said Lori should be freed. And the world heard his plea for improved human rights in Peru.

▪ New Focus

We needed to organize. Earlier in 1998 we had formed a committee, the Committee for Inter-American Human Rights. We had chosen a general name for this organization because we wanted it to work for improving human rights beyond Lori, beyond issues of lack of due process in Peru—if not immediately, then certainly as part of a longer struggle after Lori came home. But the first objective was to free Lori. In the spring, at the urging of Bob McIndoe, a supporter from Massachusetts, we decided to give this project a name to which people could immediately respond. We debated between "Justice for Lori Berenson" and "Free Lori Berenson." We were deciding whether to continue arguing for a trial or urge Lori's release. We knew that not everyone who supported a new trial would support release, but it was all too clear that a fair trial was not possible, that Lori was innocent of the preposterous charges, that she had already spent two and a half years under horrendous prison conditions, and that she should be released. Not wanting to weaken our support, we were still wavering in June when Prime Minister Valle Riestra left us with no doubt, and the Committee to Free Lori Berenson was born.

It took a few months to get this committee up and running. In the meantime, we worked to convince President Clinton to secure Lori's release. The State Department argued that because Mr. Fujimori personally helped create the image of the guilty *gringa terrorista,* it might not be easy to convince him to release Lori. They also claimed that the United States had very little influence over President Fujimori—hard to imagine, since the two countries maintained such close relations, and Peru was the recipient of millions of dollars in aid and needed U.S. approval for loans from the international banking community. We firmly believed that if President Clinton made it clear that it was important that Lori be released, Mr. Fujimori would find a way to do so under Peruvian law.

It was President Clinton's moral obligation to help Lori, and it was also his duty under an act of Congress. This act, 22 u.s.c. Section 1732, directs the president to take all necessary steps, short of going to war, to secure the release from foreign custody of an incarcerated American citizen "if it appears to be wrongful." Lori was wrongfully incarcerated.

We tried to get messages to President Clinton any way possible. We had our supporters write or phone him. We started a postcard campaign, flooding the White House with over ten thousand postcards.

We learned that the president was to be the commencement speaker at m.i.t. and we reminded him that m.i.t. was "Lori territory"—that Cambridge was her second home. Lori's supporters were at the graduation to remind him of his duty. Students, faculty, alumni, and members of the Cambridge City Council, including those sitting on the dais, wore white ribbons inscribed, "Mr. President: Free Lori Berenson, m.i.t. '91." Over four hundred members of the m.i.t. community, past and present, signed letters to the president. An open letter in the student newspaper, signed by forty-two prominent members of the m.i.t. community, reminded Mr. Clinton that it was his moral duty to seek Lori's release and his obligation under 22 u.s.c. 1732. m.i.t. president Charles Vest discussed Lori's situation with President Clinton at a private meeting. Mr. Clinton told Dr. Vest that he wanted to get her out. We did not know if this was a serious commitment, or simply a reply designed to preclude further discussion. Dr. Vest asked us not to publicize the president's remarks immediately, and promised to continue dialogue with him on Lori's behalf.

A serious commitment from President Clinton was long past due. When in March 1998 four dissidents were sentenced in Cuba, President Clinton declared, "They were tried without fair process, behind closed doors. I call on the Cuban government to release them immediately." Lori was convicted without fair process, behind closed doors. Why didn't he call on Peru to release her immediately?

Over the years Mark and I had written dozens of letters to President Clinton, asking for his help and asking him to meet with us. We knew that if he listened to us, looked us in the eye, he would no longer be able to ignore us. He was a lawyer. He would understand the lack of due process and the violation of international law in Lori's case. More importantly, he was a father. He would understand our anguish and Lori's suffering. Each letter to him described a new reason that made it more urgent than ever that he meet with us—a decline in Lori's health, observations made on a visit to Lori, changes in Peruvian politics, Peruvian newspaper stories about Lori, and on and on. But he would not meet with us. He wrote to us once, in May 1996, after he met with President Fujimori. He assured us he would monitor Lori's case closely. We didn't need him to monitor her deteriorating health. We could do that ourselves. We needed him to do his duty and secure her release.

So, on June 26, 1998, when as a result of our long efforts General Donald Kerrick called to say that Sandy Berger wanted to meet us, we saw an opportunity to get our message to the president. Sandy Berger was the president's National Security Advisor, and we had heard he was personally close to the president.

The meeting didn't take place until July 21. Unfortunately, the month-long delay and the myriad of national and international events that intervened seemed to lessen the sense of urgency and commitment conveyed in the June 26 message. Ramsey Clark and Tom Nooter went with us, as did Maurice Paprin, who helped make arrangements for the meeting. Although it was our first meeting with Mr. Berger, it was not our first visit with members of the National Security Council. We had met the year before with Eric Schwartz, Special Assistant to the President and Senior Director for Multilateral and Humanitarian Affairs, and his assistant, Scott Busby. Although nothing concrete was developed at that time, we continued to speak frequently with Mr. Busby, keeping him up-to-date on Lori's situation. He joined Mr. Berger along with other officials from the NSC.

We met for forty-five minutes, answered some background questions about Lori and her health, and made our point that we wanted President Clinton to do whatever was necessary to secure her release. Mr. Berger listened carefully and seemed sympathetic. It was a pleasant change from the stony stares we usually received from State Department officials. We were told that the relevant members of the NSC would put their heads together, consider possible approaches, and get back to us.

We met again with Eric Schwartz and Scott Busby in October. They had contacted high officials in the Peruvian government and were pleased to tell us that the conversations had been productive. They expressed surprise at the willingness of the Peruvians to resolve the situation. Unfortunately, the Peruvians suggested that Lori be transferred to a U.S. prison. It was déjà vu all over again. We had heard this from Congressman Richardson two years before, and as we knew, and the NSC should have known, if Lori transferred there was no way the U.S. government could release her. We again told our own government that transfer was not acceptable, that Lori is innocent and does not intend to spend years of her life in a U.S. prison. We urged the NSC to expedite efforts to develop a plan with Peru for Lori's release.

▪ A New Prison

On Wednesday, October 7, Lori was flown by helicopter from Yanamayo to Socabaya Prison, just outside the city of Arequipa. The Peruvian government claimed she was moved for medical tests. "Coincidentally," this was one day before Lori's petition setting forth violations of her rights was heard at the Inter-American Commission for Human Rights.

On October 8, we went with Ramsey and Tom to the OAS building in Washington for a preliminary hearing which would decide the admissibility of Lori's petition. Each side was allowed ten minutes and then a five-minute rebuttal. Ramsey and Tom used their time to point out the total lack of due process in the military tribunal system that sentenced Lori. Lawyers for the Peruvian government, rather than argue the merits of the case, chose to announce that Lori had been moved the previous day. They introduced a doctor who had flown in from Peru to describe what he called Lori's congenital circulation problem—not Peru's fault. He explained that because of concern for Lori's health, the government had moved her to Socabaya. He did not explain why the government waited until the day before this hearing to move her when they knew of this health problem for nearly three years, and the International Red Cross had recommended a variety of medical tests the previous June. The Peruvian lawyers devoted the rest of their allotted time to showing the video of Lori's press presentation. I suppose they wished the Commission to believe that because she was angry, she didn't need due process.

In December 1998, the Commission decided that Lori's petition was admissible. This meant it would rule on the petition's merits. We hoped for a full hearing at the spring 1999 session of the Commission, since it only meets two times a year. But Peru obtained a postponement, and we then hoped for the fall session. And then, in June 1999, the Inter-American Court ruled against Peru in the case of four Chileans also convicted for treason by military tribunals. The Court stated that the faceless Peruvian military tribunals were in complete violation of international law, and that the Chileans must be given civilian trials with full due process. Upon hearing that decision, President Fujimori withdrew Peru from the jurisdiction of the Court and the Commission, saying he would never give a civilian trial to the Chileans or Lori Berenson. We were not sure if Lori's case ever would get the full hearing we believed was so important for human rights in the Americas and for her freedom.

■ Visiting Socabaya

On October 24, 1998, Mark and I made the first of many trips to Socabaya Prison. We followed the same itinerary as visits to Yanamayo, including the same flight from Lima to Juliaca, only this time we deplaned at the stopover in Arequipa.

This was quite a change from Puno. For one thing, the altitude was much lower, 7,600 feet, and although this is still relatively high, it did not present a problem. And Arequipa, the second largest city in Peru, is much more Spanish and much less Indian than Puno. It is called "the white city" because of the white color of the volcanic stone used in the construction of the many cathedrals and other colonial-style structures.

We stayed at the Posada del Puente, a hotel recommended by Mary Grandfield for its quiet, relaxing atmosphere. And as I sat in the hotel garden I could even imagine I was on a leisurely vacation. The garden looked out over the river Chili running just below the hotel and across to the red-tile-roofed houses on the opposite bank. The river was calm on that first visit, unlike the rushing brown waters I viewed later during rainy season. Misti, the local snowcapped volcano and symbol of the city, dominated the skyline. The garden was filled with flowers—rosebushes were everywhere, and lilacs were in bloom. At least a dozen caged canaries were singing while the local birds were busy feeding themselves on the seeds the canaries spilled onto the grass. Alpacas were grazing down the hill, and a large turtle was fast asleep. The sun was bright, the sky clear blue, and it was comfortably warm. The setting was beautiful and tranquil—in sharp contrast to Socabaya Prison.

The prison was a half-hour taxi ride from the hotel, and on that first trip an official from the Arequipa prison system accompanied us. As we left the center of the city and headed for the district of Socabaya, the surroundings became more rural. There were acres of potatoes, corn, tomatoes, and cactus plants known locally as *tuna,* and there were fields for grazing.

Low stone walls separated the various fields, and along the way there were pyramidal piles of stones that had been collected in preparation for future building. Quite striking were the steplike terraces, *adenes,* along the mountainsides, green with vegetation—a method of farming that dates back to pre-Incan times. We also passed the large ovens where adobe was baked for use in building the local houses, many of which were in various stages of completion—some only four walls, others with windows in place, elaborate doors, gardens, and fences. Along the way we often shared the roads with cows and sheep.

But as we got closer to the prison, the paved road gave way to a dirt track, strewn with stones and pitted with holes, and before long the prison came into view. It sat on a barren flat piece of land and consisted of a tall viewing tower and two concrete two-story structures, one for women and the other for men, separated by about three hundred feet. Each was a compound surrounded by walls with small towers on each corner. Unlike the lush hotel garden, this area was desertlike, and a strong wind blew dust over everything.

The women's section held minimum-security nonviolent criminals. The men's building housed both criminal and political prisoners. Lori was the only maximum-security prisoner in the women's section, and she was placed in a separate wing apart from all other prisoners.

Perhaps because a government official accompanied us, supplies were given only a cursory inspection, the visit lasted longer than an hour, and we were permitted to see Lori "up close." We were to meet in a room with tiny chairs and tables—a playroom for the children under age three who live there with their imprisoned mothers. This was Saturday, the children were not using the room, and, in fact, the entire corridor was empty. We waited outside and watched Lori approach, accompanied by two guards. We were able to hug for the first time in a long time. Lori's walk toward us and our hug was captured on video and shown on Peruvian TV. Although government officials claimed that an overzealous newsman had broken into the prison and secretly made the tape, we knew that was impossible, given prison security. We assumed the notorious National Intelligence Service shot the footage. They may have wanted to show how humane they were in allowing us to hug—or maybe they wanted to show that Lori gets special privileges. A still photo taken from the video appeared in the *New York Times.* It showed Lori's back. She was wearing black pants and a white shirt, and she had her hair pulled back behind her ears. She looked young and small. And Mark and I were reaching out to hug her—smiling from ear to ear.

Our joy at seeing and hugging Lori was dampened when we heard how she was being treated. On October 7, she had been given only a few minutes to gather her belongings and was handcuffed, blindfolded, and taken by helicopter to Socabaya. The officer who accompanied her lifted her blindfold for a brief look at Misti, but otherwise she saw nothing of the Andes. And from the prison yard, just as in Yanamayo, the high walls only allow a view of the sky. Although she couldn't see the Andes, she could feel them. On her first night she was greeted by an earthquake, a frightening experience for her but so common an occurrence in Arequipa that no one else seemed to pay much attention.

Although ostensibly Lori had been moved for medical tests, and the media reported she was in a hospital, she was living in a prison cell. As in Puno, the cell had no heat or hot water, only buckets of cold water for washing herself, her clothes, and her environment. There was no radio, TV, or telephone. In fact, the lighting was worse than at Yanamayo, and after a few weeks, Lori was unable to see out of her right eye at night, although vision returned in the morning. Her vision had been impaired the year before during the hostage crisis, when prison officials had partially blocked the windows, keeping the cells dimly lit for most of the day, and now the poor lighting at Socabaya was exacerbating the problem. Lori said the medical facilities at Socabaya were no different from those at Yanamayo. She knew she had been moved for political reasons—because of the hearing at the Inter-American Commission—and not because of concern for her health. But she had been given a variety of tests that showed there were no problems with her heart, although her hands and face still showed the damage she incurred at the higher altitude.

There was no doubt that the physical conditions were less harsh here. The sunshine was comfortably warm, although it was cold at night and stayed cold inside the concrete cells in the day. However, it wasn't the bitter cold of Puno. And the somewhat lower altitude provided more oxygen.

But these "amenities" could not compensate for the isolation. This was a minimum-security prison for common criminals, and Lori was a maximum-security political prisoner. In order to separate her from the other prisoners, upon her arrival Lori was placed in solitary confinement. During the first nine days she was transported to and from the health clinic or the yard with a sheet over her head. She was not permitted to look at or speak to other prisoners, and they were not permitted to look at or speak to her.

We had no idea if the Peruvian government planned to keep Lori in Arequipa or return her to Puno. There were many advantages to this new prison. Certainly it was easier for Mark and me. The trip was a little shorter, the climate was better, and there was a lot more oxygen. Perhaps the simplified inspections and up-close visits might continue. And the more comfortable visits, favorable climate, and more plentiful oxygen were certainly good for Lori. But it was evident, even at that first visit, that Lori found the isolation at Socabaya a worse hardship than the physical discomforts at Yanamayo. She was more unhappy than I had ever seen her. Lori is a very social person. There was no one to speak with, no one to listen to, no one with whom to exchange thoughts, knowledge, hopes, or frustrations.

She asked us to do whatever necessary to end the isolation.

Although the Peruvian government applauded itself on its concern for human rights when it moved Lori, by placing her in isolation they incurred further criticism of human rights and church groups, and the International Red Cross. In December, Amnesty International issued an Urgent Action Alert on Lori's behalf, asking that telegrams and letters be sent immediately to Peruvian officials. The Action said in part, "Lori Helene Berenson, 29, a US citizen has been in solitary confinement for over two and a half months. Prolonged solitary confinement can cause severe and lasting physical and psychological damage, and Amnesty International is concerned that this amounts to cruel, inhuman or degrading treatment or punishment." Meanwhile, church officials in Peru were asking that Lori be allowed to go to weekly Mass with the rest of the prison population but were successful in securing permission only for the December 24 Christmas Mass. The International Red Cross arranged for the installation of an extra fluorescent bulb right outside Lori's cell to provide additional light and met often with Peruvian officials about relieving the isolation. We met with Ambassador Jett to argue the cruelty of the situation and asked that he insist on her being placed with other prisoners. In the meantime, to relieve her isolation as best we could, we increased our visits to twice a month and encouraged the embassy to visit more often and speak to Lori by phone.

If the Peruvian government was not successful in impressing the world with their concern for human rights, they were successful in diverting some of our efforts away from "free Lori" to "end the isolation." Incredible as it seemed we were looking back at the days in Yanamayo with some nostalgia. Visiting Lori every two or three weeks was taking a toll on our emotional and physical strength as well as our bankbook. The Thursday to Monday trips, with two overnight flights, followed by a return to work, were totally exhausting. Of course we thought this was a temporary change, not foreseeing that we would continue frequent visits for more than a year and a half.

The earlier visits were "up close," but soon we were meeting in the Socabaya *locutorio,* similar to the one at Yanamayo but much quieter. Although regulations specified that women could visit on Saturday and men on Sunday, for a while, when only one of us visited, we were permitted to see Lori both days. But this resulted in officials claiming Lori received "special privileges." On December 15, Lori was visited by a representative of Peruvian ombudsman Jorge Santisteban. When she once again insisted that her solitary confinement must end, his response was that the prison director told him she got special concessions—visits on Saturday and Sunday on those weekends her family came to Peru. Lori made the point that she would never be able to receive her permitted fifty-two hours per year of visits and that, more importantly, these extra visits in no way resolved the issue of solitary confinement. Mark and I certainly wanted to see her both days, but not if that was used as an excuse to avoid resolving the issue of Lori's isolation.

As 1998 drew to a close, the only good news was that on December 24, Lori was permitted to attend Christmas Mass at the prison. When she entered, which was after the other prisoners were seated, they greeted her with a rousing round of applause. She was permitted to sit with them and later told us everyone was very friendly. They also expressed the hope that Lori would be able to join them at the luncheon that followed, but the officials would not allow it.

PART FIVE

January 1999

to July 2000

■

WILL

THE

NIGHTMARE

END ?

■ Problems at the Prison

The year 1999 began with Lori still in solitary confinement. After Christmas she was not permitted to attend Mass or otherwise interact with the prison population. In addition, the officials at Socabaya were not familiar with the rules regarding maximum-security political prisoners, and Lori found herself under more stringent regulations than she had been at Yanamayo—and subjected to regulations that often seemed arbitrary and changed from day to day.

When I visited her on January 16, I learned that the prison staff had rotated and the new staff did not engage Lori in conversation. Although the Red Cross told us that they expected an agreement from prison authorities in Lima to have Lori spend her one-hour patio time with other prisoners, it never came about. The only conversations Lori had in the three weeks since my previous visit were with an army colonel who came to question her about cats. Yes, cats. As I wrote in my report to Mary Grandfield,

> At my December visit, Lori had given me (with the stamp of approval of the prison authorities) knitting instructions she had designed herself for patterns of cats. The following week she was visited by an army colonel who questioned her about this—why were there graphs and numbers, and how was it connected to the painting I had brought her that had a cat in it? Nobody had a copy of these cat patterns. Lori had given me the only copy, and the prison official who raised suspicions about them did not, to our knowledge, make a copy. Lori did, however, have books of knitting instructions and explained to the colonel why there are graphs and numbers. She also explained that everyone knows she loves cats and that she had also received a calendar with cat photos and her mother's

letters are always signed with a picture of two cats. The colonel seemed satisfied with her answers.

I attached one of the suspicious cat patterns to Mary's letter for her amusement, but reminded her "in the past equally bizarre things have been used by the Peruvian government to point to supposed wrongdoing by Lori." Sure enough, many weeks later prison officials said the cat pattern was an escape plan.

On January 22, Amnesty International issued a second Urgent Action Alert stating that, based on the evidence, they believed "the Peruvian authorities have singled [Lori] out for punishment." They added, "The conditions under which Lori Berenson is imprisoned contravene . . . the U.N. Convention against Torture and Other Cruel, Inhuman or Degrading Treatment or Punishment, to which Peru is a state party. If the Peruvian authorities are serious about following both the spirit and the letter of international as well as domestic law then Lori Berenson's isolation has to end immediately."

On January 29, after one hundred fifteen days, thanks to the efforts of Amnesty International, the Red Cross, the Catholic Church, and U.S. embassy, Lori's isolation ended when four other prisoners were moved to Lori's wing of the prison. One was a Shining Path prisoner, two were repentants, and the fourth had been recently arrested and was soon found innocent and released. Lori was permitted to spend her patio time, which had been increased to two hours for all maximum-security prisoners, with these women. Lori was no longer in solitary confinement, but she was still alone most of the time, and her problems were far from over. The repentants thought they would gain favor with the authorities by making life miserable for Lori, and some of the guards thought it would help their advancement if they did the same.

That was apparently why the colonel had come to ask Lori about the knitting pattern. On March 19, newspapers in Peru and the United States reported that prison authorities claimed to have found plans to attack the jail, and the plot implicated Lori. The guard who "discovered" the knitting plans, or prison officials in Arequipa, had decided, two months later, to go to the press. The embassy was aware this was ridiculous and told Reuters, "We have heard of the reports of the rumors and we understand that there is nothing to them and that they are false." Security was increased around the prison, and President Fujimori in a press conference assured the Peruvian public that they needn't fear, all was under control, he would not allow Lori to escape. Lori was told it was decided the drawings were an escape plan because the cats' ears were pointing up— or down—or maybe it was the tails.

At each visit Lori had another story of rumors and accusations that were being circulated by the repentants or prison guards. Whenever there was a problem at the prison, officials seemed to find a way to blame it on Lori—increased security, delayed mail, limited visits from church personnel—all Lori's fault. When an earthquake of over six on the Richter scale struck Arequipa, Mark sent the following as part of our e-mail update: "Peru is the land of the llama, coca, and a government with a wild imagination! We make no association between the coca and the government's wild imagination. However, we expect that the next rumor to circulate will be that Lori was the cause of the April 3 earthquake—why not, she is being blamed for everything else. Well, almost everything else—the government forgot to blame Lori for the *El Nino* weather phenomenon."

But the Peruvian imagination was even wilder and more malicious than we foresaw, and the next rumor was no laughing matter.

I was visiting again in April and saw Lori on Saturday morning. That evening, Mary Grandfield called to ask if Lori was okay. She said there were rumors that Lori was injured. I assured her that as of that morning she was fine. After hanging up I started to worry. Had something happened since my morning visit? But the prison authorities knew where I was staying—wouldn't they have called if there were a problem? But why did Mary sound so vague about "injuries"—what kind of injuries?

The Sunday morning newspaper reported that Lori was dead. She had burned to death in a probable suicide. I called Mark to tell him to ignore any rumors. I rushed to the prison. I insisted on seeing Lori, even though it was Sunday, a day for "men only" to visit. I showed the officials the newspaper article and told them that the U.S. embassy said I must see Lori and verify that she was alive. They allowed me to see her for five minutes. Lori had not yet heard the news of her death, and she became worried. Did Papa Al (my ninety-six-year-old father) hear this on the radio? News like that could kill him. Or what if Kathy or anybody Lori knew heard this awful report? And what if I hadn't been in Peru to assure myself she was alive? And we were both furious. Who could have started such a rumor? And why? The next day President Fujimori once again addressed the press about Lori, noting, "This is one more rumor, when the truth is she is enjoying good health."

Mr. Fujimori was right about her death being only a rumor but wrong about the good health. Her health had stabilized since coming to Socabaya, but her hands remained purple and her face remained red, both due to broken and clogged capillaries. She still had problems with her eyes, and since her time was occupied by vision-intensive activity—reading, drawing, writing, knitting—this seriously affected her well-being.

Lori was still essentially alone, and harassment was increasing. The repentants first accused Lori of death threats. Then they were allowed to work in the prison kitchen with access to ten-inch chopping knives, a situation that caused Lori to fear they would provoke an incident and try to harm her. Officials interfered with the mail. From March through June, although the letters we brought were given to Lori, she did not receive any mail that was sent directly to the prison nor was that mail, including books and gifts, returned to senders. It disappeared. The prison was very tense, and one report I sent to the embassy began with, "This visit found Lori extremely agitated due to continued harassment from prison officials and other prisoners. She asked us to visit more often. She also requests that the U.S. embassy arrange to speak with her by telephone. In general a regular schedule should be arranged but in the next few weeks she asked for calls at least once a week until the tension in the prison subsides."

Lori's letters to friends revealed both her frustrations and her will to overcome them. In an April letter that was reprinted in part in the *Albany Catholic Worker,* she wrote:

> I was in a jail [Yanamayo] where the physical conditions were much worse than this one [Socabaya] . . . but I never felt like I do now even though I have been through very difficult times. But what can I do? I have to gather strength from those who went before me and had to suffer worse conditions than mine.
>
> I have a picture of Archbishop Romero and another of two little orphans. I find strength watching them. I trust this situation won't last too long and when remembering what our Uruguayan brothers have been through, I may even consider myself lucky. . . .
>
> I believe what a prisoner in the Spanish Civil War said, "In the darkest hour of the night you can always glimpse the brightest dawn."

▪ The Committee to Free Lori Berenson

It was hard for Mark and me to decide where best to put our efforts. Visiting Lori every two weeks sapped one or the other of us of energy during and after the exhausting trip. We were also traveling to Washington to lobby members of Congress. And we were organizing The Committee to Free Lori Berenson. Everything seemed important. We had to visit Lori. We had to lobby. We had to organize. Where would we find the time?

What helped enormously were all the messages of support we received. One hears so much about the greed and selfishness of the "me" generation. But thousands of people—rich, poor, young, old, total strangers, and close friends, from all parts of the country and all walks of life—wrote or called and asked, "What can I do to help?" People we never met stood on street corners and collected signatures or handed out flyers, wrote to Lori, or sent us notes of cheer. But we needed to mobilize and organize this support to work cohesively, delivering a consistent message and focusing on the major strategies.

Ramsey was still our main adviser, and our goal was still to convince President Clinton, directly or through Congress, to secure Lori's release. But we needed advice on how best to get everyone working to achieve that goal. We looked through our lists of supporters, chose about twenty from around the country who had expressed interest in devoting more time to our efforts, and asked them to coordinate activities in their geographic regions. We also formed a steering committee of human rights activists who were willing to share their expertise.

We met Blase and Theresa Bonpane, directors of Office of the Americas (OOA) when that organization honored Lori with an award in November 1997. The OOA under the leadership of the Bonpanes had fought human rights abuses in Latin America for many years. They knew how to reach out for new support, arrange for delegations to foreign countries, and raise funds. They introduced us to James Lafferty, Executive Director of the Los Angeles Chapter of the National Lawyers Guild, who helped us form an advisory board of well-known persons that would help build support.

Through the Bonpanes we also met Frederica (Freddie) Schrider, who championed Latin-American causes in Washington, D.C. She in turn introduced us to Grahame Russell, a Canadian lawyer and director of Rights Action/Guatemala Partners, a nongovernmental organization that supported community-based development projects and human rights work in Guatemala, Southern Mexico, and Honduras. Freddie and Grahame had experience organizing demonstrations in D.C., sponsoring delegations to foreign countries, arranging speaking tours, and applying for grants.

Bob McIndoe worked for many years on outreach projects for the First Congregational Church of Winchester, Massachusetts. He had read about Lori, met with us, and became immediately involved. He was interested in drawing the business and education community into our struggle, and had many ideas for outreach and publicity.

Kristen Gardner was Lori's roommate at M.I.T. and was one of Lori's closest friends. Kristen had already organized events and speaking engagements to build up support for Lori in Northern California. She was interested in grassroots organizing and offered to help focus the regional coordinators. Blase, Theresa, Jim, Freddie, Grahame, Bob, and Kristen formed the steering committee.

And we had a new webmaster, Ken Dubberly, who took over the web site started by Jim Salem and continued by Bill Wedemeyer, Lori's friends from M.I.T. The web was crucial in providing information about Lori and telling supporters how they could help. The first thing Ken did was change the web address to one that was easier to remember: www.freelori.org.

We met with members of the steering committee and many of the regional coordinators over a cold and icy weekend in Washington in January 1999. It was really incredible to see so many people whom we had spoken with or written to but never had met. It was a long weekend of work and fun.

Tom and Ramsey had come to discuss legal issues and strategic goals. Grahame led a discussion on sending delegations to Peru. Theresa and Kristen had a workshop on grassroots organizing, and there were discussion groups on reaching the media, fund-raising, and developing alternative strategies. Monday was January 11, the third anniversary of Lori's sentencing. It was bitter cold, but we were joined by groups and individuals from Washington and Maryland, and about seventy-five of us held a rally in Lafayette Park opposite the White House. We sang songs, performed a short play about Lori, interviewed with the press, and walked back and forth demanding Lori's freedom.

The three days energized all of us for the work ahead. In the following months Grahame organized delegations to Peru; Theresa and Kristen distributed "Organizing Packets" to regional coordinators; Grahame and Kristen wrote grant proposals; Jim helped us gather an advisory board; Freddie was a liaison with the D.C. human rights community; Bob designed bumper stickers and posters advertising our web site; and Ken made the site better and better. And support grew. We got letters saying, "Saw a bumper sticker, checked out the web, what can I do to help?" More and more web visitors used the translator on the site and wrote letters to Lori.

▪ Delegations to Peru

In March, the first delegation, led by Blase Bonpane, went to Peru. He was accompanied by Reverend Lucius Walker, Director of IFCO/Pastors for Peace; Amy Goodman, host of Pacifica Radio's *Democracy Now;* Annie Bird of Rights Action/ Guatemala Partners; Patricia Todd, a California librarian and regional coordinator; and Kristen Gardner. The group met with U.S. embassy officials, including Ambassador Jett, members of the Peruvian and international press, leaders of the human rights community, and, somewhat unexpectedly, with Lori.

Long before traveling to Peru, Blase had sent a formal request to prison authorities for permission to visit Lori on Tuesday, March 2. When they arrived in Lima, there was still no response to their request. On Tuesday they traveled to Socabaya, hoping their visit would be approved by the time they arrived. They presented the prison director with a letter of support from Gustavo Mohme Llona, a Peruvian congressman they had spoken with in Lima. The director placed a call on her cell phone and then permitted a two-hour up-close visit in the yard. After Blase returned to California, he received a letter from Peruvian authorities informing him that permission would *not* be granted for the visit. The prison director was removed from her post, and Lori was blamed.

We were not certain why this group was allowed to visit. Rules limit routine visits to immediate family, although the Red Cross and religious representatives were also permitted at times. In the past, Lori had been visited by local church workers and by Rabbi Ronnie Greenwald from the United States. She had also met once with representatives of the U.N. Working Group on Arbitrary Detention and the Inter-American Commission for Human Rights. No other human rights groups or journalists had been allowed to meet her. We know that at the time Blase's delegation was in Peru, there were also visitors from the Organization of American States, and it was possible that prison officials confused Blase's organization, the OOA, with the OAS, which in Spanish has initials OEA.

On his return, Blase summarized his visit. ". . . the effects of the cold and high altitudes were apparent in her red complexion and purple and swollen hands. She maintains her innocence and would like to be released. She continues to be concerned about the social injustice in Peru, including the level of poverty, the lack of due process for many arrestees, and the prison conditions. . . . She would prefer to be released, rather than being granted a new trial, because she assesses that she could not receive a fair trial within Peru due to the negative, distorted media coverage [there] . . . she does not want to ask for a transfer [to a U.S. prison] because it assumes her guilt, and she maintains that she is innocent."

Kristen, who knew Lori well, expressed her concern that Lori had been separated from the world for over three years, the world she loves, and separated from her work for social justice. All members commented on Lori's continued concern for others and her wish that the delegation make it known that there were many other Peruvian prisoners who were convicted as she was, held under the same inhumane conditions, and whose health was even more precarious than hers.

The delegation had nothing good to say of their meeting with Ambassador Jett. He was determined to continue asking for a new civilian trial—despite the scathing State Department report that described the Peruvian judicial system as corrupt and easily manipulated by the executive branch. The ambassador was upset that the delegation had been allowed to see Lori, but not once in the almost two-hour meeting with the delegation did he ask how she was.

Lori was thrilled to have sat in the sunshine and chatted with a group of friendly people. She, as I, was amazed that these men and women, most of whom had until recently been total strangers, would give so much of their time and energy, would travel so far, just to see her.

However, the firing of the director made it clear that future delegations would have a difficult time visiting Lori. With that in mind, we limited the next trips to members of the religious community, believing Peru would find it harder to deny them entry. Rabbi Greenwald, who had seen Lori in Yanamayo, saw her again in Socabaya. In May, she was visited by Rabbi Marcelo Bronstein of Congregation B'nai Jeshurun in New York City, Reverend William Nottingham of Indianapolis, retired president of the Division of Overseas Ministries of the Christian Church (Disciples of Christ), and Sister Eileen Storey of Sisters of Charity in New York City. In September Lori met with Bishop Thomas J. Gumbleton, of the Archdiocese of Detroit.

Blase Bonpane, Bill Nottingham, and Sister Eileen reported on their visits at a Congressional Briefing of the Human Rights Caucus of the House of Representatives on "Human Rights in Peru: The Lori Berenson Case." Reverend Nottingham said, in part,

> I recognized in [Lori] the kind of person the churches had sent by the score as mission interns and volunteers during the 1970s and 80s to Latin America, Southern Africa, South Korea, the Philippines and Eastern Europe. That is when I was a mission executive for the Christian Church (Disciples of Christ) in the United States and Canada and for the United Church of Christ. These young people were well educated, politically aware, non-violent, deeply committed to social justice for the poor, and motivated by faith. I did not know if Lori Berenson was a religious person, but I had no doubt that her understanding of the suffering and oppression of the Third World was the same

as ours. It came from the same protest against injustice which dignifies the human spirit by God's command to love thy neighbor and to seek justice for the poor. . . .

One realizes that judgments are made about her even though her story has not been heard. She told us that much said about her is not true, even absurd. Not only are there unsubstantiated charges but also rumors and speculations which have woven around her name a myth of sinister or naive collaboration with terrorists. Some people even are under the impression that she confessed to her accusers, which simply proves the degree of misinformation that confuses what is real and unreal in her situation.

He also reported that the group had fifteen interviews with Peruvian religious leaders—Catholic, Protestant, and Jewish—and human rights officers, as well as members of the U.S. embassy staff. He said, "These interviews convinced us that a fair civilian trial is unthinkable under present circumstances, although that is what we thought was a reasonable expectation. No one saw that as a serious possibility, because there is not an independent judiciary."

▪ The Congressional Campaign Continues

In spite of President Clinton's expression of concern the previous spring at his meeting with M.I.T. President Vest, and in spite of assurances from the NSC that they were looking for a solution, we knew we needed even stronger pressure from Congress.

Congresswoman Maloney circulated another Dear Colleague letter, this time addressed to President Clinton urging Lori's release. It referred to the president's obligations under Title 22 U.S.C. Section 1732, and the finding of the U.N. High Commission on Human Rights, that Lori was wrongfully arbitrarily deprived of her liberty. It goes on to say, "Lack of leadership and effective action on Lori's case could endanger U.S. citizens not only in Peru, but in many other countries. It sends the unfortunate message that the United States will not act when its citizens are wrongfully imprisoned in foreign countries. In addition, lack of strong action in this case would jeopardize the importance of the office of U.N. High Commission on Human Rights and denigrate the cause of justice and human rights throughout the world."

We wanted a similar letter sent from the Senate, but Senator Moynihan preferred to write again to Madeleine Albright. He asked his colleagues to join him in telling the secretary of state, "We now believe that Ms. Berenson's deteriorating health warrants humanitarian release from prison and urge you to use your authority to secure Ms. Berenson's release before her health further deteriorates." Writing to the secretary was not nearly as effective as writing to the president, but at least the emphasis was "release."

By June, one hundred eighty members of the House signed the letter telling President Clinton it was his duty to secure Lori's release. And thirty-three senators asked Secretary Albright to seek a humanitarian release. In July, Mr. Clinton responded, writing that the embassy in Lima continually urges a fair trial, and ending with, "The administration continues to explore all options to resolve Ms. Berenson's case, and we are committed to achieving a just outcome." Also in July, the president sent Governor Buddy MacKay, his special envoy to the Americas, to speak to Mr. Fujimori.

Meanwhile, Congresswoman Maxine Waters proposed an amendment to a State Department authorization bill. The amendment asked Congress to support democracy and human rights in Peru and investigate the lack of press freedom and judicial independence. It also stipulated that, "in deciding whether to provide economic and other forms of assistance to Peru, the United States should take into consideration the willingness of Peru to assist in the release of Lori Berenson."

The debate on the amendment was shown live on CSPAN. We were glued to the TV. The usual sleep-inducing atmosphere of dull congressional speeches was changed suddenly into a dynamic argument on the fate of Lori Berenson. Congresswoman Waters spoke passionately in favor of the amendment. Congressman Christopher Smith from New Jersey led the opposition. Congressman Gary Ackerman of New York also asked to speak against the amendment but deferred to Congressman Smith when time became an issue.

Congressman Smith agreed, saying, "The procedures used to convict Lori Berenson of aggravated terrorism were egregious. Lori Berenson certainly deserves due process and to have her case tried by an open, civilian court in Peru." He then went on to oppose Lori's release on the grounds that "we must avoid commenting, even implicitly, on the serious evidence against her." (Of course he couldn't say what constituted that "serious evidence," because the Peruvian government never has shown any evidence.) He then went on to discuss the violence of the MRTA. He suggested that Congresswoman Waters consider changing the amendment to ask for a fair trial rather than release.

In rebuttal, Representative Carolyn Maloney pointed out that Lori proclaimed she is innocent, that President Fujimori had refused all past requests for a new trial, and had "announced that he would not respect the OAS decision on Lori's appeal regardless of the outcome." Congressman Jim McGovern pointed out "even the State Department concludes that it is still impossible to receive a fair trial, to undergo a just process in Peru's current judicial system. So asking for a new trial in Lori's case is very problematic, because it is impossible to get a fair trial in Peru today." Congresswoman Cynthia McKinney added, "If Lori Berenson is not going to get a fair trial, and she is not, then she deserves to be set free. That is what we would do here for people who are tried unfairly, and we have no right letting a foreign government get away with less when Americans are involved." Supporting remarks were also presented by Representatives Clayton, Delahunt, Hinchey, Meek, and Morella.

Mr. Smith again insisted on changing the focus to fair trial. A vociferous debate continued, and then Congressman Sam Gejdenson suggested a short break during which Representatives Smith and Waters would work to reword the amendment.

Our phone rang. It was Maxine Waters. She wanted to know if she should change the wording to something like, "Lori should have a fair trial according to international standards, within a year, and failing that, that she should be released." Or should she leave the amendment as originally written. We had to decide instantly. There was no time to speak with advisers or carefully weigh the pros and cons. We knew a fair trial was impossible, which is why we insisted on release now. "Release now" was the message we wanted sent to Peru. On the other hand, we knew the amendment could pass unanimously if Mr. Smith agreed to the new wording. It might lose otherwise. And, on the plus side, the new wording specified that the trial must meet international standards and set a time limit, after which the demand would be release. But we still wondered who would guarantee that the trial met international standards. It was a difficult decision. We told the congresswoman to propose the new wording.

The representatives returned to the House floor. We returned to cspan. The congresswoman proposed the word change. But Mr. Smith refused to agree to any time limit for a trial or any use of the word "release" in the amendment. He repeated that he did not know if Lori was innocent, and once again went into a long discussion about the terrors of the mrta. As a result the wording remained as originally written—without reference to a trial—and the amendment was defeated by a vote of 233 to 189.

We were disappointed. But 189 votes meant a lot of support. When we compared the list of those who voted for this amendment with those who signed the letter asking President Clinton to secure Lori's release, we found that there were differences. Some had signed the letter but voted "no" on the amendment and some had not signed the letter and voted "yes." When we combined results we found that a total of 225, a majority, of the 435 voting members expressed their support for Lori's release via the amendment and/or the letter to President Clinton.

When we told Lori of this she was both thrilled and surprised. Mary Grandfield had visited and told her that the amendment lost, and Lori had assumed it had received only a few votes. But 189 votes told Peruvian officials that they should beware. And the possibility of a majority would be a real concern. Peru understood that the U.S. Congress held the purse strings on aid to Peru. Lori told us, and we were to see clearly over the next months, that Peru watched the actions of the U.S. Congress very carefully. They even went so far as to invest hundreds of thousands of dollars to hire two well-known

U.S. firms, Patton Boggs and ssk (Shepardson, Stern and Kaminsky), to lobby our Congress in order to improve their image.

▪ August 1999

August was quiet. Congress was on recess, and most of our friends were away. But we continued with our routine, spending much of the day responding to e-mail and other letters and reading and translating the Peruvian newspapers. I was considering writing a book and started keeping notes on what we read and what we wrote. So, for example, on August 26, among the dozens of e-mails and letters, we received the following:

- A note from Len Strickman, a high school friend of Mark's, who had just learned about Lori's plight and who as dean of the Law School at the University of Arkansas, knew Bill and Hillary Clinton and wanted to know how he could help.
- Two résumés from applicants for the position of National Organizer of the Committee to Free Lori Berenson. (Our efforts to bring Lori home had become so overwhelming that we needed a professional organizer with an office in Washington.)
- A newspaper column by Amelia Fletcher in Baldwin County, Alabama, in which she connected Lori's situation to that of Bonnivard, a political prisoner in Chillon in a sonnet by Lord Byron, intercutting quotes from the poem and details of Lori's case.
- A letter from Hillary Clinton, responding to one handed to her in June by friends of ours when she was the commencement speaker at our alma mater, the City College of New York. Mrs. Clinton's letter said, "The President and I share your concerns about Lori's case . . . Please know that we continue to seek a just and expeditious outcome of Lori's case."
- A request for twenty-five posters for an event planned for September 23, sponsored by an Amnesty Inter-

national chapter in Montclair, New Jersey.

- ▪ A copy of a petition signed by fifty supporters at a rally in Northern California.
- ▪ A copy of a letter to the editor in defense of Lori by Gary James Boyle that appeared in the *Boston Herald.*
- ▪ A photo and poem for Lori from a St. Louis supporter, along with a request for a bumper sticker for his guitar case.
- ▪ A letter for Lori from a Brazilian anthropologist.
- ▪ A book of cartoons, in Spanish, for Lori from a New York supporter who sends gifts nearly monthly.
- ▪ A flyer announcing a street performance of "What You Do: the Story of Lori Berenson" by the theater group Great Small Works, scheduled for September 8 at Union Square Park, in New York a show that included a fifteen-foot puppet of Lori that had been performed in the summer of 1998 at the Bread and Puppet Theater in Vermont.

And our perusal of the Peruvian press revealed articles about the arrival in Peru of United States "Drug Czar" General Barry McCaffrey who was there to discuss coca growth. We hoped he would also tell authorities that the United States is seriously concerned about Peru's treatment of Lori and that, after three years and nine months without benefit of a proper trial, the Peruvian government must release her and send her home. This would be a good followup to the trip of President Clinton's special envoy, Buddy MacKay, who discussed Lori on his visit to Peru the previous month.

The newspapers also announced the expected arrival of the new U.S. ambassador, John Hamilton. We had met Ambassador Hamilton before he left for Peru and expressed to him our hopes that he would actively seek Lori's release.

In the afternoon I sent out thank-you letters to donors and packets of information to potential supporters and then we spent the evening with Suzy Baer, who filmed some footage for a documentary about Lori.

It was summer and it would have been nice to visit the beach or take a ride in the country, but we chose not to. Taking time off only would result in work piling up, and there always seemed to be something that had to be completed instantly. And although we tried not to admit it, even to ourselves, after almost four years, we still hoped that the next phone call, e-mail, or letter would contain the message that would lead to Lori's freedom. And we wanted to be there when the message came in.

■ New Evidence

In September we received a message from the NSC that they had important information for us that they could not discuss over the phone. We met on September 29. Peruvian officials had informed Ambassador Hamilton that they had evidence that would cause the military courts to set aside Lori's conviction. The ambassador asked the NSC to notify us. The evidence was provided by three high officials of the Peruvian government and one high official of a foreign government. These four men had concluded from information that had become available to them that Lori was not a leader of the MRTA. Because leadership is an essential element of the crime of treason, such evidence would require the military courts to void her conviction. Lori was urged to present the Supreme Council of Military Justice with a *recurso de revision,* a petition to reevaluate her case based on its new evidence, and, obviously, the highest officials in the Peruvian government approved such action.

Wow! The Peruvian government conceded it made a mistake—a big mistake. Filing a *recurso* held forth the potential for Lori's release. But we were cautious—there might be a trap. After the military court set aside Lori's conviction, the civilian courts could decide to try her for other crimes. And we were very concerned because, according to human rights organizations and the U.S. State Department, the civilian courts do not meet international standards of openness, fairness and due process and are not impartial and independent. They are controlled by the executive branch. So this could mean a corrupt show trial, one with "pretend" due process, scripted to find Lori guilty.

But we focused on the positive. We wanted the Peruvian government to publicly admit its mistake and throw the case out of the military courts. Then we would press Peru on the next admission—that Lori was not even a member of the MRTA, that she was innocent of any and all charges, and that she would be released.

Our immediate concern was to speak with Lori. We asked Ambassador Hamilton to secure permission for Ramsey Clark to visit her so he could discuss the ramifications of these new proposals. We also requested that the ambassador arrange for us to meet members of the Supreme Council of Military Justice so they could explain the procedure for filing a *recurso* and assure us of its purpose.

The trip to Peru on the weekend of November 6 was even crazier than usual. I went to Socabaya on Saturday and outlined the latest events for Lori. Ramsey joined me there on Sunday and we both visited Lori. We returned to Lima that night and joined Mark for a meeting with Ambassador Hamilton and Mary Grandfield in the ambassador's residence. Monday morning the five of us met with the Supreme Council of Military Justice and then Ramsey and I returned to Socabaya Monday afternoon to update Lori. I spent a lot of time in airports, but it was different from the usual grind—it felt like something really important was happening.

The meeting with the president of the Supreme Council of Military Justice and his staff of generals took place in one of the most beautiful old Spanish colonial buildings in Lima. With Ambassador Hamilton acting as translator, the president of the supreme council, joined by others from time to time, described the necessary procedures. They agreed that although a *recurso* was often written and submitted by a Peruvian lawyer, Lori could submit *pro se*—writing and submitting on her own, naming the four witnesses. The supreme council would then secure affidavits from them. Both the petition and the affidavits were to address only the question of leadership since that was the only question relevant to the military court proceedings. Upon receipt of this new evidence, actually prepared by the Peruvian government and court investigators, Lori's conviction for treason would be set aside and her case dismissed from the military courts. We were told that new proceedings might be initiated in the civilian court system for alleged crimes within its jurisdiction. That decision might be made by civilian authorities, based on their independent investigation, but only after dismissal of all charges in the military courts.

Lori, of course, was very excited by the new possibilities and very anxious to file the *recurso* as soon as possible—although she was also aware of the possible risk of a staged civilian trial. She and Ramsey outlined what the petition would say and after we returned to New York, Ramsey and Tom Nooter wrote a draft. It simply stated the facts: that Lori was convicted of acting as a leader of the MRTA; that during the entire judicial proceeding she consistently maintained that she was never a leader and therefore the conviction against her was not valid, and the charges against her could only be dismissed. It named the four witnesses—Jorge Valdez Carillo, Vice Minister of Foreign Affairs (later appointed permanent representative of Peru to the United Nations); Francisco Tudela Van Breugel-Douglas, permanent representative of Peru to the United Nations (and more recently elected Vice President of Peru); retired Admiral Luis Giampetri Rojas, President of the Peruvian Institute of the Sea (IMARPE); Jorge Gumacio Granier, the Bolivian ambassador—and pointed out that she would not have been convicted if the military courts had knowledge, during the trial, of the information that these witnesses could now provide.

Tom went to Peru, he and Lori made some final corrections, and U.S. embassy officials delivered the petition to the Supreme Council of Military Justice on December 6.

We kept this all very quiet, not telling anybody, waiting nervously for the supreme council to act. But news leaked out in early December, when Peruvian Prime Minister Alberto

Bustamante and other officials visited Washington D.C. and were interviewed by the *Washington Times*. The *Times* reported, "Peruvian officials for the first time say new evidence about Lori Berenson's role in a revolutionary Marxist group is prompting them to consider a new trial . . ." It goes on to say that members of the prime minister's entourage said, "there are provisions in Peruvian law to introduce 'new evidence' if someone has been wrongly convicted. If the military court accepts the new evidence, Berenson could get a trial before Peru's Supreme Council of Military Justice." We were greatly surprised to hear that the prime minister had revealed this information to the press. We worried that premature disclosure might hinder the process.

Although the *Times* wrote about "a trial before Peru's Supreme Council of Military Justice," we knew they were referring to the council's evaluation of the affidavits accompanying the *recurso*. And we were waiting for those affidavits to be submitted. If the *recurso* had been drawn up by a Peruvian lawyer, the affidavits would have been collected by the lawyer and submitted along with the petition and the petition would reflect the substance of the affidavits. Because Lori filed without a lawyer, the affidavits were to be collected by the supreme council, and the petition was written to reflect what Lori had been told the affidavits would address—only questions of leadership. In mid-December we were horrified when we were shown a copy of an affidavit signed by three of the witnesses. While it forcefully stated Lori was not a leader, contrary to what the supreme council had told us, the affidavit went on to assert she was guilty of a lesser crime—of aiding the MRTA. As an attachment to Lori's *recurso*, this would be construed as an admission of guilt when, in fact, Lori adamantly proclaims her innocence and would refute any such charges.

We immediately informed Peruvian officials of our objections and they quickly agreed the affidavits were inappropriate. We were assured the witnesses would submit new ones promptly.

We could only speculate on why the affidavits were written as they were. We thought possibly these dignitaries were worried that they would be called soft on terrorism if they didn't claim Lori was guilty of something. Perhaps they hoped to end Lori's case with what in effect would have been a guilty plea, although to a lesser crime.

We anxiously awaited the new affidavits and the decision of the supreme council. Every time the phone rang there was a chance it was Ambassador Hamilton, or the NSC, or a reporter who heard that the supreme council had reversed Lori's conviction. Peruvian officials hinted that the action could come before government offices closed for the Christmas holidays. It did not happen. Instead we encountered one delay after another.

▪ Christmas 1999

On December 21, I said good-bye to my students and good-bye to Nassau Community College. It was time to retire. I could no longer continue teaching and do all the work necessary to help Lori. It was a difficult decision. My time in the classroom, immersed in a discipline governed by logic, had become my escape from the unpredictable chaos that Lori's arrest had brought to my life. I knew I would miss the classroom, the students, and conversations with my colleagues. But I just couldn't continue.

Mark and I spent December 24, our thirty-sixth wedding anniversary, traveling to Peru. We brought around one hundred cards and letters, many with multiple signatures, including some from Italy, Chile, Israel, Canada, and Ecuador. People had sent boxes of stationery, warm socks, and books. Mark and I had searched for the perfect holiday gift and decided on a book of embroidery patterns, all based on pictures of cats and complete with graphs—though no escape plans! Lori appreciated both the humor and the practical value of the book.

Among the numerous greeting cards was one from President and Mrs. Clinton, addressed to Lori and reading, "Our family wishes you and yours a blessed holiday season filled with treasured memories of past traditions and joy and peace in the new millennium." Somehow Lori's name had gotten on the "important person mailing list "at the White House. The censors were so impressed they allowed Lori to have the card, even though it was in English.

In return, Lori sent a handmade card with the thread drawing of a Peruvian boy in colorful, traditional garb holding a bunch of flowers and a message, in Spanish, for a happy Christmas and a prosperous New Year. She also added, "I'm sure knowing that I am innocent, Mr. President, your administration will do all that is possible to secure my freedom in the year 2000."

Lori tried to exude holiday cheer. She was wearing the burgundy turtleneck shirt that Kathy had brought last month for her birthday under a flannel jacket and blue and gray sweater. The gray in the sweater brought out the gray in her hazel eyes. Her hair had been recently trimmed and hung just below her shoulders.

She talked about her latest knitting projects and gave us three pairs of tiny booties for friends who had recently had babies. Lori loved knitting baby clothes. She loved being reminded of children. Although she still could not mix with the general prison population, on a few occasions the children living at the prison wandered by her cell and spoke with her. She always had stories, like the time that a little boy stopped to ask where she slept. When Lori pointed to her mattress, he thought for a moment and then asked, *"¿Y tú mamá donde duermo?"*—"But where does your mama sleep?" He and his question "made Lori's day," and Lori had looked so happy just telling me about it.

At Lori's suggestion we came to the prison with a huge bag of festively wrapped toys, chocolate Santas, and children's clothing. The clothing was collected by Elizabeth Mandeville, a high school student in New Hampshire, who like Lori was deeply concerned about the hardships faced by the children and their mothers.

Holiday banter was interrupted by a serious discussion of Lori's case. We were all very disappointed that the Supreme Council of Military Justice had not yet made progress on her recurso. The best we could tell Lori was that Ambassador Hamilton believed everything was still on track. But we were very worried that delays would bring us too close to the Peruvian election, which was scheduled for April 9, and that the Peruvian government would prefer to slow down the process until after that date. President Fujimori was expected to declare his candidacy the following week—no surprise after all the maneuvering he had done to allow himself an unconstitutional third term.

Lori remembered how closely she had followed the 1995 elections. She very much wanted to follow this campaign—and to hear other news of Peru, news of the United States, and news of the world. For several months she was awaiting permission to have a radio. She knew that Peruvian law did not forbid radios, had heard that prisoners at Yanamayo and other maximum-security prisons now had them, and the Peruvian ombudsman told her she could have one. But Socabaya authorities continued to say no.

Sometimes prison guards placed a radio, tuned to music, so that Lori could listen. But, as she indicated in a letter to Daniel Radosh, Lori would have preferred to make her own musical selections. Daniel was Lori's friend since seventh grade. I always knew when Lori was on the phone with Daniel because of all the laughter. His ability to make her laugh, and his close friendship throughout the years, was a source of strength for Lori. In the December 20 edition of *The Nation,* Daniel wrote:

> According to my old friend Lori Berenson, life in a Peruvian prison is even worse than I had thought . . . I've known Lori since junior high when we passed notes behind the teacher's back. Today we correspond only in Spanish so her guards can monitor what we say. She is not allowed to write much about her circumstances, which are appalling, or her health, which is deteriorating, but it wouldn't be her style to complain. In her most recent letter, however, Lori does write of a new affront to her dignity. Her prison wing has been given radio privileges which to her horror, means disco music: "I can put up with a regimen of isolation and confinement," she says, "but nobody said when they

sentenced me that I was going to have to listen to 'Won't you take me to Funky Town.'" After four years, Lori's sense of humor helps keep her strong. Reading between the lines, I know she's counting on our sense of outrage to set her free.

Yes, Lori's sense of humor helped keep her strong. And her strength helped keep me strong.

Lori had made a card for Mark's fifty-eighth birthday, only a few days away. It had a caricature of Mark's face, the caricature that Mark and Lori had been sending back and forth in letters for years—a round face, bald head with little side tufts of hair, glasses, beard, and mustache. And Lori referred to him as "the numbers doctor"—a reminder of the day when Mark received his Ph.D. and we had a cake congratulating "Dr. Mark." Lori was very young at the time and not too fond of doctors, who were always pricking or prodding her. Mark reassured her that he only treated sick numbers, not sick children.

On the front of the birthday card, Mark was smiling. The caption read *"El Doctor de Números de pone a pensar . . ."*— "The numbers doctor is thinking . . . " In the cloud above his head, the number doctor was thinking "365(1999-1941) + (1999-1941)/4." Inside, the left page had a smiling Mark thinking "21,184–21,184 *días,*" and saying *"ha vivido 21,184 días . . . "*— "I have lived 21,184 days . . . " The right page showed Mark aghast, OY! as he contemplated "21,184 days!" It was signed *"Feliz Cumpleaños Dad! Te quiero mucho!*—Happy Birthday Dad! I love you very much. Lori."

Lori had withstood four years of imprisonment. The Peruvian government incarcerated her under conditions that compromised her physical well-being, and, as Lori wrote, sought to "morally and psychologically destroy those prisoners who do not renounce their principles." But, as I said good-bye to Lori and wished her a Happy New Year, I knew that in spite of everything, she was still the same Lori. She was still joking with Daniel, still designing "mathematical" birthday cards, and still worried about the health and happiness of children.

▪ A New Millennium

Another new year, in fact, a new millennium. The Committee to Free Lori Berenson now had an office in Washington, run by our recently hired national organizer, Gail Taylor. Gail was a graduate of Syracuse University, where she majored in International Relations, concentrating on U.S. foreign policy and Latin America. She had studied in Chile, was fluent in Spanish, and had worked at the Center for International Policy in Washington. She organized our ever-growing grassroots support and increased the number of regional coordinators to forty-five, so that most of the country was "covered." She was also a constant presence in Washington—meeting with human rights leaders, religious groups, congressional aides, and government officials. Now there were three of us, Mark, Gail, and I, who were working endlessly, missing sleep and hardly eating.

January 11 marked four years since Lori's sentencing, and it was commemorated by vigils in over a dozen cities across the country, including one in Fairbanks, Alaska, where the temperature was thirty-five degrees below zero. Student chapters of Amnesty International in Wisconsin and New Jersey collected hundreds of signatures on huge banners and sent them to President Clinton. Students, staff, and the administrators at Norwell High School in Massachusetts organized a twenty-four-hour fast to draw attention to Lori's plight. And we planned yet another congressional campaign.

As always, Mark and I were busy writing, reading and speaking about Lori. But our number one concern was the Supreme Council of Military Justice. Ambassador Hamilton still insisted the process was "on track." But when would they announce they had thrown out Lori's conviction? We prepared news releases to distribute after the declaration was made. Several times a week we called Ambassador Hamilton in Peru and

Wendy Patten who had replaced Scott Busby at the NSC, anxious to know if they had heard anything new.

At the end of January, representatives of the Peruvian government, including the prime minister and foreign minister, visited Washington. They met with officials at the State Department and the NSC and members of Congress, particularly those who had influence over financial aid for Peru. We were told that, at these meetings, Lori was a key topic of discussion and Prime Minister Bustamante explained that it was now clear Lori was not a leader of the MRTA. Important witnesses would be submitting affidavits to this effect. Based on these affidavits, Bustamante expected her conviction would be reversed. Similar messages were given to other members of Congress when Peruvian officials returned a few weeks later.

The Peruvians even proposed an approximate timetable, expecting that the council would act by the end of March. In mid-February three new affidavits had been submitted and an official from the U.S. embassy viewed them and verified that they addressed only the relevant evidence—that Lori was not a leader of the MRTA. That was the good news. The bad news was that we still had to wait for the fourth affidavit.

Meanwhile, Peru was immersed in its presidential election campaign. We were following events very, very intently, and so was the international community. Election monitors from human rights groups descended on Peru and reported on widespread corruption and dirty tricks—some of which were all too familiar to us.

We recalled that for several weeks after Lori's arrest the news kiosks had been covered with unflattering photos and ridiculous, ever-changing, unsubstantiated accusations designed to convince the public she was guilty. Now on these same kiosks the front pages of the Fujimori-controlled press featured unflattering photos and ridiculous, ever-changing accusations designed to discredit the two main opposition candidates—Alberto Andrade and Luis Casteñeda. In addition, the government and, therefore, Mr. Fujimori had control of eight of the nine TV stations and denied opponents airtime. When the opposition held rallies, suddenly the power would be cut on the loudspeaker system or a military band would appear and drown out the speaker.

Newspaper headlines around the world used the words "fraud," "irregularities," and "foul" in describing the election process. Monitors from the Organization of American States, the Carter Center for Human Rights, and other international human rights organizations were highly critical. And President Clinton approved a resolution passed by the U.S. Congress threatening to modify political and economic relations with Peru unless the elections were free and transparent.

As the campaign progressed, Alberto Andrade and Luis Casteñeda fell by the wayside along with five other candidates, their campaigns devastated by dirty tricks. But Alejandro Toledo, a Peruvian of mixed Spanish-Indian lineage with strong Indian features, gained strength. He campaigned against Mr. Fujimori's authoritarian ways and, having been raised in poverty, promised to be "the president of the poor." In return, and despite an agreement not to offer inducements for votes, Mr. Fujimori gave away parcels of land and bags of rice as he campaigned around the country, particularly in the rural Indian areas that had given him strong support in the past.

There were more cries of "foul" and reports that ballots and tally sheets disappeared for hours without explanation while votes were counted in undisclosed locations. Astonishingly, there were 1.4 million more ballots counted than there were eligible voters. The final count, which dragged out for days, showed 49.87 percent for Mr. Fujimori and 40.24 percent for Mr. Toledo with the remaining votes distributed among the other candidates. Because no candidate received more than 50 percent, a runoff between the two leaders was scheduled for May 28.

And we were still waiting for the supreme council to act on Lori's *recurso*. We had hoped that after the election, there would be movement. Now we didn't expect movement until after the runoff—although we kept pushing U.S. officials to press for a resolution.

Meanwhile, both Mark and I, and our supporters, took advantage of the U.S. media coverage of the election mayhem to write letters to the editor and op-ed pieces. We pointed out that Lori was a victim of the same types of false claims and dirty tricks that were used in the political campaign against opposition candidates. And while we applauded the commitment of President Clinton and the Congress to fair elections in Peru, we also wanted them to press demands for human rights—particularly Lori's rights.

In mid-April, in a particularly strong column in the *New York Times,* Anthony Lewis wrote, "When the Serbs captured three U.S. soldiers during the Kosovo war a year ago, President Clinton warned President Milosevic of Yugoslavia: 'Make no mistake—America takes care of its own.' It is a fine sentiment. But the President has signally failed to apply it in a case that should nag at his and the country's conscience. It is the case of Lori Berenson." He went on to say that Lori's "flagrantly illegitimate trial makes President Clinton's passive posture on the case puzzling." I couldn't agree more. Surely the case of an innocent young woman enduring years of deprivation and abuse in a Peruvian prison should weigh on President Clinton's conscience. And I cannot believe that he would want to end his term with Lori still in prison—to have as part of his legacy that he neglected to take care of America's own.

Meanwhile in Peru, despite the many important issues that could affect the future of that country and its people, at times it seemed that the only issue of significance was the future of Lori Berenson. On April 28, the *New York Times* reported, "Without promising to release her from prison, the opposition presidential candidate Alejandro Toledo held open the possibility of a legal appeal for Lori Berenson . . . In New York, Mr. Toledo said that under judicial reforms he favors, Ms. Berenson's lawyers would be allowed to present evidence that she was judged unfairly."

Immediately Mr. Fujimori's supporters cried "soft on terrorism." By the next morning, papers noted that Mr. Toledo "clarified his position." He would not release terrorists, regardless of nationality. No way would he review Lori's case—it is a closed case. He emphasized that his government would be even stronger against terrorism than President Fujimori's. This started a flurry—actually a huge storm—of articles and TV interviews focused on Lori. On April 29, each of the Peruvian newspapers had several items, and *Expreso* alone had more than a dozen different articles discussing Lori. Meanwhile, TV coverage was accompanied by unflattering clips of Lori's 1996 press presentation.

Of particular concern were the comments by high-ranking members of the Peruvian judiciary who joined in the political fray. Jurist Mario Amoretti said that a *recurso de revisión* is not applicable in the case of Lori Berenson because a *recurso* is only possible for someone who wishes to prove her innocence, but Lori confessed—and the confession made due process irrelevant. Marcos Ibazeta, President of the [civilian] Superior Court for Terrorism said Lori's sentence is a settled matter and there could not be a new trial. Pedro Infantes, President of the Superior Court of Lima, said she was already judged and sentenced. And, preposterously, Mr. Infantes declared that due process was respected in her case. Even the Peruvian ombudsman, who is supposed to be independent of government and political influence, said, "I do not see why she has to be in a distinct position from the other terrorists. I do not believe that her situation should be different." Many articles made a point that there would be no special favors for a U.S. citizen. Statements from Fujimori supporters featured Lori but were directed at the United States for its criticism of the electoral process.

The demagoguery aimed at Lori was beyond belief. But one thing was made perfectly clear. Respected members of the civilian justice system had already prejudged her. They said she was guilty, had confessed, and her case was closed. Perhaps even more incredibly, they insisted she had due process. They simply confirmed once again that Peru lacked an impartial judiciary, that Peru was incapable of providing a fair trial for Lori.

▪ Election Turmoil Continues

In the midst of the election turmoil, Kathy and I went to Peru for Mother's Day. Lori had requested that we have an up-close longer visit—the type of special Mother's Day visit that is permitted in all other prisons, even Yanamayo. Her request was denied. We met in the *locutorio* for one hour and we made the best of it. This was the first time in many years I spent Mother's Day with both my daughters, and we weren't going to allow the prison officials to spoil things. Lori borrowed a guitar (she had left hers in Yanamayo), and the three of us, ignoring the screens that separated us, sang songs that we had sung together when Lori and Kathy were children and the guitar was in my hands. Lori selected the first song, and saying, "I bet you haven't heard this one in over twenty years," she broke into the chorus of "The Gypsy Rover." I realized I had never told her about singing it at the January 1996 "folkfest" in our hotel room in Lima with John Richardson, Mr. Achahui, and Tom Nooter. I wondered how much else I had never told her—how much she never learned—because one hour every few weeks and censored letters in my poor Spanish is simply not enough.

As a small concession for the holiday, Kathy and I were allowed to hug Lori before we left. And in spite of the difficult good-bye, we left smiling—at least momentarily. But as the taxi pulled away from the prison we realized once again how sad it was that we were dependent on the whims of the Peruvian authorities for such small things—an hour visit, a few songs, and a hug.

As the May 28 runoff drew near, Peru was making news around the world with stories of the same dirty tricks that characterized the April 9 election. Alejandro Toledo was still denied access to TV coverage and was still slandered in the Fujimori-controlled press. And there were questions about the reliability of new computer software to be used to tally votes. Mr. Toledo threatened to withdraw from the race. Eduardo

Stein, leader of a monitoring team from the Organization of American States, tried to mediate a solution whereby the election could be postponed to give foreign observers time to test computer software to make sure the counts were transparent and clean. But the Fujimori government refused to postpone, and on May 18 Alejandro Toledo said he would not participate in the runoff, claiming the computer system was susceptible to fraud and that Fujimori's control of newspapers and TV denied him a fair chance to win. On May 26, Mr. Stein, saying, "The Peruvian electoral process is far from one that could be considered free and fair," ordered his monitoring team and observers to leave Peru. Other monitoring groups, including the one from the Carter Center, also withdrew. President Clinton issued a statement: "Free, fair and open elections are the foundation of a democratic society. Without them, our relationship with Peru will inevitably be affected."

On May 28, although Mr. Fujimori was the only candidate, voters went to the polls. By Peruvian law voting is obligatory and neglecting to do so is a crime punishable by a heavy fine. Mr. Fujimori won barely 50 percent of the ballots. Toledo supporters either voted for him despite his withdrawal, wrote "no to fraud" on the ballot, or turned it in blank. If the total of those who expressed their support for Mr. Toledo on their ballots is added to the number of people who did not vote at all, nearly 60 percent of eligible voters did *not* vote for Mr. Fujimori.

On May 29, the United States joined other nations in criticizing the fraudulent election. The State Department issued a statement that "No president emerging from such a flawed process can claim legitimacy. In view of the refusal of the government of Peru to accommodate international observers' complaints . . . we do not see the election as being valid. This problem is a serious threat to the inter-American system and its commitment to democracy." I was a bit surprised and impressed by this strong statement of condemnation. But I was not surprised the next day when a State Department spokesman backpedaled, refusing to endorse the statement of the previous day. He preferred to simply express the administration's concern and "regret." Ah yes, the U.S. government expresses "regret"—that was a lot more typical of the weak response that I had learned to expect from our State Department. I am sure that Mr. Fujimori wasn't surprised, either. When he was asked by a reporter for the *Washington Post* about possible sanctions by the international community, he said, "For us, there is no fear that they could apply sanctions . . . We will get through this in a few days."

Sure enough, at a June meeting of the OAS, over the objection of the United States, member nations voted not to call for new elections or sanctions against Peru. They voted instead to send a mission to Peru to work to strengthen democracy. U.S.–Peruvian relations remained strained. And we were still waiting for the supreme council to dismiss Lori's case.

▪ New Hopes

Ever since our meeting with National Security Advisor Sandy
Berger we had kept in close contact with the NSC—speaking
frequently first with Scott Busby, Director for Multilateral and
Humanitarian Affairs, and then with his replacement Wendy
Patten. We also spoke and met occasionally with the Senior
Director, Eric Schwartz. But as the months wore on without
signs of progress on Lori's *recurso*, we asked to meet again with
Mr. Berger. We feared that the process in the Supreme Council of Military Justice was stalled, perhaps dead, despite consistent assurances from the government of Peru—up until the
time this book went to press—that it was "on track." There is
much more to be said about the Peruvian government's admission that Lori was never a leader of the MRTA, its initiatives
to have the conviction of treason dismissed, and the many
delays in the promised action, but I cannot jeopardize Lori's
release by revealing them as I write this.

Mark, Ramsey and I met with Sandy Berger at the White
House on June 14. He was well apprised of Lori's situation and
we were thrilled when he expressed his determination to secure her release. He made it clear that he and his staff would
work to bring Lori home in the next six months, before President Clinton left office. He informed us of the U.S. decision
to send a high-level delegation to Peru that would discuss many
of the issues relevant to U.S.–Peruvian relations, including Lori,
making it clear that resolution of Lori's situation was a high
priority. And we all hoped that the process in the Supreme
Council of Military Justice would be completed by the time
that the delegation arrived in Lima so that the focus could be
on Lori's subsequent release.

Once again we were impressed by Sandy Berger's sincerity
and humanity. As we were leaving and thanking him, Mark
expressed his hope that Lori would soon be able to thank him

in person. Mr. Berger replied that he would love to be on the plane that brought her home.

We left the meeting excited but nevertheless concerned. After four and a half years of inaction or, at best, weak initiatives that had only guaranteed Peru's ability to defy international law with impunity, *finally,* it seemed that the U.S. government would make an all-out effort to resolve Lori's situation. *Finally,* there seemed to be a commitment—not a commitment to secure a fair trial, which everyone agreed was impossible, but a commitment to secure Lori's release. But we knew there were no guarantees, and time was rapidly running out on the Clinton Administration.

We met again with the NSC in July. This time we met with Eric Schwartz who, like Mr. Berger, was determined to press for Lori's release, indicating that Lori's situation needed to be raised strongly and often with the Peruvian government. He also suggested that perhaps two missions be sent to Peru—a delegation to discuss Lori among other issues and a special emissary to discuss only Lori. He pointed out that other issues—democratization, freedom of the press, revamping of the Peruvian justice system and electoral process—were long-term efforts that required many meetings and negotiations. The release of Lori Berenson was different—it should be settled on immediately. The delegation would go to Peru at the end of August and then a decision would be made about sending a special emissary soon after.

On our next trip to Washington, Mark, Kathy and I met with Hillary Rodham Clinton at the White House. Our meetings with Sandy Berger were in the west wing. We had never been in the main building, the place where Presidents greeted dignitaries and banquets were held for heads of state. We were in awe of the majesty of the rooms, and as we waited for the first lady we reflected on how much our lives had changed.

Five years ago, none of us would have ever imagined such a meeting and we didn't know quite what to expect. But as soon as Mrs. Clinton sat down and began to speak, we relaxed. She was completely informed about Lori's situation and was very concerned about her well-being. She offered to work with the NSC, however they deemed would be best for Lori, and promised to do whatever she could to bring Lori home. We were very touched by her compassion and thankful for her commitment.

And as July drew to a close, we had more good news—this time from the congress. On July 27, Congressman Joe Moakley of Massachusetts spoke on the floor of congress, stressing that "it is time that President Clinton demands Lori's release at the highest levels—it is time this nation stands up for Lori—it is time for Lori to come home." And then, on July 28, a letter signed by forty Senators and another signed by two hundred twenty-one members of the House of Representatives were sent to President Clinton, urging him once again to secure Lori's immediate release. In a press statement Congresswoman Carolyn Maloney said, "It is unbelievable what has happened to Lori Berenson . . . I am hopeful that with the support of Congress, President Clinton will continue his efforts to free Lori Berenson from prison and to work for human rights in Peru and throughout the world." And in a separate statement, Congresswoman Maxine Waters wrote, "I am proud that the majority of the members of the House of Representatives have joined me this year to call for Lori's immediate release. Now is the time for the President to act."

Also on July 28 President Alberto Fujimori was inaugurated for a third term.

So once again we are waiting and hoping—waiting for the Supreme Council of Military Justice to act on Lori's *recurso*, waiting for the U.S. missions to visit Peru, hoping that they, as representatives of President Clinton and the U.S. government, will demand Lori's release and that the Peruvian government will realize that there is no alternative, that Lori must be released. And while we wait for governments to act, and hope every moment for Lori's freedom, we will continue to work long hours every day, travel wherever support can be found, and journey regularly to visit and be strengthened by Lori. And I can say, as Lori said just before her sentencing, "[I] never will lose the hope and confidence that there will be a new day of justice in Peru."

■ July 30, 2000

Today marks four years and eight months since Lori's arrest. 1705 days. I still have very vivid memories of that first phone call that brought such horrifying news and prefaced this totally unimaginable chain of events. I never could have imagined that more than four-and-a-half years later I would still be waiting for the call saying Lori is coming home. If I had known that then, I might not have thought myself capable of enduring such a long struggle. But now I know I can continue for as long as it takes.

On that first night, and for quite a while after, I was terrified. But the terror was gradually replaced by a more complex mix of emotions—sadness, anger, and frustration, with occasional periods of profound fear and a few of hopeful anticipation. Mostly I worry. Between visits I still agonize, "Is Lori all right?" I still get knots in my stomach when I travel to see her and my heart breaks at the end of each visit as I say good-bye.

Our lives have changed dramatically. Physics, dancing, even knitting, are things of my past, as statistics, jogging and watching football are of Mark's. I am amazed at the things that now seem routine—meeting with government officials, speaking on TV and radio, receiving mail from all over the world, traveling to Peru every few weeks. And I am also amazed that I have written this book. I was always such a private person and here I am telling my story to all who will listen.

I have learned so much—and not just about lobbying or sound bites. I have become much more aware of the pain and suffering endured by so many throughout the world because of disregard for justice and basic human rights. And I never before fully appreciated how many wonderful, compassionate people there are who take time out of their busy lives, time away from their own families or interests, to help right the wrongs against humanity. I could never adequately thank the thousands and thousands of people who have devoted words, deeds, and prayers towards comforting and encouraging us. They have told everyone who would listen that Lori Berenson is innocent and must be freed. They have helped me maintain my strength when exhaustion seemed almost overwhelming and helped Lori maintain her strong spirit, despite the extremely harsh conditions of her imprisonment.

This past January 11, Lori asked that the following letter be read at the many vigils around the country commemorating the fourth anniversary of her sentencing. She wanted to thank her supporters for their help and for their commitment to human rights. And she also wanted them to know that the years of wrongful imprisonment had not changed who she was or what she believes.

Dear Friends:

Thank you all for coming today and for all the help you have given me these past four years.

I admire the dedication of people like you to the cause of human rights, social justice, and freedom. I am immensely grateful for your efforts to see me free. These efforts certainly will benefit those who live in similar and in worse circumstances.

The violation of human rights in Peru isn't only a problem of lack of democracy, freedom of speech and press, and the existence of judicial systems that are completely subordinate to political power. The foremost violation is the institutional violence that relegates the vast majority of people to living in misery. The right to food, health, education, and employment are human rights that are consistently violated in Peru, and we cannot be silent when we see and live these violations, when we know that there is spreading hunger and misery—and far too many deaths resulting from neglect.

In addition, the judicial systems in Peru have sentenced thousands, falsely accused as I was, to live in prisons under horrendous conditions. This includes the civilian courts, whose judges are appointed by the President and the secret military courts, both of which often fulfill a more political than judicial function. In Peru's jails today, as Amnesty International has pointed out, access to better conditions is contingent on prisoners' denials of their own beliefs and their denouncing of those who refuse to betray their beliefs.

Over these last four years I have become more convinced than ever that in the presence of social injustice and abuse, silence is almost as harmful as the injustice itself. To be silent is to be an accomplice. We will not be silent, we will not be quiet, until this changes, until there is justice and respect for human rights in Peru. And we will keep the faith that justice will prevail.

I thank you again for your help and efforts to better the situation of human rights and to see to my freedom.

Thank you,

Lori Berenson

Perhaps the most important thing I have learned over these years is that I will not be an accomplice. I will not be silent. I will shout until Lori is free—and then I will not be quiet until there is justice and respect for human rights everywhere.

Please join me.

EPILOGUE

SOMETIMES, IN THE MIDST OF A NIGHTMARE,

TO YOUR RELIEF, YOU FIND YOURSELF HALF

AWAKE, ESCAPING THE HORROR. BUT

THEN, EVEN BEFORE YOUR HEART CAN SLOW

TO ITS NORMAL RHYTHM,

SLEEP RETURNS AND

THE NIGHTMARE BEGINS AGAIN.

■

▪ Sunday, August 27 to Friday, September 1

On Sunday, August 27, 2000, we were feeling pretty good. We had learned that President Fujimori would be visiting the United Nations the week of September 4. National Security Advisor Sandy Berger would be meeting with him to discuss Lori's situation. We hoped he would make it clear that President Clinton wanted her to be released immediately. We were also the focus of renewed media attention, with an appearance on *Oprah* scheduled for August 30. On Monday, August 28, we received a phone call from the U.S. embassy in Peru. The Supreme Military Council had, on the basis of Lori's *recurso*, dismissed the charges against her.

Finally.

The world was surprised, but we had been waiting for this announcement since last December.

But as we had feared, that same day, a prosecutor for the civilian courts announced that Lori was under arrest for terrorism. She would be tried by the civilian antiterrorism courts and would be sentenced to at least twenty years. President Fujimori immediately concurred—at least twenty years. Other government officials and members of the Peruvian Congress chimed in, confirming her long sentence. This was *Alice in Wonderland*— "Sentence first, verdict afterward."

Within five minutes of the announcement we were deluged with calls from the media. No one understood why this was happening. No one knew that Lori had filed a *recurso* in December 1999 and that this decision was based on that *recurso*. In Peru, President Fujimori was accused of and castigated for giving in to U.S. pressure by offering Lori a new trial. Suddenly the press saw Lori's case as political. But why hadn't they seen that in December 1995 when Mr. Fujimori gleefully waved Lori's U.S. passport? Didn't they realize that everything about Lori's case was about U.S.-Peruvian relations and not about Lori?

Meanwhile in the United States, many people cheered, believing Lori would finally have a fair trial. But we and all those familiar with the Peruvian justice system knew better. President Fujimori already pronounced her guilty, and we all knew what that meant. The *New York Times* wrote, "Human rights officials . . . warned that in a country whose court system has been sharply criticized, the decision did not mean the new trial would be fair." The article went on to quote José Miguel Vivanco, executive director of the Americas division of Human Rights Watch, who said that under the antiterrorism laws, "the definition of terrorism is so broad and so vague that almost any activity could qualify as terrorism" and that the new trial could be influenced by political concerns whether or not the law was used. "If there is one serious problem in Peru, it's lack of rule of law. The World Bank has suspended its programs on judicial reform in Peru because there's no evidence of an independent judiciary." Even State Department spokesman Philip Reeker said, "There remain serious concerns about the openness and fairness of trial proceedings . . . in cases related to terrorism in civilian courts."

My stomach was once again in knots. Fear started taking hold. The nightmare was beginning again.

Once again our phone rang all day and night with requests for interviews. We were running on nervous energy, with little time to eat and too much anxiety to sleep. Once again one of us—me, this time—traveled to Peru with Ramsey Clark to hire a lawyer. Once again the Peruvian news kiosks were covered with headlines about the *"gringa terrorista,"* and Ramsey and I barely escaped stampedes by the Peruvian media. And once again Lori was to be tried by a system that was incapable of providing due process.

Mark and I spent the rest of the week giving interviews, trying to explain what happened and what might happen. We were also in constant contact with the embassy.

Lori would be moved to a prison in Lima—but when? How was she taking the news? How was she being treated? When we learned on Thursday that Lori was moved to Santa Monica Prison in Chorrillos, I immediately reserved a flight to Peru for the next night, arriving in Lima Saturday morning, in time for visiting hours at the prison.

■ Saturday, September 2 to Wednesday, September 13

Yet another prison. Yet another *locutorio*.

Yet another set of rules and regulations. The prison, like the rest of Lima, was cool, damp, and gray. Lori was dressed in jeans and a heavy blue sweater. This prison did not permit clothing with any black, green, or red, so much of her clothing was returned to me. I immediately pulled out a sweater in an Andean design with forbidden bits of black and green and layered it above my other sweaters in an attempt to keep warm. I knew I would have the opposite problem in Lima's summer when hot and humid would be the norm.

The *locutorio* was filled and very noisy with ten visitors speaking to ten prisoners in the all-concrete confined space. Lori and I each leaned in close to the screens and struggled to hear each other. Lori was outwardly calm, but at times I noted the tension in her face. She told me about her trip from Socabaya—handcuffed but not hooded, the first time in over four and a half years that she saw anything of the world beyond prison walls. I wondered what it was like for her to see trees, mountains, buildings, flowers, life, after years of seeing nothing but concrete and sky. I wanted to know what she saw and what she thought, but there wasn't time enough to discuss the trip or the new prison, and there was certainly no time for gossip. She was glad that the Supreme Military Council had finally nullified her conviction, but she knew that the newspapers, the prosecutor, and President Fujimori already considered her guilty and were discussing a twenty-year sentence. She knew that she would have a trial in which the verdict and the sentence were predetermined by politics rather than decided by guilt or innocence.

It was already clear that there was no hope for internationally accepted standards of due process. As soon as Lori had arrived at Chorrillos on Thursday afternoon, August 31, the prosecutor and a judge had come to question her "for the record." She had refused to answer without a lawyer and they had accepted her refusal, saying they would return the following Wednesday. They had insisted that if Lori did not have a lawyer by then, they would provide a public defender whether she wanted one or not. And they were already taking testimony from witnesses. This was all done despite the requirement of the American Convention on Human Rights, as well as Peruvian law, that prisoners have the right to counsel of their own choosing, a right to adequate time and means to prepare a defense, and a right for the defense lawyer not only to be present when witnesses testify but also to question them.

As I understood the process in the antiterrorism civilian courts, during this first phase, the "instructive" phase, the instructive prosecutor and the instructive judge have thirty working days, possibly extended an additional twenty, to gather any evidence and obtain testimony from Lori and witnesses. At the end of that phase, the prosecutor would determine whether there was sufficient reason to bring the case to trial—sort of like the grand jury phase in the United States—except there is no jury. The courtroom phase would have a panel of three trial judges, but still no jury. Lastly, there would be an appeal to the Supreme Court, regardless of the verdict. Lori would appeal if she was found guilty, and the prosecutor would appeal if she was found not guilty.

Lori needed a lawyer. Ramsey arrived in Peru on Monday morning. We started immediately meeting with lawyers and with influential people who might recommend lawyers. Many of those we spoke to wanted nothing to do with the case. Others did not have the appropriate experience. The rules for terrorism cases in the civilian courts were different than for other criminal cases. On the other hand, we did not want someone like Grimaldo Achahui, who had defended so many alleged "terrorists" that his clients were automatically assumed guilty. We also wanted a lawyer familiar with human rights issues.

Ramsey had filed a new petition with the Inter-American Commission on Human Rights on Lori's behalf. It cited all the violations of Lori's rights to due process and referred to a ruling in April 2000 on behalf of Carlos Molera Coca and others, wherein the Commission determined that violations of rights to a fair trial are inherent and inescapable in criminal proceedings in civilian courts under Peru's antiterrorism laws. The petition also pointed out that the judgment of the Supreme Military Council nullifying Lori's conviction constituted an acquittal, which under the American Convention on Human Rights and principles of double jeopardy precluded Peru from trying Lori again for the same conduct. In September 1997, in a similar case, the Inter-American Court ruled that Peru must free Maria Elena Loayza because her right to protection against double jeopardy had been violated. I was in Peru a month later when the justice minister announced that Peru respects its international obligations and would abide by the decision of the Inter-American Court and free Professor Loayza.

We needed a lawyer who understood all these issues. Although we had many meetings with lawyers, by Monday afternoon it was clear that there was no way we could hire one before the judge returned to question Lori on Wednesday.

On Tuesday, Ramsey, Consular Officer Mary Grandfield, and I visited Instructive Judge Romel Borda. We brought him a signed petition from Lori in which she requested that all proceedings be stopped pending fulfillment of rights guaranteed by the American Convention on Human Rights. The petition listed these rights and stated that Lori would respectfully refuse to answer any questions until she had a lawyer of her own choosing. Ramsey explained to the judge that we had not had adequate time to hire a lawyer and that even if we had hired one, he or she would not have had time to meet Lori, let alone prepare a defense. Ramsey noted that on the judge's desk was a copy of that infamous two-thousand-page file that DINCOTE had assembled four years and nine months earlier. Pointing to the enormous file, he commented that it would take quite a bit of time to read through it. The judge replied that a good lawyer needed only two hours.

Two hours? He must have been kidding.

Ramsey asked that the judge postpone his questioning of Lori and also desist from interviewing witnesses until Lori's lawyer could be present. Judge Borda responded that he was on a tight thirty-day schedule and there was no time to wait, even if that meant forgoing due process. He would continue taking testimony from witnesses, but he agreed to postpone the questioning of Lori one week, until the following Wednesday. After we left he apparently changed his mind, or perhaps someone changed it for him, because when he saw Lori on Wednesday he gave her only two days, saying he'd be back on Friday and she'd better have a lawyer by then.

So Ramsey and I continued interviewing prospective lawyers, and on Thursday we met with José Luis Sandoval. He was highly recommended by some members of APRODEH, a well-respected Peruvian human rights organization. He had tried several terrorism cases wherein human rights were at issue. He had won half of them. On Friday he met with Lori, and she agreed we should hire him. He immediately arranged for Lori's questioning to be postponed until the following

Wednesday, September 13. But clearly he would not have adequate opportunity to consult with Lori about the defense or have anywhere near sufficient time to read the file carefully by then.

I flew home Wednesday night. I was so tired that I felt like I was sleepwalking. I wondered how I would get through the next months. Would I be able once again to sleep through the night or have a few minutes without my stomach in knots? I was, as usual, worried about leaving Lori. I knew she was under tension, subject to harassment, isolated from the other prisoners, and in need of visitors. I wanted to be in Peru with Lori, but I also wanted to go home.

■ Amazing Changes, Thursday, September 14 to Saturday, December 9

On Thursday, September 14, a video was broadcast in Peru showing Vladimiro Montesinos, President Fujimori's key advisor and head of the National Intelligence Service, bribing an opposition congressman to join Mr. Fujimori's party. All of Peru was in an uproar. The opposition parties were screaming for Mr. Montesinos's arrest and President Fujimori's resignation. On Saturday afternoon, the Organization of American States said the allegations of top-level corruption in Peru were of "utmost seriousness" and demanded "quick and severe action" from the president.

At 10:30 Saturday evening, September 16, President Fujimori held a press conference at which he said, "After deep reflection, I have decided first to deactivate the National Intelligence Service and, second, to call for a general election immediately, in which I will not stand." President Fujimori was going to step down.

Over the next several weeks, the news from Peru continued to amaze. Rumors circulated that Montesinos would mount a coup. Several foreign governments tried to lure Montesinos from Peru by finding a country that would give him asylum. No country wanted him. Montesinos secretly left Peru, secretly returned, and then once again left under cover of darkness. TV cameras recorded President Fujimori, dressed in combat boots and a leather jacket, heading a convoy of vehicles as he personally set out to find Montesinos, searching everywhere—from army installations to supermarkets.

In November, Mr. Fujimori attended an economics conference in Brunei. He was scheduled to follow that with a trip to Panama. Instead he went to Japan and faxed his resignation to Peru. The Peruvian Congress refused to accept it and instead dismissed him for "moral incapacity."

As time went on, officials found thousands of videos, secretly taped by Montesinos, like the one that started it all on September 14. Dozens of prominent Peruvians, politicians, judges, bankers, media moguls, and businessmen were seen in compromising situations with Montesinos, arrested and jailed. Montesinos taped everyone and everything. Every day new videos were released. Peruvians were glued to the TV. "Vladi videos," named for Vladimiro Montesinos, drew more viewers than the afternoon soap operas.

Among the tapes was one from January 1998, soon after Lori filed a petition with the Inter-American Commission on Human Rights. In it we saw Montesinos telling the then foreign minister, "Right now I could tell the Supreme Council of Military Justice to bring [Ms. Berenson] from Yanamayo. We don't need to consult with anyone." He went on to describe how Lori could be retried in a civilian court and sentenced to ten to fifteen years and then pardoned and sent home. It was just as we had always thought: Montesinos and Fujimori used Lori however and whenever it was politically convenient. They could dictate the verdict and sentence, and they did not have to consult with anyone.

Montesinos was accused of numerous crimes including arms trafficking, drug dealing, money laundering, bribery, rigging elections, organizing death squads, and robbing the country of hundreds of millions of dollars. Fujimori was accused of absconding with millions and ordering the murders of innocent people. But Fujimori found it useful to claim Japanese citizenship, and Japan will not extradite a Japanese citizen accused of a crime in a foreign country. The Peruvian government has not given up efforts to bring him to justice. But meanwhile, he lives very comfortably in Japan on the money he allegedly stole from Peru.

An interim government was established, and new elections were scheduled for April 2001. Valentin Paniagua, a well-respected member of the Congress, assumed the presidency; former United Nations secretary general Javier Pérez de Cuéllar was appointed both prime minister and foreign minister; and Diego Garcia Sayan, a well-known human rights activist, was named justice minister. Lori, in her January 1996 press presentation, had expressed her hope for "a new day of justice in Peru." By the end of November 2000, that new day seemed near.

Kathy and I visited Lori on December 9 and were surprised to learn that two days earlier, the justice minister did away with the special rules that governed political prisoners. Lori and the other prisoners were now permitted out of their cells from 6 a.m. to 10 p.m. They could go to the yard whenever they wished and could eat meals or work together on the benches in the corridor outside the cells. Lori was no longer isolated, which made her prison life so much more bearable.

Visiting was now from 9 a.m. to 5 p.m. "up close" in the yard, for as long as we wished. Women could visit on Wednesdays and Saturdays and men on Sundays. And visiting was no longer limited to immediate family. Kathy and I had come expecting a one-hour visit in the dark *locutorio* and instead spent hours with Lori out in the yard. That first visit under the new rules was incredible. We could hug. We did not have to rush through reading our notes. We could talk leisurely about books, music, and news events. We could hug again, as often as we liked. The yard was filled with prisoners and visitors. Sometimes some women sang or played a guitar or a *zampoña*. Those who had no visitors sat chatting among themselves, knitting. Families who hadn't hugged or touched hands for years huddled together.

I've spent many hours with Lori under these new rules. During the first few visits, a real sense of euphoria existed amongst the prisoners. But the exhilaration soon faded. Conditions were a little better, but Lori and the others were still in prison.

In the midst of all these events, Lori's trial plodded on. Judge Borda and the instructive prosecutor, Maria Peralta, continued gathering testimony. Lori's lawyer, José Sandoval, continued recording due process violations. On October 13 we attended a hearing at the Inter-American Commission on Human Rights. Lori's lawyers argued that her trial must be stopped. They cited as precedents the 1997 ruling for Professor Loayza on double jeopardy and the ruling from April 2000 that concluded that the special terrorism courts lacked due process. Javier Llaque represented the Peruvian government and told the three commissioners that Lori would be guaranteed full due process including an open hearing where "she could prove her innocence." The commissioners immediately protested. According to both the American Convention on Human Rights and the Peruvian law, the prosecution must prove guilt. Lori should not have to prove her innocence. Mr. Llaque mumbled something about having misspoken, that of course he meant to say the prosecution would have to prove her guilt. But his correction did not seem to impress the commissioners. They probably knew that "innocent until proven guilty" is written in the Peruvian Constitution, but it is not imprinted in the Peruvian minds or practiced in the Peruvian courts. And this was only one of many, many problems with Peruvian "justice."

We were somewhat optimistic that the Commission might take quick action. But a few weeks later, when Mr. Fujimori fled and an interim government was installed, the Commission seemed reluctant to rush ahead. Perhaps they wanted to give the new government a chance to make changes.

Peruvian human rights leaders had long called for the elimination of Fujimori's antiterrorism laws and the terrorism courts. We met several times with Justice Minister Diego Garcia-Sayan and he readily acknowledged the shortcomings of the terrorism courts and agreed that they needed reform. But he insisted that although the interim leaders were intent on rooting out corruption and improving human rights, they would not in any way interfere with an ongoing judicial process. After all, a major criticism of the Fujimori-Montesinos administration was its control of the courts. We argued that we were not asking him to interfere with a legitimate judicial process. We were asking him to stop a corrupt process that had begun under Fujimori's rule and was continuing with Fujimori laws and Fujimori personnel—a process that was condemned by major human rights groups and the Inter-American Court. The international community would be watching this trial, and if changes weren't made, they would criticize the "new Peru" for continuing Fujimori injustice.

■ Another New Year

On January 16, four days before he was to leave office, President Clinton called Peruvian president Paniagua and asked him to find a "good resolution" to Lori's case. Mr. Paniagua replied that the courts would guarantee a fair legal process and he would not interfere.

Although President Clinton had also spoken to Mr. Paniagua soon after he took office the previous November, and Sandy Berger had spoken to Mr. Fujimori in September shortly before his administration fell, overall the efforts of the Clinton administration amounted to "too little, too late."

January 20 brought the Bush administration to Washington. In anticipation, we had sent packets of information to Secretary of State Colin Powell and National Security Advisor Condoleezza Rice. We were surprised and pleased that they both responded—and quickly. Secretary of State Powell wrote that he was awaiting the results of the trial. He added, "Embassy officials . . . will continue to emphasize to the Government of Peru the importance the United States Government places on this matter." National Security Advisor Rice wrote, "I want to assure you that the Bush Administration shares your hope that her case can be resolved as quickly as possible, consistent with humanitarian principles and the rule of law. In fact, Mike Hammer, Director for Western Hemisphere Affairs, has already conveyed our views on this to [Peruvian] Ambassador Alzamora." We had been concerned that we would have to start all over again, climbing the ladder of power. It had taken us years to reach the top of the Clinton administration, and we had never received any response from Madeleine Albright. We were encouraged by the immediate messages of support from the Bush administration.

Meanwhile, we were waiting for the open hearing, the courtroom phase of the judicial proceeding that most people consider "the trial." In September everything had been rushed. Judge Borda started proceedings before Lori could hire a lawyer. We were told that Peruvian law allowed a maximum of fifty days for the instructive phase. But the fifty days stretched into four months, and the trial was still was not scheduled.

On January 16, Prosecutor Peralta finally forwarded her report to the Superior Court for Terrorism. She concluded that

Lori was not a leader or member of the MRTA, nor did she participate directly in acts of terrorism, but she recommended that Lori be tried as a collaborator. On February 15, Superior Court prosecutor Walter Vivas charged Lori with facilitating the rental of the house in La Molina used by the MRTA; renting an apartment where she "hid" Nancy Gilvonio; preparing and delivering food and giving "indoctrinating" lectures to MRTA members living in the La Molina house; purchasing office equipment for the MRTA; and obtaining press credentials for Nancy and herself with the intention of assisting an MRTA plan to attack the Peruvian Congress. Although Prosecutor Peralta had concluded that four months of gathering testimony did not produce any evidence that Lori was a member of the MRTA or had participated in acts of terrorism, Mr. Vivas included the charge that she was a militant of the group. He asked for a sentence of twenty years. We knew there was no evidence to support any of these charges, and we waited impatiently for the trial to begin.

In the next weeks, Mr. Vivas was replaced by another Superior Court prosecutor, Carlos Navas. Perhaps this change was made with the foreknowledge that Mr. Vivas would be relieved of his duty in April when the government removed judges and prosecutors it deemed corrupt or incompetent. We never found out if he was fired for corruption, incompetence, or both. But his charges against Lori formed the basis of the courtroom trial.

The Superior Court prosecutor was joined by *Procurador* (state prosecutor) Mario Cavagnaro from the Department of the Interior. The *procurador* represents "the public" and seeks civil reparations. Mr. Cavagnaro had been the *procurador* in the military tribunal five and a half years ago, and his accusations relied on the tainted testimony and DINCOTE reports from that time.

Although the charges and a compendium of the purported evidence had been officially filed on February 15, the Superior

Court for Terrorism did not send them to Mr. Sandoval until the evening of Thursday, March 15. Lori first saw them on Friday, only four days before the March 20 trial date.

▪ The Public Trial Begins

Mark and I arranged to go to Peru for the duration of the trial, which we assumed might be four to six weeks. We went to Lima a week early so we could visit with Lori, consult with Mr. Sandoval, and hold press conferences. We wanted to tell the Peruvian public that we were not looking to impose a U.S. justice system on Peru. We were only asking Peru to meet the standards and guarantee the rights it had agreed to in international treaties.

But most Peruvians were unaware of what these standards were or what rights were guaranteed. The Peruvian media certainly did not understand the presumption of innocence, that a decision of guilt can only be made *after* not *before* the trial. The press referred to Lori as "the terrorist," rarely using the words "alleged" or "accused." And it wasn't only the press. We were appalled to learn that even respected members of the human rights community saw nothing wrong in assuming she was guilty. On March 19, a day before the open hearing began, Ronald Gamara, a leading human rights lawyer, told the *New York Times*, "Our evaluation is that she deserves a correct, fair trial, but that in a free court she would be condemned."

And perhaps even more disturbing than prejudgment by the press and the human rights community was prejudgment by the presiding judge, Marcos Ibazeta.

Mr. Ibazeta was officially named presiding judge when the trial date was announced. But his name, and his interest in the case, had been bandied about ever since a new trial was ordered the previous August, and it was the secretary from his court, Javier Llaque, who had represented Peru at the Inter-American

Commission in October. Mr. Ibazeta was also a candidate for the Office of Human Rights ombudsman, a prestigious and politically connected position. Of course, some judges might see running for office while serving as presiding judge on a high-profile televised case a conflict of interest, but not Judge Ibazeta. He saw it as a golden opportunity to enhance his campaign. The election for ombudsman was to be held in the Congress, and the Congress had not changed after Fujimori's departure. Members of Congress who had been calling Lori "guilty" for years would be casting the votes. If Judge Ibazeta was looking for Lori's trial to help him win, then it would be beneficial to find her guilty and deliver a harsh sentence.

Our concerns about the judge were deepened when Ramsey came across a two-year-old article in the Peruvian newspaper *La Republica*. In it, Mr. Ibazeta harshly attacked Lori for filing a petition with the Inter-American Commission on Human Rights. Even though the judge admitted he did not know the "details," he repeatedly described Lori's petition as "irrational" and "escaping the rational." He referred to Lori as a "terrorist," even saying she was a member of the "bureau" or highest governing body of the MRTA, although she was never charged as such. In other words, without knowing the details, he believed she was guilty and that the military tribunal procedures and decision were appropriate.

Ramsey thought it would be inappropriate to discuss this article in public before giving Judge Ibazeta the opportunity to either demonstrate it was in error or withdraw from the case. Ramsey met with him on March 15, and the judge defended himself. He claimed he was misquoted and a check of other sources would so verify. Ramsey checked other sources. The only other report was in the newspaper *Expreso*, and it only confirmed the prejudicial statements quoted in *La Republica*. Ramsey sent the articles to the Inter-American Commission on Human Rights.

As time went on, we also learned there were Vladi videos wherein Montesinos referred to Marcos Ibazeta as "a member of the team." And there were records of Mr. Ibazeta speaking at the Inter-American Commission on Human Rights in 1998 on "The Autonomy and Independence of the Peruvian Courts." In 1998, there was no one in Peru who did not know that the courts were controlled by Fujimori and Montesinos. Only "a member of the team" would say otherwise.

The days leading up to the trial were almost unbearable. Mark, Lori, and I were bundles of nerves. We could not sleep. Each day brought us less confidence that the trial could possibly be fair. We were worried about the impartiality of Judge Ibazeta and had some concerns about the other two judges as well. Rumor had it that Judge Eliana Araujo was a close friend of Judge Ibazeta and Judge Carlos Manrique was a Montesinos appointee. We also anticipated a circuslike atmosphere with Judge Ibazeta as ringmaster.

The trial was to be held in the courtroom at Lurigancho Prison on the outskirts of Lima. It is usual in Peru for trials to take place in a courtroom at the prison where the accused is being held. But officials had decided that the courtroom at the Chorrillos Prison was too small for the anticipated crowd. There was a lot of talk about how the trial was open to "the public." But "the public" was reluctant to attend the trial, perhaps because entering a prison was intimidating or because Lurigancho was too far from the center of Lima. Lurigancho was chosen to accommodate the media, including Channel N, a local cable station that was to air the trial live.

On Monday night, March 19, we were joined by Tom Nooter and the first two of many legal and human rights observers who would attend the trial and report their observations: Anna Gallagher, professor of law at Georgetown University, and Sergio Widder of the Holocaust Museum in Buenos Aires, Argentina. The U.S. embassy would be sending personnel to monitor the trial, but only consular officers, not staff more appropriately specialized in law or human rights issues. We wanted observers who had the expertise to comment on the fairness of the proceedings, and fortunately several well-respected specialists volunteered their time.

At 7:15 a.m. the next morning, Tom, Anna, and Sergio hailed a taxi, and Mark and I joined Consular Officer Mary Grandfield, her assistant, and three security guards in the embassy van. We all set off for Lurigancho Prison, forty-five minutes away. Throngs of reporters and photographers were waiting at the entrance. Mark and I pushed through the mob and through the metal detectors into a large yard equipped with speakers and a giant viewing screen to accommodate an overflow crowd. The back of the courtroom was open to the yard, and we could see rows of plastic white chairs and, farther forward, wooden benches. We were led down to the front where four straight-backed chairs had been placed for the embassy officials, Mark, and me. We were seated immediately behind the waist-high Plexiglas partition that separated the public area from the official proceedings. To our left, extending from the partition and covering almost half of the public viewing area back to the yard, was a raised platform that had been specially built for the press. The press had followed us in and were busy installing tripods and microphones. The platform, which was approximately twenty feet by thirty feet and had no chairs, was crowded with equipment and people, some of whom hovered over Mark's left shoulder. The ringing of cell phones, combined with the murmur of phone conversations and discussions among reporters, created a din that I assumed would end when the proceedings began. I assumed wrong. The concept of "order in the court" was as foreign to Peruvians as "due process" and "fair trial."

Court officials sat behind tables along three sides of the room on the other side of the Plexiglas partition. The prosecution team had their backs against the partition, their backs to the press platform. The defense lawyer sat on the far side of the room, facing the prosecutors and the audience behind them. The three judges sat at a long table along the third side, with the prosecutors to their right and the defense to their left. The judges faced a "wall" of floor-to-ceiling bars. Behind the bars were concrete steps. The bars and steps gave the appearance of a circus cage.

At 9 a.m. Lori was led from an underground cell directly into the cage. A blinding flash from dozens of bulbs and TV lights was directed at her face.

Judge Ibazeta rang a handbell, and the proceedings began. Lori stood behind the bars for approximately ninety minutes while the prosecutor's charges were read and the case file was described. Mark and I did our best to follow the Spanish. I watched Lori as she stood as still as possible. She was wearing a print skirt and white blouse. Small fish, carved out of bone, hung on the end of the dangling earrings that a friend had made especially for her. It was crowded and very hot. Ceiling fans whirled and paper fans waved. We had brought bottles of water, and a court employee served water to the court officials and Mr. Sandoval. No water was offered to Lori.

Unlike U.S. courts, in Peru the defense attorney does not make an opening statement to counter the prosecutor's remarks. However, Judge Ibazeta permitted Lori to address the court. She stated that she was innocent of all the charges, that all the alleged evidence had been fabricated by DINCOTE, and that her case was highly political and she was being judged under the Fujimori antiterrorism laws that had been broadly criticized. She ended by saying, "One more observation—the fact that you are questioning me behind bars violates the principle of presumption of innocence. You are presenting me to the press as if I am guilty, thus violating my right to be presumed innocent."

Judge Ibazeta commented that he wasn't treating her differently from Peruvians similarly accused. Apparently he was unaware, or chose to ignore, the Peruvian Constitution that guarantees the right to be presumed innocent and Article 212 of the Peruvian Criminal Procedures Code that states: "In all trials the accused will appear without ligatures nor imprisoning objects, only accompanied by the necessary police members to avoid an escape." And the courtroom at Chorrillos, where the trial could have taken place, does not have a cage or bars.

Pictures of Lori behind bars appeared in newspapers around the world, sending a message that Judge Ibazeta refused to respect the American Convention on Human Rights and the Peruvian Constitution. But in Peru the photos sent a different message: Judge Ibazeta was protecting the public from a monster terrorist. *La Republica* referred to Lori as "The Tamed Beast." Fujimori was gone, but the demonization continued.

At the next hearing on March 22, at the request of the prosecutor, Lori was brought out of the cage and remained in front of the bars for the duration of the trial. But the image of "The Tamed Beast" behind bars continued to appear in the Peruvian press.

▪ New Routines

Mark and I rented a furnished apartment on the eleventh floor of a building in the Miraflores district of Lima. When we moved in at the beginning of April, we had a distant view of the Pacific Ocean and, although we could not see the prison, we could see the district of Chorrillos marked by a large crucifix on a cliff jutting into the ocean. As the months passed and the seasons changed, all we could see was the Lima fog.

I visited Lori on Saturdays and, if there was no court hearing, Wednesdays. I spent all day at the prison. We tried to ease each other's anxieties. We went over the week's trial events and discussed the press reports. We diverted ourselves by reminiscing. We chatted with other prisoners.

All the women in Lori's section of the prison were charged under the antiterrorism laws. Some were admitted members of subversive groups, and others proclaimed their innocence. Most had sentences that seemed far too long for the crimes for which they had been tried. All had horrendous stories to tell about their arrest and imprisonment. Many of them had been tortured.

Some of the women were mothers, and their visiting children brought much joy on their arrival and much sadness when they left. Nancy Gilvonio was also imprisoned at Chorrillos. She hadn't seen her sons since her arrest. In 1995 DINCOTE had threatened to torture them if Nancy didn't "cooperate," and they were quickly sent to live with relatives in France, where they were granted asylum. They were safe, but they could not visit their mother without losing their asylum status. Nancy missed them enormously and spoke of them constantly—how well they did in school, how they were growing. She had albums filled with their photos and letters.

While sitting and talking in the prison yard, it was so easy to forget these women were prisoners. But then I would leave, and they would have to stay.

Trial days were the most hectic and anxiety ridden. The embassy no longer drove us, so we left by taxi at 7:45, arriving at Lurigancho at 8:30 for a 9 a.m. start. Mark and I listened intently to the proceedings, but we missed a great deal. Although our Spanish comprehension was improving, it wasn't nearly good enough. At times the audience would laugh, or a judge would express anger and we didn't know why. The frustration was enormous. We would watch Lori's face to try to gauge if things were going well or not. We had to wait until we returned to our apartment to find out exactly what had happened. Our legal and human rights observers were all fluent in Spanish. They would take notes and then go over them with us later in the day. We were very grateful to Anna, Sergio, Angela, Mark, Abelardo, Marie, Martha, Lucian, and Grahame for traveling so far and sharing their expertise. They translated, they advised, and they provided moral support. They filed reports with their parent organizations, human rights groups, and the U.S. Congress. They helped us cope with our frustration, anger, apprehension, and exhaustion.

Lori's days were also exhausting and, of course, emotionally draining. She awoke at 5 a.m., washing and dressing in the dark. At 6 a.m., she was taken to the court in a motorcade of seven cars and several motorcycles. The security precautions were discussed in the press to assure the public that the MRTA would not be able to ambush the motorcade and allow Lori to escape. But the press neglected to report that there are probably no MRTA in Peru except those in prison. One day the press claimed that a truck had mysteriously stopped in front of the motorcade. The next day Lori traveled by helicopter. The leading Peruvian newspaper, *El Comercio*, had a front-page photo of the helicopter, guarded by soldiers with guns held at the ready, along with more accounts of the mysterious truck and the tightened security measures. It was just another reminder that Lori was considered guilty and dangerous.

Lori arrived at Lurigancho before 7 a.m. and spent the next two hours waiting in a cell. Shortly before proceedings began, she was brought to the courtroom to a chair placed in front of the bars. Our front-row seats were only about twenty feet from her, but we were not permitted to speak. Her lawyer, José Sandoval, was about twelve feet beyond. But unless Judge Ibazeta granted special permission, Mr. Sandoval was not allowed to speak with her either. At best, she could look at him when she wanted to alert him to testimony she believed needed to be addressed. But even this was against the rules. One day

when she turned sideways to look at him, Judge Araujo criticized her for "disrespecting the court" because she looked away
from the judges.

Whenever possible, Mr. Sandoval would meet with Lori
after she returned to Chorrillos. But there were a few weeks in
April when the hearings were four days a week, lasting until
late in the afternoon, after lawyers' visiting hours ended and
no meetings were possible. Perhaps not coincidentally, those
were days when key witnesses testified, a time when meetings
would have been most valuable. And also perhaps not coincidentally, these long days provided maximum television coverage for Judge Ibazeta immediately before the election for
ombudsman. After two congressional hearings during which
none of the five candidates received the requisite eighty votes,
the election was postponed until August, when new congressional representatives would take office.

■ The Trial Routine

Each trial day began with Mr. Llaque, the court secretary, reading aloud the proceedings from the previous session. This was
extremely time consuming, lasting anywhere from one to three
hours. But Judge Ibazeta explained it was necessary to protect
the rights of the defendant—Lori had a right to hear what was
entered into the official court record and make any corrections she believed were necessary. What a joke. Lori was supposed to listen to a transcript of what had occurred anywhere
from one day to five days previous, and she and Mr. Sandoval
were to note any discrepancies between what they were hearing and what they remembered. They could not interrupt.
They could only make suggested corrections at the end of the
reading. So Lori tried to remember what was said in the previous session, and then tried to remember all the errors so that
she and Mr. Sandoval could point them out when the secre-

tary finally finished reading. Until the fifteenth session, she wasn't even permitted pencil and paper. This certainly did nothing toward protecting Lori's rights. It simply forced Lori and her lawyer to put a stamp of approval on an official record that they could never be sure was complete or accurate. Amazingly, Lori often spotted errors and omissions, some of which would have been harmful if left uncorrected.

Meanwhile, because the court had an official videotape of all proceedings, it would have been easier and more accurate to have the interested parties check the written record against the video. But reading the transcript aloud was part of the pretense of providing due process.

As the next order of business, the prosecutor, *procurador*, or Mr. Sandoval could submit new evidence or object to evidence that others submitted. *Procurador* Mario Cavagnaro almost always had something to offer. Among other things he introduced as so-called new evidence was an article from the newspaper *Expreso* that was a translation of portions of a 1996 article in the *Village Voice* describing the journalist's view of Lori's activities in El Salvador. Another time, he submitted a letter from the director at Chorrillos Prison who claimed that he heard from some of the personnel that Lori was not a model prisoner—a hearsay claim that was false, irrelevant, and designed to prejudice. Mr. Cavagnaro objected to the bank records I had submitted to verify that the money in Lori's account did not belong to the MRTA. He claimed that because I was Lori's mother, I had reason to falsify the records. He objected to the affidavits from *Third World Viewpoint* and *Modern Times*, attesting to the legitimacy of Lori's press credentials and the articles Lori was writing. He claimed they must have been false because Lori did not have a degree in journalism and, therefore, could not have been writing for the magazines. This brought guffaws from the press in the audience, many of whom did not have degrees in journalism either. And there were many other examples of hearsay or irrelevant evidence and ridiculous objections. It was up to Judge Ibazeta to decide whether or not to accept what was submitted, and he always decided to reserve his decision until the end of the trial. But that did not stop the press from describing these submissions as if they were accepted truth.

▪ Lori Testifies

Lori was the first to testify. Prosecutor Navas questioned her on March 22 and, at the succeeding hearings, she was questioned by each of the three judges, *Procurador* Cavagnaro, and finally, her own lawyer. She testified for twenty-five hours over eight days between March 22 and April 9.

She told each of the questioners that she met Panamanian Pacífico Castrellón in Panama and traveled with him to Peru, stopping briefly in Ecuador. They rented the large house in La Molina, shared the house and the rent, and were initially pleased to have so much room at a reasonable price. They each hoped to have visitors from home. But when the opportunity presented itself, they decided to sublet the fourth floor of the house to an engineer named Tizoc Ruíz, and he subsequently hired a live-in housekeeper. It wasn't until after her arrest that Lori learned that Ruíz was Miguel Rincón, an MRTA leader. Lori moved out of the La Molina house in August 1995, before other members of the MRTA moved in, and only visited the house occasionally after that time. And when she did, she never visited the fourth floor. The design of the house, with its different levels and wings, was such that one couldn't hear fourth-floor activity on the lower floors.

When Lori sought to write articles about poverty in Peru for U.S. magazines, Ruíz recommended a Bolivian photographer, Rosa Mita Calle, who subsequently was revealed to be Nancy Gilvonio. In preparation for these articles, Lori interviewed several members of Congress in their offices and attended plenary sessions of the Congress.

Lori denied knowing that the house was used by the MRTA, denied that she helped them in any way, and insisted that her trips to Congress were only as a journalist.

The bulk of the questioning came from the judges, particularly Judge Ibazeta. He started at the end of the session on March 22 with a twenty-minute speech giving his version of the history of Central America after 1980—focusing on El Salvador, Nicaragua, and Panama. He emphasized the violence in those countries and the U.S. involvement there. He said he was developing "the context" for the line of questioning he would pursue at the next hearing. Indeed, at the next hearing he questioned Lori extensively on her interests in Latin America before coming to Peru. She recounted her work on behalf of the people of El Salvador from 1988 to 1992, years during which El Salvador was in the midst of a civil war. In 1991, during the peace negotiations, Lori worked as a secretary for Salvador Sanchez Ceran, who was then in the political and diplomatic wing of the Farabundo Marti Liberacion Nacional Front (FMLN), and who is now a prominent member in the Salvadoran Congress. Mr. Sanchez Ceran sent an affidavit to the court, testifying that Lori's duties were strictly secretarial and that she had no involvement with military activities or violence.

Much of that session and many of those that followed focused on who Lori was—or at least who the judges thought she was. The courtroom discussions and the subsequent coverage in the Peruvian press pointed up numerous cultural differences that prevented understanding. Judge Ibazeta seemed amazed that in the United States, eighteen-year-olds live away from home when they attend college. The court was not aware that thousands, if not millions, of U.S. residents supported the plight of the Salvadoran people during their civil war and others in need around the world. And no one could understand why a young, middle-class woman would leave her comfortable home and come to Peru to help the poor. In Peru, few college students live away from their families, and even fewer become involved in global actions. And they do not usually concern themselves with the plight of the poor. Not many speak publicly about poverty and injustice other than the church and members of subversive groups.

For five and a half years, in spite of extreme difficulties, Lori somehow managed to remain strong and even maintain a sense of optimism. And no one understood that either. After Clifford Krauss of the *New York Times* visited Lori at the prison in Chorrillos, he reported, "Her jailers say her bright disposition is part of being a disciplined, hardened cadre of the Túpac Amaru. But she had another explanation: 'I think if I wasn't cheery, I'd be miserable, and I don't know how people can last when they are miserable.' " But in Peru, a cheery prisoner must be a hardened terrorist. To convince the judges or the people that she was innocent, or at least that she was worthy of release, she would have needed to confess and repent. But Lori would never confess to something she didn't do, even if that was what Peruvian culture expected. As she told a reporter from Reuters, "I'm very sad and sorry people have died in Peru [as a result of violence over the past twenty years] but I'm not responsible and I won't say I am so they can let me off."

The judges and prosecutors questioned Lori extensively about her beliefs and opinions, implying that a person who supports social change would be likely to collaborate with "terrorist" groups. She was even interrogated about her interest in the music of the Chilean songwriter Victor Jara, a known socialist who was brutally tortured and killed by General Pinochet's death squads.

Another time she was asked about terrorism. She clearly said she condemned terrorism whether committed by individuals, groups, or the state, but that the word "terrorism" is used much too loosely in Peru as a label for any activity the government doesn't like, including writing articles or stating opinions or beliefs opposed to the government. Lori insisted that it was Peru's responsibility to form a Truth Commission to evaluate twenty years of actions by the so-called subversive groups, the government, and individuals to determine what should be considered as terrorist and what should not.

Although the style of questioning, emphasis on beliefs rather than acts, and prejudice of the court did not seem to bother mainstream Peruvian journalists, some Peruvian intellectuals felt otherwise. The newspaper *Liberacion* printed an article by Peruvian writer Eduardo Gonzalez Viaña comparing Lori's trial to the Spanish Inquisition in Peru, when the accused were asked to renounce their beliefs and condemn others. Gonzalez Viaña wrote, "The civilian court that currently judges her emphasizes her ideological beliefs more than irrefutably demonstrating her participation in a criminal act. The court's judges appear to ignore the fact that no democratic country punishes a person for thoughts, as rebellious as those thoughts might be." Winston Orrillo, a poet and professor at Lima's San Marcos University, wrote an article highly critical of the justice system and Judge Ibazeta, saying, "We have seen the very young and upright Lori Berenson . . . face the gibberish, the legal enticement, and the little tricks that the Court president sets for her. All he wants is to make his career! On account of this, he never will heed justice but rather his sordid interests." And more than a hundred scholars, writers, and university professors from around the world signed a letter from Peruvian writer Alfredo Pita to the Peruvian government, criticizing Judge Ibazeta for subjecting Lori to humiliating practices and trying to intimidate her into renouncing her ideas, convictions, and personal ties.

Questioning Lori's beliefs was only one of many problems. Of greater concern were comments that showed soon after the trial began that the three judges had already concluded Lori was guilty. To our dismay, early on Judge Ibazeta told Lori, "You had come to Peru to be the 'sun' around which the MRTA revolved." Judge Manrique declared that Lori may not have been a leader of the MRTA, but she was a militant. And Judge Araujo stated, "We consider you to have been the financier of the MRTA," even though Lori wasn't even charged with this. Although I never expected a fair trial, I had expected that the judges would at least pretend to reserve their conclusions until after they heard all of the evidence.

The judges sounded exactly like prosecutors, and they acted like prosecutors. They came into the court every morning and greeted the prosecutors with handshakes or hugs. They ignored Lori's attorney. U.S. congressman Joe Scarborough visited the trial on April 18. He noted that the prosecutor, *procurador*, and three judges all wore red sashes, chatted with each other, and appeared to be friends. They all treated Lori as if she were guilty. Mr. Sandoval wore a blue sash, sat by himself, and defended Lori's innocence. Mr. Scarborough said there was no way Lori could get a fair trial. It was stacked five to one.

▪ Other Testimony

The prosecution's star witness was Pacífico Castrellón. In 1995 he had "cooperated" with the police and implicated Lori in the hopes of a lighter sentence. The DINCOTE file included a statement from him asserting that he cooperated because of those hopes. I'm sure he was very angry when, after confessing, repenting, apologizing, and incriminating others, he was given a thirty-year sentence. But at least he never had to endure the horrors of Yanamayo. He was imprisoned in Lima with others who had repented. He spent his time painting, and his work was displayed in Lima art shows. In January 2001 he filed a *recurso* with the Supreme Council of Military Justice, asking that his case be revised. On April 6, his case was remanded to the civilian terrorism courts for a new trial. This was just a few days before answering the questions of the judges, prosecutors, and Mr. Sandoval, in three very long sessions on April 10, 11, and 17.

Castrellón described what he termed "a sad story that led to my misfortune." He was an artist and student of architecture who had been unemployed for several months in 1994 when a Panamanian named Brito offered him a job working in Peru on a socioeconomic study. He did not explain why an artist/architect would be recruited for such a job. Before he left for Lima, he met Lori, they traveled to Peru, and they rented a house that was later partly sublet to an engineer named Tizoc Ruíz.

Castrellón and Lori agreed on most of their testimony but differed on some important details. Castrellón claimed that he did not meet Lori by accident, that the meeting was arranged, and that in Ecuador Lori introduced him to a man named Carlos. While detained at DINCOTE, police showed Castrellón a "badly drawn sketch," which he identified as Carlos. The police told him the sketch was of MRTA leader Nestor Cerpa. Castrellón also described a woman named Isabel, whom he said he and Lori met in Ecuador and again in Lima, where she helped them look for an appropriate house. According to Castrellón, Isabel joined them when the lease to the house in La Molina was signed.

Lori said she did not know Carlos or Isabel, although there was a woman who was helping them with real estate agents. At a later court session, the real estate agent and landlord of the La Molina house gave testimony that agreed with Lori's. The agent said that a woman rode in the van with Lori and Castrellón when they first came to see the house, but his description of her was totally different from Castrellón's description of Isabel. The landlord never saw "another woman," and he and the agent agreed that only Lori and Castrellón attended the lease signing. As Lori's lawyer pointed out in his summary statement, there is no evidence that Brito, Carlos, or Isabel ever existed other than in Castrellón's mind.

Castrellón claimed he was first duped into helping the MRTA and then threatened when he wanted to quit. He was "forced" to draw maps of the streets around the Peruvian Congress and build a model of the Congress building, and he drove the van that brought MRTA members from the countryside to the La Molina house. But he insisted he knew nothing of arms hidden in the house or plans to attack the Congress.

Castrellón did not claim that Lori collaborated with the MRTA. He said he never heard her talk about politics or the group, and he emphasized that the only people who went up to the fourth floor of the house were Ruíz/Rincón and the housekeeper, supporting the testimony of Lori, Rincón, and those who lived on the fourth floor, all of whom said that Lori did not give food or indoctrinating lectures to those hidden upstairs.

It was very upsetting to watch the court and the Peruvian press fawn over Mr. Castrellón. Judge Ibazeta used a kinder, gentler, more respectful tone when questioning him. At various points he expressed sympathy with him, with phrases such as, "We understand one another," "You were trapped," "You were forced."

The Peruvian press spoke of Castrellón's testimony as "ratifying" the accusations of the prosecutors and confirming Lori's guilt. The foreign press was much more skeptical. Clifford Krauss of the *New York Times* reminded readers that Castrellón was hoping "that his own future trial will reduce his sentence" and that "many parts of his story appear vulnerable to cross-examination." It was Castrellón's word against Lori's, and according to Peruvian law, "doubt must favor the accused." But Castrellón had repented and apologized, whereas Lori refused to repent or apologize for something she had not done. In Peru this automatically made Castrellón's testimony more acceptable than Lori's, even though it was clear that he was just trying to save himself.

The testimony of Miguel Rincón clearly brought Castrellón's story into question. Rincón took everyone by surprise on April 19 when he told the court that Castrellón was a longtime, important member of the MRTA who used Lori without her knowledge to cover up MRTA activities. Rincón claimed that Castrellón's statements were all carefully crafted to reduce his sentence and that he was "simply trying to implicate a person that he himself involved, to be able to unload his responsibilities on that person." In addition, Rincón emphasized that Lori did not know who he was or his connection to the MRTA when, as Tizoc Ruíz, he lived in the La Molina house. And she did not know how Castrellón used her. She was not a member of the group. She was not a collaborator with the MRTA.

Other witnesses included the two doormen from the apartment house where Lori moved in August 1995. They agreed that Lori was a "normal tenant," and neither recalled seeing Nancy Gilvonio at the building.

For two days experts testified as to whether or not it was Lori's handwriting on a hand-drawn seating plan of the Congress and a typed document entitled "Plan Brady" that had a few handwritten editorial and spelling corrections, written by several people. Two of the prosecution experts were from DINCOTE and two others from the National Police, even though a textbook written by none other than Prosecutor Navas advised that to avoid conflict of interest, prosecutors should use only civilian experts. The defense experts were university professors of criminology specializing in handwriting analysis. The prosecution concluded that the numbers on the seating chart and some of the editorial comments on "Plan Brady" were Lori's, and the defense said that it was impossible to conclude that the writing was Lori's.

Neither of these documents was even important. The seating plan simply showed squares arranged as the seats in Congress, consecutively numbered by hand. It was difficult to see how it would be useful in planning an attack on Congress, especially since it wasn't nearly as detailed as the photos that appear regularly in the press that showed members sitting in their seats, guard posts, doors, and so on. "Plan Brady" described the MRTA's view of the economic plan by which the U.S. government guarantees loans to Third World countries. Attached was a history of the MRTA and its socio-politico-economic platform. But there was nothing related to any plans for an attack on Congress. Judge Ibazeta asked that the entire forty-two pages be read aloud, probably to remind the public of the MRTA ideology—an ideology the judge assumed was not popular with the public. And the press referred to "attack plans," although these were nothing of the sort.

Procurador Cavagnaro requested that Luis Díaz, an aide to a Peruvian congressman, be called to testify. Mr. Díaz worked in Congress as a press aide and had met Lori in the second-floor press gallery. His phone number was on Lori's beeper at the time of her arrest. From his observations, Lori was only doing what every other member of the press was doing—writing notes on what she saw and heard. Mr. Cavagnaro had called Mr. Díaz to court assuming he would testify that Lori was "casing" the Congress. When it became clear that he wasn't reporting that Lori acted unlawfully or even suspiciously, the judges and prosecutors turned on him. They reminded him several times that he was under oath, as if to imply that he was not telling the truth. They badgered him repeatedly. But he remained calm and stuck to his account.

This kind of treatment was not new. When other witnesses did not support the prosecution, the interrogations became intimidating. But it was the worst with Mr. Díaz. I found it extremely painful to watch. I wanted to shout, "Stop!" Earlier in the trial, Lori had told the court she would not give the names of her friends in Lima because she was afraid that under the antiterrorism laws, they would be harassed or worse. The treatment of Mr. Díaz certainly didn't change her mind.

▪ Meanwhile in Peru

During our three and a half months in Peru, we sensed the new political climate. The departure of Mr. Fujimori and Mr. Montesinos brought a tremendous sense of freedom. On April 8 there was an election for president and Congress, and Fujimori's party won only 4 of the 120 congressional seats. None of the presidential candidates received a majority, necessitating a runoff between Alejandro Toledo, who had the election stolen from him by Fujimori in 2000, and Alan García, who had been president from 1985 to 1990. On June 3, Mr. Toledo was elected president.

Lima started to feel like home. Mark and I discussed the weather with neighbors in the elevator and said hello to the familiar faces on the street. Folks at the supermarket, the restaurants, the Internet cafés, the newspaper stands, and the laundromat considered us part of the neighborhood. Strangers were always stopping us on the street to express their support for Lori and for us.

But many Peruvians believed Lori was guilty and should remain in prison. That wasn't really surprising, given the slant of the Peruvian media. Few Peruvians could view the cable TV broadcast of the trial, and most Peruvians had vivid memories of the "angry Lori" at her 1996 press presentation. And no matter what Lori did, the press was unfavorable. If she smiled, it was labeled a "defiant smile"; if she didn't smile, she was "emotionless."

Lori knew that it was important to change her image. Her lawyer arranged for her to be interviewed on *Panorama*, the most popular show on Peruvian television. The show was aired on Sunday, March 25, after the first week of the trial. *Panorama* showed Lori in quiet conversation with the interviewer, explaining who she was and what she believed. She appeared sincere and compassionate. I am sure many Peruvians remained unconvinced. But others started to forget the image sold by government propaganda and see the real Lori, such as the taxi driver who told the *Washington Times*, "Lori is a sensitive person who feels the injustice in the world."

Lori wanted to do as many interviews as possible with Peruvian and international media. NBC's *Today Show* arranged for an interview, and dozens of television and print journalists sent requests to the Ministry of Justice. But just as the *Today Show* crew was ready to come to Peru, the justice minister announced that there would be no interviews until the completion of the trial, including appeals. It was a tremendous disappointment. Justice Minister Diego Garcia-Sayan was internationally known for his strong support of human rights, and yet it was he who was determined to deny Lori the right to speak. We could not comprehend this ruling, and we circumvented it as best we could. Lori refused to remain silent. On visiting day I would bring Lori questions from reporters and then bring them her answers. Some reporters were able to visit Lori as "friends" and write about their visits. But the public needed to see Lori and hear her voice.

▪ The Trial Drags On

On April 19, in a radio interview, Judge Ibazeta opined that the verdict and sentence would be given within three weeks.

So when the last of the witnesses testified on April 27, we thought the end of the trial was possibly two weeks away. Wrong again. Ten more sessions dragged out over the next six weeks.

At one session, the video of Lori's January 8, 1996, press presentation was shown along with TV coverage that interlaced Lori's press statement with commentators' impressions, pictures of armaments, and scenes of bloodshed. This was Lori's first view of the event, and when asked to respond, she apologized for appearing so aggressive. She explained that her anger was brought on by the stress of her detention at DINCOTE and particularly her eleven-day confinement with a seriously wounded prisoner who was deliberately denied medical attention. The next day, the 1996 photos returned to the local newspapers, but there was no mention of the horrors of DINCOTE or the wounded prisoner.

Five long sessions were spent reading testimony that had been provided to Judge Borda in the earlier instructive phase. There were statements from many MRTA prisoners who did not appear in court, all of whom confirmed that Lori never went to the fourth floor of the La Molina house. Members of the Peruvian Congress attested to the legitimate interviews Lori conducted. Former vice president Francisco Tudela said that when he was a hostage in the Japanese ambassador's residence in 1997, he never heard the MRTA discuss Lori. And when Mr. Tudela was asked whether Nestor Cerpa had included Lori on the list of those to be released from prison, he replied that he heard demands for the release of two founders of the MRTA and Cerpa's wife, Nancy, and no one else.

Document after document in the case file was read aloud: pages of sales receipts, lists of items found in the La Molina house, newspaper articles, parts of the 1995 U.S. State Department report and the El Salvador peace accord, and long policy documents of the MRTA. It seemed endless. The press stopped coming to the trial, and Channel N stopped televising. Every week there would be a report that the verdict would be decided in two weeks. But it went on and on through June 5. Then all that was left were the closing remarks of the prosecutors and the defense.

Prosecutor Navas proclaimed that loads of evidence showed that Lori was not only a collaborator but also a member of the MRTA. He asked for a twenty-year sentence and a fine of twenty thousand soles—approximately six thousand dollars. He stressed that he could not ask for less because Lori was unrepentant and continued to insist on her innocence.

Procurador Cavagnaro continued to refer to the "evidence" from the case file assembled by DINCOTE in 1995, even though much, if not all, of that testimony was tainted, taken after the shootout at La Molina from MRTA members who had no lawyers and were either tortured, threatened with torture, or had their loved ones threatened. Most of them, even in 1995, stated they never met Lori until after their arrest, and the few who said anything against Lori retracted their statements at the present trial, insisting that DINCOTE had forced them to sign false statements. But Mr. Cavagnaro ignored the recent testimony in favor of the old and told the press he still believed Lori was a leader of the MRTA. He asked for a penalty of twenty million soles—approximately six million dollars.

Mr. Sandoval spoke for over four hours and, point by point, tore apart the prosecution's case. He concluded that there was no testimony and no document that demonstrated Lori was guilty of any of the charges. The Peruvian press had long articles discussing the statements of the prosecutors. There was no news coverage of Mr. Sandoval's refutations.

At the end of the session on June 11, Judge Ibazeta announced the court would recess until June 20 so the judges could prepare the *sentencia*, a long document giving the verdict and sentence along with explanatory matter. Lori was told she would be permitted to make a final statement, and at first we assumed that would occur before the recess, so her words could be taken into consideration as the *sentencia* was being written. But that wasn't the Peruvian way. She would speak the morning of June 20, after the *sentencia* was written but before it was read out.

As June 20 approached, we were flooded with e-mails and calls of support. The media was fighting over who would meet us first. We were booked for pre-verdict and post-verdict interviews. Since we had little reason to be optimistic, we prepared ahead of time a press release lamenting the verdict and sentence and decrying judicial prejudice and the lack of due process.

We were helped through these unbelievably trying days by an ecumenical delegation that came to "bear witness" at the reading of the *sentencia*. Father Bill Bichsel, Rabbi Steven Jacobs, Reverend Dr. James Lawson, and Reverend Dr. William Nottingham met with Lori. Rabbi Jacobs told the press, "If she's a terrorist then I'm a terrorist."

▪ Wednesday, June 20, 2001

On Wednesday morning, June 20, Mark and I went to the courtroom in Lurigancho Prison for the last time. Once again we fought our way through the crowd of press, passed through the metal detectors into the yard, and took our seats beside the embassy representatives in the front row of the courtroom. Our visitors sat immediately behind us. It was exactly three months since the start of the proceedings. On March 20 we waved fans and drank bottles of water to keep cool. Now we were layered in jackets and sweaters to ward off the damp chill.

At 9 a.m. Lori entered, dressed in black slacks, gray turtleneck, beige jacket, and the fish earrings that she had worn throughout the trial. Judge Ibazeta rang his handbell, and the session convened. After the transcript of the previous session was read, Lori was permitted to speak.

> I am innocent of all charges against me. Neither of my trials, in the civilian or military court, has proven me guilty of any crime. The charges against me are still based upon the hearsay of a fellow detainee who is trying to be freed at my expense.
>
> Since the very day of my arrest I have been called a terrorist, a term that has been used and abused in Peruvian society for far too many years, mostly because of the psychological impact of a concept that brings to mind indiscriminant violence designed to terrorize; irrational destructive violence; deadly, senseless terror. I am not a terrorist; I condemn terrorism; I always have.
>
> It is necessary to understand the past to construct a better future. During the years of political violence, if there have been acts that could be deemed terrorist acts, it's important to know the exact magnitude of what happened, why it happened, and how it happened and know who was responsible for it, albeit the state or one or more of the subversive or paramilitary organizations. This knowledge is essential for a society's well being. Under dictatorships or repressive states, society is subject to propaganda campaigns and outright misinformation designed to advance the state's interest. History must be constructed on the basis of truth and I'm hoping that truth will be known in Peru.
>
> I feel very sad for all direct and indirect victims of violence. The damage to a society goes beyond the physical and psychological impact of violence on its victims and their families. It leaves deep wounds, painful wounds, and it is very sad to watch a people en-

dure it. Political violence harms a society because it is interconnected with the institutionalized violence criticized by important church authorities in the second half of the twentieth century. El Salvador's martyred Archbishop Oscar Romero gave his life in 1980 because of his criticism of what he called institutionalized violence, as did Bishop Juan Gerardi martyred in Guatemala. Hundreds, perhaps thousands of clergy and lay workers were assassinated for defending the poor and speaking the truth against social injustice and the institutionalized violence of hunger and poverty that is the horrendous daily peril of millions.

Thousands of Peruvians have suffered persecution, detention, torture, and death as part of a state policy violating the human and fundamental rights of its population. After ex-President Fujimori's self-coup in 1992, constitutional law was violated by executive decrees made during a state of emergency. The congress and universities were closed, all forms of social organization and opposition were prohibited. The unconstitutional legislation included the antiterrorist laws that destroyed due process in civilian and military courts.

But today in Peru and throughout the world it is common knowledge that the Peruvian state did more than violate human rights by closing democratic institutions and stomping on labor and social rights and leaving its people hungry. It is now common knowledge that behind the unconstitutional legislation and the manipulation of public opinion around certain issues like political violence was an extremely corrupt government that profited from the blood and sweat of its citizens, condemning them to live in hunger and misery. The dictatorship manipulated the judiciary to ensure the cover-up of human rights violations and corruption. It wasn't an issue of particular judicial authorities, but the system itself and the legislation. In the cases of those tried for "terrorism" or treason, they were often condemned on the basis of hearsay and fabricated evidence. People were sentenced for refusing to admit guilt—regardless of whether or not they were guilty. They were condemned for not fingering others and for rejecting the psychological and social stigma of being called a "terrorist." Hearsay, supposed intentions, finger pointing or lack thereof, personal and political opinions—none of these constitute proof of any crimes.

I am aware that much of the Peruvian public has a very negative image of me, which in part is because of the anger I expressed, how aggressive I came across, when I was illegally presented to the press in January 1996. And I am aware how that image and those statements were manipulated to create a monster larger than life, so that later I personified twenty years of insurgent and state violence. This was part of the propaganda designed to make people forget how government policy and corruption impoverished the Peruvian people.

As I have stated in this trial, I regret having come across as such an angry or aggressive person, especially if it confused or offended the Peruvian people whom I really respect and love. The anger I showed was the result of my indignation upon seeing not only the violation of human rights and fundamental rights of the Peruvian people, but also the suffering I witnessed in dincote and the farce of a trial I was undergoing. The mistreatment and outright torture of my fellow detainees form only a short chapter of the history of torture in DINCOTE or army bases that was a state policy. Even so, I think it was wrong of me to have expressed myself in that way, so angry. However, I believe I was punished more for what I said. Not only was I given a life sentence, but also for over five years my name and image were used as a symbol of so-called terrorism. The punishment was for not cowering to the system of injustice and for expressing my beliefs.

I am innocent of the charges against me. Even with the limitations of ex-President Fujimori's anti-terrorism legislation that will sentence me today, this court has not proven the contrary.

Yes, I jointly rented a house with another person, but I did not do so with the idea or intent of doing so for the MRTA and there is no evidence to the contrary.

Yes, I did rent an apartment later that year, once the house had been sublet. I rented it and lived in it as witnesses from the apartment building have confirmed. I did not rent it to hide anyone or for any reason related to the MRTA, and there is no evidence to the contrary.

Yes, I did know on a social, human basis, several people who wound up being part of, or somehow related to the MRTA. I knew them with other identities and I had absolutely no reason to doubt the truth of who they said they were. They did not act in any way to make me think otherwise. Perhaps there is a cultural difference here, but it goes against my upbringing to snoop around in someone else's belongings or covertly visit their rooms, to interrogate them or pry into their private lives. I had already lived in several communal environments, both in the United States and abroad, and there is an issue of mutual respect, respect for other's space and privacy. One must mind one's own business. For these reasons, after subletting,

I never went to the fourth level of the house, nor did I go into any other room that was sublet. I never cooked for the MRTA nor brought food upstairs. I never led nor participated in indoctrination courses—not with or without a hood. No one has testified to the contrary. In fact the young people who had lived there all said—as do I—that they first saw me in DINCOTE or in prison.

Among my personal belongings the police found my computer, beeper, and the cell phone I rented. I used these things for work and recreational purposes. Unfortunately the books, the tapes, and my writings "strangely" disappeared. They would have provided concrete evidence of studies I was conducting and the articles I was writing. I did not obtain any "communications equipment," beepers, or computers for the mrta and there is no evidence to the contrary.

I did not come to Peru to cause any harm. I was and am interested in Peru's history and Peru's future. The reason I wanted to write articles about Peru was precisely because I thought it was very important that people in the United States and elsewhere know more about Peru. Peru's cultural richness should be more greatly appreciated by all. I believe that cultural history should be considered useful in the present and looking toward the future. I was seriously writing those articles. The editors of the magazines have confirmed it. My notes, my interviews with various people prove it. I knew nothing about any supposed plan the MRTA may have had to seize the Congress. To this day I know nothing about such a plan or even if it existed, and if it existed, I certainly had nothing to do with it.

After hearing Miguel Rincón's testimony in this courtroom and the reading of Pacífico Castrellón's statements at different phases of this process, I am absolutely certain that Castrellón has told lies to save his own skin, not simply to hide any real participation he may have had in all of this, but especially to seek his own release by condemning others. His statements were the only basis of my sentence in the military court and were the basis of the prosecutor's accusations here. It is very common to shift responsibilities to others when trying to secure your release. Castrellón admitted to knowing many people who he described in detail and pointed a finger at. I don't know if he really knew these people or if they even existed because the only evidence of their existence is in Castrellón's statement. But certainly I have never, ever met any of the people he claims he met through me. Such claims are absolutely false. Some of the contradictions between Castrellón's statements and those of the other detainees support what Miguel Rincón said about Castrellón in this courtroom. When Castrellón was asked why Rincón called him an international collaborator, Castrellón said "Oh, that's part of their jargon, the same way he would have considered me to be a traitor." The concept of betrayal denoted having belonged to or shared something with a group of people or cause.

I am innocent of the prosecutor's charges of being a member of and a collaborator with the MRTA. In fact, by definition one cannot be both a member and a collaborator. I am neither and there is no evidence to the contrary.

I did not come to Peru to cause harm or damage to anyone or anything. I have always been deeply concerned with issues of poverty and social justice, and if I was interested in Peru's history and its people, it was with my best intentions. When I spoke about poverty five years ago during my press presentation, it was because the human suffering caused by social injustice is unfair, inhumane, and downright immoral. Poverty in Peru has gotten worse since my detention. Now people talk about more sectors of poor and higher percentages of extreme poverty. And no one can deny this. Not only that, politicians, the church—everyone speaks of it. I have been very open and honest about this because it has been part of my way of life for many years—I believe that when things are wrong, one should say they are wrong. One should speak out when faced with injustice. I am grateful I was raised that way, as I am also grateful that my family continues to support and promote those social and moral values, for all people. I am grateful for the help of my family and friends and especially for the presence of my parents in this courtroom throughout this trial.

I haven't hidden my opinions or my beliefs. I have been honest and transparent when expressing who I am and what I think. It has been a tremendous honor for me to be involved in social issues for many years. It has also been a great honor for me to work in a country like El Salvador, work with refugees, with students, and, particularly, on the peace process. I have nothing to be ashamed of. If I describe my work in El Salvador or say I like the music of Victor Jara who was cruelly assassinated by a dictatorship because of his beliefs, that does not make me guilty of a crime. On the contrary, I think that it makes it clearer who I am and what I believe. I have nothing but love for the Latin American and Peruvian people. I've been in jail many years now, but I still have great hopes and I'm still convinced that there will be a future of justice for the people of Peru and all humanity.

The court recessed until late in the afternoon.

It took four hours to read the *sentencia*. The judges declared that Lori was not a terrorist, not a member of the MRTA, and did not participate in acts of violence. But they ruled that she collaborated with the group by renting a house and an apartment and posing as a journalist, all to help them in their plan to attack the Peruvian Congress. Lori was sentenced to remain in prison until November 29, 2015, at which time she would be expelled from Peru. She was fined a hundred thousand soles—approximately $28,500.

I watched Lori as the sentence was read. It was heart-rending. Although she knew it was unlikely, she had hoped that she would be released, that she would come home. She had told Clifford Krauss of the *New York Times*, "I think about walking by the ocean, even taking the New York City subway, everything to do with being free."

I couldn't hug her or even offer words of comfort. But she knows I will not rest until she is indeed free. And I have great faith that she will be home long before November 2015.

It has been more than five and a half years since Lori's arrest—years that were often exhausting and filled with pain. But there was a lot more than the anguish. These were years in which Lori and I became very close and grew to understand and help each other in a way that might not have been possible under other circumstances. My whole family has become closer, and I have made so many wonderful new friends. Also, over these years, I have become even more aware of the suffering, hunger, misery, and injustice in Peru and other areas throughout the world. I have been honored to meet so many people who devote a large part of their lives to protesting the economic, political, and social policies that promote this misery, and I hope that Lori's story has inspired others to join their ranks, that Lori's plight and her strength of conviction have encouraged them not to remain silent.

.AFTERWORD

This is an understated story of stunning heroism, understated because it never intended, and is unaware of, the courage it reveals. Mother Courage is the highest form of courage, because its source is love. It acts selflessly, without cunning, as it must. This is the story of two heroic women, a mother and her daughter.

It is a story of the struggle for truth over power, innocence against false witness, of a Good Samaritan traveling by choice and unafraid in a very violent, repressive place. Lori Berenson is one of those persons opposing violence in all its forms, and like many in the Peace Corps, human rights witnesses, or people doing missionary work among the poorest and most oppressed, she sought the opportunity to relieve the suffering and achieve the dignity and fulfillment of those who have no power. She was thus considered dangerous by governments that dominate and exploit the many for the profit and glory of the few. President Alberto Fujimori understood that by arresting a *"gringa"* and seeming to defy the United States, he would be setting an example that is always—and for good reason—good politics in Latin America. It is no coincidence that Madeleine Albright could demonstrate her total opposition to terrorism by distancing herself from Lori's case just as a generation ago Alexander Haig and Jeane Kirkpatrick had virtually condoned the murder of American nuns in El Salvador.

This is also a story about tyranny, the struggle for truth and freedom, the corrupt uses of claimed democracy, the abuses power inflicts through control of the media, the cowardice and destruction that political ambition and foreign policy breeds, the hypocrisy and impotence that infects the struggle for human rights in the face of economic and political will, and, finally—on a much larger scale—why war afflicts humanity worldwide.

Rhoda Berenson may deny that her book is about so many things. Though she is an intellectual, a scientist, an academic, and could have addressed any or all of these vital concerns outright, she has written a very human story of a terrifying personal experience. And her direct, simple, true account of her struggle to free Lori speaks more clearly and more powerfully about the failures of governments, leaders, militarism, and economic self-interest than libraries of scholarly studies, because it reveals in the most intimate way how all these affect the individual human being.

You have read the most positive and generous presentation of the roles played by the many actors and institutions that appear in these pages. That is Rhoda Berenson's nature. During the long years I watched her quest, in times of greatest adversity and danger when, exhausted from days of travel, confrontation and negotiation with hostile government officials, police and prison guards, media harassment, constant tension and sleepless nights, Rhoda Berenson never lost her perspective, commitment, self-control, sense of humor, or personal dignity. And with all her inner strength, she never committed a mean or harmful act. And so it was with Lori.

But to find the full value of this book, some questions inherent in the story, though not explicitly addressed, must be asked.

What drove Lori Berenson from childhood to care so much for the poor, the oppressed, indigenous peoples, their culture and music, that no threat, physical or psychological torment, demonizing and defamation, or enticement could break her will, her determination to help the meek and abused wherever she was, however she could? Though often learning the hard way that you cannot do good for humanity with impunity, how could she yet maintain her love of music, children, cats, knitting, and writing distant friends, father, sister, mother, and never lose her courage or dignity? Realize that despite the coolness of Rhoda's account, Lori was surrounded by the cruelest deprivations, murderous violence, torture, and constant crippling physical hardship, ever since her arrest, and she never ran from it.

What drove Rhoda Berenson, at the height of a successful and satisfying professional career, the contentment of home and husband, to set all that aside without a thought, to exhaust herself in personally painful pursuits of presidents, ambassadors, generals, and military judges? Where did she summon the strength to deal with the often hostile and harassing media, addressing audiences of strangers, composing and broadcasting letters, articles, pamphlets, and pleas, seeking to persuade human rights organizations in the United States, Great Britain, and Peru, the United Nations High Commission on Human Rights in Geneva, and the Inter-American Human Rights Commission of the Organization of American States in Washington? How could she endure the long journeys to strange places, the all-night flights to Lima and back with connections to Puno and Arequipa—often alone—the predawn Amtrak treks to Washington to face difficult, sometimes dangerous challenges? How did she manage, in the midst of chaos, incoherence, intimidation, and against seemingly hopeless odds, to be undeterred and remain always ready for a song, or a good laugh in her struggle to free Lori?

Why could the President of the United States not find one moment over years of pleas to stand up publicly, or even meet privately, with Lori's parents, knowing Lori had never had a trial and was a political prisoner held under life-impairing, if not threatening, conditions? Why, having seen President Fujimori wave Lori's passport before the international media when she was arrested, did her own President remain silent, the same man who proudly proclaimed—when politically advantageous—"we take care of our own"? The selfsame president was obligated by law to seek Lori's release. Where were the staff and officials who should have urged him not to remain silent?

It is difficult to believe that the Congress of the United States is incapable of any initiative to protect the human rights of an American citizen wrongfully imprisoned abroad. Respect for the rights of others means peace. Some members, like Congresswomen Carolyn Maloney, Maxine Waters, Constance Morella, and Cynthia McKinney; Congressmen Jim McGovern and Jim Leach and Senators Patrick Leahy, Jim Jeffords, Christopher Dodd, and Paul Wellstone spoke the truth to their colleagues on the floor of Congress. But why did others insist that Lori accept transfer to an American prison, thereby admitting guilt to crimes she did not commit, or that she seek a fair trial in a civilian court in Peru, knowing that a fair trial is impossible under present conditions? Why did a republican floor leader, Christopher Smith, reputedly a champion of human rights, refuse an amendment to a bill that would require Peru to provide a fair trial within a year or else release Lori and why did a democrat, Gary Ackerman, work the floor vigorously to defeat an amendment demanding Lori's release?

Why have the U.S. media overwhelmingly approved of President Fujimori despite an international consensus that Peru has among the very worst human rights records in the Western Hemisphere? The Fujimori government enforces policies that exacerbate growing poverty and concentration of wealth, and has been contemptuous of democracy, constitutional government, electoral processes, freedom of the press, and human rights and dignity. President Fujimori has suspended and then manipulated Peru's Constitution for years while ruling with an iron fist, excluding political opposition from TV and most media, manipulating voting requirements and election dates, using government programs to secure votes, seizing TV stations and arresting and exiling media opposition, and creating at least the appearance of rigged vote counts—all this— while generally ignoring the patent adjudicated illegality of Lori's conviction and the inhumanity of the conditions of her confinement. Yet the U.S. media have characterized Lori in terms used by President Fujimori himself, repeatedly using unattractive pictures of her coerced and staged press presentation by DINCOTE and rarely taking up her cause, with a few recent exceptions such as an Anthony Lewis column in the *New York Times* and a Mary McGrory column in the *Washington Post*. Are media that act so subserviently to dominant economic and political interests the major obstacle to the truth that might set us free?

Why did the U.S. Department of State fail to immediately demand justification by the Fujimori government for Lori's arrest knowing that it was first announced in an obvious political show and repeatedly thereafter by President Fujimori himself? Why did it consistently act to impede simple justice for Lori by pushing for her to transfer to a U.S. prison to serve her life sentence, thereby abandoning appeals of innocence? How could our own Department of State raise doubts about the role Lori actually played, instead of calling for her release, even when the prime minister of Peru did? Why does it consistently answer congressional mail concerning Lori with negative comments, even challenging her right to humanitarian release, and call for a new trial in Peru's civilian courts at the very time it criticizes those courts for corruption and inability to provide fair trials in political cases?

Why does the U.S. Department of State degrade the role of human rights in foreign policy, favoring military force and economic exploitation?

Why have the president, the Department of State, the Congress, the media and even human rights groups been all too willing to presume Lori's guilt until she proves her innocence despite the failure of the Peruvian propaganda machine to identify the acts which they claim support her conviction of treason?

What would have happened to Lori if her family had not fought so valiantly for her freedom?

What would you have done if Lori were your daughter, or if your closest friend had met with Lori's fate?

This book is about two remarkable women and what they did. Though the voice is nearly always Rhoda's, Lori is present in every page. And the book tells the story. Lori and Rhoda may seem more like sisters in appearance, interests, and the way they act toward one another. But this history is powerful support for the old adage that your mother is the best friend you ever have. Not that Lori's sister, Kathy, and father, Mark, haven't been heroic too. Their stories will have to wait for another book. But it is hard to believe that any other relationship could have brought forth the mutual strength, faith, support, laughs, and determination that these two generate in each other. Lori loves her "Doctor of Numbers," a known statistician and educator, passionately, and Mark would make any sacrifice for Lori and has sacrificed at least as much as Rhoda. But when the worst crises came, it was Rhoda's presence that turned shared anguish into laughter and relief, and transformed the sense of powerlessness that often overwhelms in time of maximum peril into belief that we shall overcome. And thus can the human spirit prevail and Lori will be free.

Ramsey Clark
Former Attorney General of the United States